Two Solicitudes

MARGARET ATWOOD
VICTOR-LÉVY BEAULIEU

Two Solicitudes

CONVERSATIONS

Translated by Phyllis Aronoff and Howard Scott

Originally published by Éditions Trois-Pistoles as *Deux Sollicitudes*,
copyright © 1996 by O. W. Toad Ltd. and Victor-Lévy Beaulieu

English translation copyright © 1998 by Phyllis Aronoff

Canadian Cataloguing in Publication Data

Atwood, Margaret, 1939–
Two solicitudes : conversations

Translation of: Deux sollicitudes : entretiens.
Includes bibliographical references.
ISBN 0-7710-0836-8

1. Atwood, Margaret, 1939– – Interviews. 2. Beaulieu, Victor-Lévy, 1945– Interviews.
3. Authors, Canadian (English) – 20th century – Interviews.* 4. Authors, Canadian
(French) – Quebec (Province) – Interviews.* 5. Authors, Canadian (French) –
20th century – Interviews.* I. Beaulieu, Victor-Lévy, 1945– . II. Aronoff, Phyllis,
1945– . III. Scott, Howard, 1952– . IV. Title.

PS8501.T86Z5313 1998 C813′.54 C98-930380-2
PR9199.3.H88Z46313 1998

The translation of the text was completed with the support
of the Canada Council for the Arts Translation Grant.

We acknowledge the financial support of the Government of Canada through the Book Publishing Industry Development Program for our publishing activities. We further acknowledge the support of the Canada Council for the Arts and the Ontario Arts Council for our publishing program.

Every reasonable effort has been made to contact copyright holders of material used in this book. The publisher would welcome any information regarding errors or omissions.

Typeset in Minion by M&S, Toronto
Printed and bound in Canada

McClelland & Stewart Inc.
The Canadian Publishers
481 University Avenue
Toronto, Ontario
M5G 2E9

1 2 3 4 5   02 01 00 99 98

CONTENTS

ACKNOWLEDGEMENTS

"Untitled" from *Power Politics* by Margaret Atwood (Toronto: House of Anansi, 1971). Copyright © 1971 Margaret Atwood. Reprinted by permission of Stoddart Publishing Co. Ltd., 34 Lesmill Rd., Toronto, Ontario, M3B 2T6.

"He Is last seen" from *Power Politics* by Margaret Atwood (Toronto: House of Anansi, 1971). Copyright © 1971 Margaret Atwood. Reprinted by permission of Stoddart Publishing Co. Ltd., 34 Lesmill Rd., Toronto, Ontario, M3B 2T6.

"The Blue Snake" from *Interlunar* by Margaret Atwood (Toronto: Oxford University Press Canada, 1984). Copyright © 1984 Margaret Atwood. Reprinted by permission of Oxford University Press Canada and Margaret Atwood.

"They eat out" from *Power Politics* by Margaret Atwood (Toronto: House of Anansi, 1971). Copyright © Margaret Atwood 1971. Reprinted by permission of Stoddart Publishing Co. Ltd., 34 Lesmill Rd., Toronto, Ontario, M3B 2T6.

"The Immigrants" from *The Journals of Susanna Moodie* by Margaret Atwood (Toronto: Oxford University Press Canada, 1970). Copyright © 1970 Oxford University Press Canada. Reprinted by permission of Oxford University Press Canada.

English translation of the excerpt on p. 128 copyright © 1973 Marc Plourde, from Victor-Lévy Beaulieu's *The Grand-Fathers* (*Les grands-pères*) published by Harvest House. Reprinted by permission of the University of Ottawa Press.

English translation of the excerpt on p. 151 copyright © 1982 Raymond Chamberlain, from Victor-Lévy Beaulieu's *Jos Connaissant* (*Jos Connaissant*) published by Exile Editions. Reprinted by permission of Exile Editions.

English translation of the excerpt on p. 182 copyright © 1975 Sheila Fischman, from Victor-Lévy Beaulieu's *Jack Kerouac: A chicken-essay* (*Jack Kérouac: essai poulet*) published by Coach House. Reprinted by permission.

English translation of the excerpt on p. 235 copyright © 1984 Raymond Chamberlain, from Victor-Lévy Beaulieu's *Monsieur Melville* (*Monsieur Melville*) published by Coach House. Reprinted by permission of Dewey Dimsdale for The Estate of Raymond Chamberlain.

PREFACE TO THE FRENCH EDITION

I remember one day I was in New York with a friend who was doing radio reporting and we ran into the artist Andy Warhol in the streets of Manhattan. We were carrying a tape-recorder, and we had the audacity to stop him and ask him to give us an interview. Unfortunately, Andy Warhol did not speak French. Radio gives you a licence for audacity, but it has its limits. You have to speak the same language.

Perhaps it was the dining room with its indigo walls and the portrait of Margaret Atwood painted by Charles Pachter that took me back to the streets of New York when we visited her in early March 1995. Margaret Atwood has always travelled a lot. After growing up in Abitibi–Témiscamingue, she has lived in Boston, Ottawa, Vancouver, Edmonton, and Montréal, where she learned French.

And here I was, finally, in the Toronto writer's spacious house, one step away from carrying out the project we had thought up four years before, excited and nervous, and silently thanking her for her ability to speak French, which finally made this radio adventure possible.

Margaret Atwood began her writing career with poetry, self-publishing her first poems when she was eighteen, printing the books herself and selling them through small bookstores. It was in the eighties that I came to know her, through her novels *The Edible Woman*, *Surfacing*, and *Life Before Man*. I discovered an extraordinary artist.

Poet, novelist, essayist, short-story writer, author of some thirty books that have been translated into thirty-four languages, Margaret Atwood is a major figure in the panorama of modern literature and a source of inspiration for many. She has broken new ground. In *Cat's Eye*, for example, she showed that hierarchy (relationships of dominance and submission) also exists in the world of little girls. Her novel of speculative fiction, *The Handmaid's Tale*, published in 1987, sold more than three million copies and was brought to the screen, with a script by Harold Pinter and with Faye Dunaway in a starring role.

That morning in March 1995, in the dining room with the indigo walls, in a state of joy, excitement, and nervousness, I came back to that Charles Pachter portrait of Margaret Atwood – solitary, mysterious, vibrant, and a little sad – as if it held the key to the author of *Snake Poems*. Just as in Trois-Pistoles at the home of Victor-Lévy Beaulieu, another literary giant, I had been fascinated by a huge painting by Tibo that dominated the living room, depicting his Satan Belhumeur, a screaming devil with a twisted red tongue – a very striking work.

Toronto, March 1995, the first morning of recording. I'm a nervous wreck. I'm scared. How will the interview go? Knowing that it's impossible to plan everything, I wonder about the quality of the conversation that will develop between these two exceptional individuals, writers from different worlds, bearing the distinctive stamps of their respective cultures. Sitting anxiously in the big dining room with the indigo walls, I feel my heart pounding when Joe Mahoney starts the tape-recorder and Victor-Lévy Beaulieu asks Margaret Atwood the first question – and she responds with a burst of laughter. That sets the tone, and they tell their stories to each other in a spirit of comradely sharing. I pinch myself. It isn't a dream, but the beginning of a fascinating adventure in radio.

Doris Dumais
Producer of the radio series "Deux sollicitudes"
Rimouski, 1996

INTRODUCTION

Margaret Atwood

Seven years ago I was sitting on some steps in Trois-Rivières, Québec. I was there for the francophone poetry festival – poets from Québec, French poets, Belgian poets, Haitian poets, Swiss poets, and the occasional odd anglophone Canadian poet: occasional and odd, because not many anglophone Canadian poets speak French, even as badly as I do. The Trois-Rivières Festival takes place here and there all over town – in bars, restaurants, cafés, and so forth – and is a thing of variety and eccentricity, which was just as well for me. We anglophone Canadians usually sweat a little when speaking French, and particularly when speaking it in Québec – there is sometimes an atmosphere of testing which can get querulous, and which differs from the mere impatience we occasionally encounter in France – but the Trois-Rivières audiences had been patient and benign, and I was feeling some relief.

Beside me on the steps was sitting Doris Dumais, a producer from Radio-Canada in Rimouski. She was making me an offer I couldn't refuse. Her idea – which would be a "first" for radio in Québec – was that I and a Québec counterpart of my own generation – the redoubtable Victor-Lévy Beaulieu – would interview each other, and that she would then fashion the results into a radio series. We would have a lot to talk about, she thought. We'd both been connected with cultural nationalism in the sixties and seventies, we'd both worked with small literary publishers, we'd both come from a small place to a metropolis, we'd both written in several modes. I said, in my bad French, that I thought my French was too bad. However, I was planning to spend some time in France, and perhaps after my return it would be better;

although even if it was better, it would still sound peculiar: even my *English* sounds peculiar, or so I've been told, and my French is so slow it gives the impression that someone has tampered with the tape-recorder.

Doris was not put off. She indicated that she could always snip away the really impossible bits, and patch things together so it would come out all right. This was a little like your hairdresser telling you that wigs can do wonders these days, but nevertheless I was reassured. Making a fool of yourself in English is one thing – you usually know you've done it – but second languages are notoriously booby-trapped, and I didn't want to find that I'd made some arcane sexual blunder when I'd intended only to comment on the weather.

Doris promised that she would save me from myself, though only in this context, and I believed her. We shook hands on it. This took a certain amount of courage on both our parts: mine, for going out on a limb linguistically, and hers, for shooting the rapids politically: airing an anglo-Canadian on French-language radio was bound to raise a few eyebrows in some purist quarters.

Doris arranged for me to meet Victor-Lévy Beaulieu during one of my visits to Montréal, before the series began recording. He was a formidable figure, with a beard like Edward Lear's, a throwaway sense of humour, a mind full of literature, a past not unconnected with separatist philosophy, a purple shirt, and a tie ornamented with miniature Goofies. We eyed each other over glasses of orange juice, and exchanged pleasantries. Then we galloped off to read each other's works. I had the lengthier task: VLB, as he is known, has written a great deal indeed, and in every possible form except poetry: novels, plays, essays, scripts for *téléromans*, and some other things you can't exactly classify. A translator I know has called him the Victor Hugo of Québec literature, and there's something to that. Not only that, as the radio series was to be in French, VLB had only to make his way through those of my books that had been translated, whereas as I had, you might say, the entire universe to choose from.

It was a complex and fascinating journey, and I was not at all ready when the series was due to begin recording. The first half wasn't too difficult; it took place in Toronto, where the team expressed a little surprise that nobody had scoffed at their English accents. (I pointed out that

Torontonians are used to hearing English spoken in at least a hundred different ways, so nothing is too astounding for them.) We recorded in the dining room; VLB asked the questions, and all I had to do was answer them as best I could.

The second part, however, was quite a workout. Doris, team member José Bruneau, and VLB picked me up in Québec City, and we drove along the St. Lawrence, past huge flights of snow geese, to VLB's home town, the origin of his richly ornamented literary universe. There I spent the evenings writing out my questions in French, the mornings going over them with Doris and with José, who helped make them more elegant, and the afternoons sitting in VLB's huge study trying to pronounce these more elegant questions into the microphone. The team cheered me on, with the mingled hope and exasperation of those trying to push a car out of a snow-filled ditch, and I would back up, breathe deeply, and take another run at it.

After duty hours, VLB showed me around. I saw his own enclave, which includes a summer theatre and a museum. I also got a lightning tour of Trois-Pistoles: its history, its ghosts, its magnificent cathedral all done up in faux marble, and finally its bowling alley, where I am sorry to say I did not uphold the honour of Toronto very well: my score was dismal, and I broke two fingernails. At the end of the week, I had a lot to think about, many warm memories, and much gratitude for Doris Dumais, without whose persistence I would never have had this experience. I was left with a sense of parallel journeys, and a renewed appreciation of the effort it must have taken VLB to change himself from a small-town boy growing up in a poor milieu that had no understanding of his artistic interests into the literary prodigy he has since become.

The series, when it aired, was an unqualified success, thanks in part to lively montage work by Doris – "Sainte Doris, l'Ange des Ondes," I christened her: St. Doris, the Angel of the Airwaves. It was VLB who came up with the name for the series: "Deux Sollicitudes" ("Two Solicitudes"). This is of course a play on Hugh MacLennan's famous observation about Canada's "two solitudes," and it captures the true spirit of that remark – a remark which was originally used as an epigraph, but often taken out of context. It comes from Rilke's *Letters to a Young Poet*, and reads as follows: "Love consists in this, that two solitudes protect and touch and greet each other."

In our conversations, I believe we acknowledged the solitudes. We also acknowledged the greeting. If there were more solicitude, on both sides of the great linguistic divide, we would all be a great deal better off.

Toronto, 1998

Toronto

VICTOR-LÉVY BEAULIEU
You say in your novel *Cat's Eye* that knowing too much about other people gives them a hold over you – they have rights over you, you're forced to understand the reasons for their actions, and that makes you vulnerable. I'd like to begin our conversation with that idea, first of all because I'm a Québécois reader and you're a major English-Canadian writer and there are all kinds of things I don't know about you and your work. Your writing is so polyphonic that one can approach it in different ways, beginning at the end, for example, or jumping right into the middle. Any way you do it, you're sure to get a lot out of it.

However, I'd suggest that our discussion centre on childhood. Childhood is the basis of reality. It's through childhood that the future is formed, that we really become what in fact we have been from the beginning. As a Québécois, I don't know much about your childhood, except for a few bits of biography provided by your publishers. I know that you were born on November 18, 1939, in Ottawa, that your father was an entomologist and professor, and that as a child you lived in Sault Ste. Marie, Toronto, and northern Québec. But that's so little. I'd like to learn more, if only to better understand *Surfacing* and *Cat's Eye*, those two great books you've written on childhood.

Since, as you probably know, we're a bit fanatical about genealogy in Québec, my first question will be about your parents' background. Where did your mother and your father come from?

MARGARET ATWOOD

My father and mother are both from Nova Scotia. It all started with Puritans from New England who came up during the American Revolution and Huguenots who came from France in the eighteenth century, and who also settled in Nova Scotia. And there were also Scots, driven out by the English, and a few Irish. And also people from Wales. All sorts mixed together. In Nova Scotia, there are a lot of little villages all along the coast, and in each village there's a different kind of people. My father comes from the southern coast, my mother from the Annapolis Valley. They had to leave during the Depression. Confederation had not been all that great for the Maritime provinces.

We're used to seeing our father in windbreakers, battered grey felt hats, flannel shirts with the cuffs tightly buttoned to keep the blackflies from crawling up his arms, heavy pants tucked into the tops of woollen work socks. Except for the felt hats, what our mother wore wasn't all that different.

Now, however, our father wears jackets and ties and white shirts, and a tweed overcoat and a scarf. He has galoshes that buckle on over his shoes instead of leather boots waterproofed with bacon grease. Our mother's legs have appeared, sheathed in nylons with seams up the backs. She draws on a lipstick mouth when she goes out. She has a coat with a grey fur collar, and a hat with a feather in it that makes her nose look too long. Every time she puts on this hat, she looks into the mirror and says, "I look like the Witch of Endor."

– Margaret Atwood
Cat's Eye

Margaret Atwood, aged thirteen, at Niagara Falls, 1953.

VICTOR-LÉVY BEAULIEU
Even then?

MARGARET ATWOOD
Yes. It started with Confederation, and also with the construction of the railway. Because before that, we had major ports, in Halifax and so on, but with the railway it became possible to transport goods by train, and the ports became less important. That's the ancient history of my people.

VICTOR-LÉVY BEAULIEU
But when your family was in Nova Scotia, did your grandparents work for the ports?

MARGARET ATWOOD
My mother's father was a country doctor in a tiny little hamlet in the Annapolis Valley. My father's father was a very, very small farmer, what you'd call "land poor" – they had land, but that was all. So their house, in the middle of the twentieth century, was like a nineteenth-century house: no electricity, no running water, a pump, a cow. They made butter, they made everything they needed. I remember all that. So I was touched by your play where they were selling the farms, the implements . . . that's the story of our time. I've lived in the country in Ontario. I've seen a lot of that.
My mother was a tomboy: she liked horses and hiking more than housework.

VICTOR-LÉVY BEAULIEU
A country woman. But your father?

MARGARET ATWOOD
My father was self-taught. He got his schooling by correspondence, and then he won a prize and went on from there.

VICTOR-LÉVY BEAULIEU
When you talk about correspondence school, are you talking about elementary school and high school?

MARGARET ATWOOD
High school.

VICTOR-LÉVY BEAULIEU
He did it all by correspondence?

MARGARET ATWOOD
Yes. The farm was very isolated and there was no high school in the area. During the Depression, he was so poor he lived in a tent and earned money cleaning rabbit cages for laboratories. My parents met in Normal School, where they were training to be teachers.

VICTOR-LÉVY BEAULIEU
Still in Nova Scotia?

MARGARET ATWOOD
Yes. In Truro. My father first saw my mother as she was sliding down a banister, and he said to himself, "That's the woman I want to marry."

VICTOR-LÉVY BEAULIEU
How old was your mother?

MARGARET ATWOOD
Nineteen.

VICTOR-LÉVY BEAULIEU
Did he marry her right away?

MARGARET ATWOOD
No. As I said, it was during the Depression. So it took time. They didn't get engaged right away. They got married when my mother was twenty-seven, I think. My father was an impoverished student and my mother wasn't rich either. So, like a lot of people, they had to wait. They spent the year after their marriage in Montréal. Because it was very cheap, they rented an apartment in the red-light district. They were so naïve that they didn't know.

My life's no different from the lives of others. I came into the world, I didn't ask for it. Once I'd grown up, I got married. The old man gave me his land. I just continued to do what he'd done before me. I expanded, it was easy, there was plenty of land, it belonged to no one, it only asked to be farmed. I went from two horses to eight, then from eight horses to two tractors. Instead of ten cows, I was feeding a hundred. That didn't change anything because I still did it all alone. Cécile gave me two kids, but they were kids who didn't like the land. They went to the city, Bérangère to become a nun when they didn't need nuns any more, and Castor to find ways to reforest what I'd spent my life clearing. I stayed 'cause I had nothin' else to do. Pretty obvious. Now I'm done in. I've put in my time. Like the mailbox. Besides, you should know, Blanche, there's nothing to understand in a life. It's lived, that's all. Then once you've lived it, it rots. There's nothin' else.

– Victor-Lévy Beaulieu
La maison cassée [The broken house]*

VICTOR-LÉVY BEAULIEU
What year was that?

MARGARET ATWOOD
1935. My brother was born in 1937 and I was born in 1939. Twelve years later I had a sister.

VICTOR-LÉVY BEAULIEU
So, three children. What did your father do when your parents lived in Montréal? Those were hard times.

---

* Where not otherwise noted, translations of excerpts from works by Victor-Lévy Beaulieu are by Phyllis Aronoff and Howard Scott.

MARGARET ATWOOD

He was a graduate student at Macdonald College, an agricultural school. He was a forest entomologist. He specialized in insects that eat trees. Very important for Canada.

VICTOR-LÉVY BEAULIEU

And during that time, was your mother working? Or was she studying, too?

MARGARET ATWOOD

No. She'd had her first child. And during the Depression, only one person per family had the right to work.

VICTOR-LÉVY BEAULIEU

They couldn't both have worked?

MARGARET ATWOOD

No, no, no. That wouldn't have been right. You're so young, Victor-Lévy, you don't remember any of that!

VICTOR-LÉVY BEAULIEU

Hey, I'm not that young!

MARGARET ATWOOD

The Depression and the war were very hard times from a material point of view.

VICTOR-LÉVY BEAULIEU

Yes. Some Québec authors have written about that. Like Roger Viau in *Au milieu, la montagne* [In the middle, the mountain], which describes the whole world of the Depression – the poverty, the people who didn't have glass in their windows and who put in cardboard instead, who would steal dead branches from Lafontaine Park to make a fire. Of course, I didn't experience those hard times, because I wasn't born yet, but in French-Canadian literature, there's a lot about them.

MARGARET ATWOOD

A lot of things were rationed. You had a little card and you would mark each week that you'd received your little piece of cheese. My mother had an envelope. Every week, she would put in a certain amount of money, and that was all for the week. I think she'd put in five dollars. Of course, a dollar bought a lot more than it does today, but still, it wasn't much.

VICTOR-LÉVY BEAULIEU

In most of your novels, you talk more about brothers than sisters. For example, in *Surfacing*, and again in *Cat's Eye*. Elaine is at school but she knows nothing about the world of little girls because she lives practically in symbiosis with her brother, Stephen. Was your real brother like the character of the brother you invented?

MARGARET ATWOOD

I would say yes. He says no!

VICTOR-LÉVY BEAULIEU

Why does he say no?

MARGARET ATWOOD

I guess he doesn't want to be in a novel. But there are a few details that are authentic. Of course, it's not exactly my brother. My brother is a neurologist at the University of Toronto. He works with marine animals. He's an expert in the synapse, in what happens chemically between two branches of your nerves. It's a very specialized field, and I don't understand anything about it. My brother is the head of the international synapse team. (Laughs.) The biologist at the U. of T. is not the same as the brother in *Cat's Eye*. But I have a nephew in the same profession as the brother in *Cat's Eye*.

VICTOR-LÉVY BEAULIEU

An astrophysicist?

MARGARET ATWOOD

Yes. When I see him I ask, "How's the universe today?" He answers, "Today, it's made of big bubbles." "Okay. And next time, how will it be?" He

answers, "And the next time it will be made of very thin pieces of string."
It's very reassuring! (Laughs.)

VICTOR-LÉVY BEAULIEU
He traded the synapses in the brain for the synapses in space.

MARGARET ATWOOD
Yes. That nephew is an extraordinary mathematician. He scribbles equations while he's watching TV. Not very reassuring for you, sir, who write for television. (Laughs.)

VICTOR-LÉVY BEAULIEU
Well, it's no worse than people who do housework while they watch TV! (Laughs.) With Stephen in *Cat's Eye* – he's a very important character – and in *Surfacing*, too, there's a kind of intimacy that exists between the female character and the male character, between brothers and sisters. They could even be twins. Did you have that strong an emotional attachment with your older brother? You tell how he collected stamps, hockey cards, all kinds of things.

MARGARET ATWOOD
When we were little, we spent most of the year very isolated in northern Québec, in our house all alone in the woods. There weren't many other children.

VICTOR-LÉVY BEAULIEU
Exactly where in northern Québec was it?

MARGARET ATWOOD
I'd rather not say exactly where. (Laughs.) It was near Témiscamingue. When my brother was born, it was only accessible by train. There was a very big lake, thirty miles long, a thousand miles from the coast. It was a lake with a lot of islands, a lot of bays.

VICTOR-LÉVY BEAULIEU
You spent the summer there?

MARGARET ATWOOD

Spring, summer, and fall. The insects' active period. We'd spend the winter in Ottawa. I have photographs where you can see us in a big sleigh, crossing the frozen lake. In our little house, there was no electricity or running water. We used a hand pump, kerosene lamps, and candles. All the cooking was done on a wood stove. Because of our situation, we did all kinds of work you don't have to do in the city. But it was the city that seemed strange and bizarre to us. As a child, I was scared of flush toilets; they made an incredible noise! (Laughs.) They terrified me!

VICTOR-LÉVY BEAULIEU

You didn't have them in Témiscamingue?

MARGARET ATWOOD

No. It was a very, very small town.

On my way back to the motel I detour to the store, the one where they're supposed to speak English: we will need some food. I go up the wooden steps, past a drowsing mop-furred mongrel roped to the porch with a length of clothesline. The screen door has a BLACK CAT CIGARETTES handle; I open it and step into the store smell, the elusive sweetish odour given off by the packaged cookies and the soft drink cooler. For a brief time the post office was here, a DEFENSE DE CRACHER SUR LE PLANCHER sign stamped with a government coat of arms.

– Margaret Atwood
Surfacing

VICTOR-LÉVY BEAULIEU

When you were in northern Québec, didn't you have any neighbours?

MARGARET ATWOOD

We could see a little village from the house. We would paddle there once in a while in a canoe. We also had a small motorboat. But the war was on and fuel was rationed. It was a typical old Québec village: a little church, a little priest – very little – a little general store. That's the store I described in *Surfacing*. And five or six houses, and that's it. The people who lived there usually worked repairing the railway through the forest.

There were lumberjacks too. (Laughs.) They worked the old-fashioned way. They would cut down the trees during the winter and pull them onto the ice with horses. When the ice melted, the trees would float. They'd gather all the floating logs in a big boom, then, with a little boat, they'd tow the timber to the falls. They'd push the trees into the river and let them float down to Témiscamingue, where there was a sawmill to cut the logs and make sawdust. (Laughs.)

VICTOR-LÉVY BEAULIEU
And besides the lumberjacks and railway workers?

MARGARET ATWOOD
There were also a few Indians. Once there were more Indians, but a lot of them were killed by tuberculosis at the end of the nineteenth century, and by influenza.

VICTOR-LÉVY BEAULIEU
Did you have any contact with the Indians?

MARGARET ATWOOD
Not much, because, as I said, our house was very isolated and the Indians' houses were very isolated, and the lake was very big . But we would see them go by from time to time.

VICTOR-LÉVY BEAULIEU
In *Surfacing*, you often talk about the Americans. They're always there in the background.

MARGARET ATWOOD
Yes, but that was later. I described the first five years of my life in *Surfacing*, during the war. The Americans came after the war, during the tourist period.

VICTOR-LÉVY BEAULIEU
So it's the American tourists you're talking about in *Surfacing*.

MARGARET ATWOOD
Yes, definitely.

In the mornings we do our schoolwork, in our workbooks. Our mother tells us which pages to do. Then we read our school readers. Mine is about two children who live in a white house with ruffled curtains, a front lawn, and a picket fence. The father goes to work, the mother wears a dress and an apron, and the children play ball on the lawn with their dog and cat. Nothing in these stories is anything like my life. There are no tents, no highways, no peeing in the bushes, no lakes, no motels. There is no war. The children are always clean, and the little girl, whose name is Jane, wears pretty dresses and patent-leather shoes with straps.

These books have an exotic appeal for me. When Stephen and I draw with our coloured pencils, he draws wars, ordinary wars and wars in space. His red and yellow and orange are worn to stubs, from the explosions, and his gold and silver are used up too, on the shining metal carapaces of the tanks and spaceships and on the helmets and the complicated guns. But I draw girls.

– Margaret Atwood
Cat's Eye

VICTOR-LÉVY BEAULIEU
When you left northern Québec, your family spent some time in Sault Ste. Marie.

MARGARET ATWOOD
Yes. My father set up a lab to study insects there. That lab still exists. In the spring, summer, and fall, we lived on the shores of Lake Superior, in the woods again. All those houses were built by my father, plank by plank.

When my father was growing up on a small farm in Nova Scotia, everyone knew how to build a house. Another time, we moved back to Québec and he built there, too. In all, my father built seven houses.

VICTOR-LÉVY BEAULIEU
And how was life in Sault Ste. Marie? Were there a lot of francophones?

MARGARET ATWOOD
No. There were francophone names. For example, Pointe-Duchesne. And Pointe-aux-Pins. Those names remained, like Sault Ste. Marie, but there weren't a lot of francophones. There were a lot more in North Bay.

VICTOR-LÉVY BEAULIEU
You were very young. Did you have any francophone or French-Canadian friends in Sault Ste. Marie, or anywhere else?

MARGARET ATWOOD
I made some friends after a while, because my father built a little road to the shore of Lake Superior, and some families had summer cottages near that road. We lived there or vacationed there until I was ten. After that, we moved again, but farther from everyone. We were more and more isolated.

VICTOR-LÉVY BEAULIEU
What did your mother think of all those moves?

MARGARET ATWOOD
My mother didn't like housework. She preferred living outdoors. She liked those houses in the woods because she had no vacuum cleaner and no household appliances. What she enjoyed was gardening. We always had a vegetable garden. During the war, it was essential.

VICTOR-LÉVY BEAULIEU
The vegetable garden in *Surfacing* is very important. It comes up a lot in all kinds of ways.
Right after the war, in 1946, I think, you moved to Toronto.

MARGARET ATWOOD

Yes. My father accepted a position as professor of entomology at the University of Toronto.

VICTOR-LÉVY BEAULIEU

And that was in Toronto?

MARGARET ATWOOD

In the beginning, we lived on the edge of the city. A little house in a field full of mice. I remember because my brother and I would chase the mice. We caught quite a few of them. (Laughs.)

VICTOR-LÉVY BEAULIEU

What was Toronto like back then? Was it, as you say in *Cat's Eye*, "provincial, self-satisfied, boring"?

MARGARET ATWOOD

It was a very Protestant city; that is, with laws on alcohol and everything. It was a city with a provincial attitude. It was mockingly called "Toronto the Good." It was too good! For example, there was a law on beer. The bars were divided in two: one part for men alone, the other part for ladies and their escorts. And it was forbidden to drink in a place where you could be seen by passersby. It was always dark in those bars. Singing or playing games was not allowed. All sorts of regulations. But all that has changed. And the mythical city was Montréal, "where you can drink wine with your meals!"

VICTOR-LÉVY BEAULIEU

But that's a leftover from the Puritan past.

MARGARET ATWOOD

Yes, it's Victorian. But Toronto started out as a frontier town. In the beginning, it was a French town. And in the very beginning it was an Indian town. So, Indian, then French, and then British. In the nineteenth century, there were lots of bars, lots of taverns, lots of alcohol, and lots of prostitutes in Toronto.

The fact is that I hate this city. I've hated it so long I can hardly remember feeling any other way about it.

Once it was fashionable to say how dull it was. First prize a week in Toronto, second prize two weeks in Toronto, Toronto the Good, Toronto the Blue, where you couldn't get wine on Sundays. Everyone who lived here said those things: provincial, self-satisfied, boring. If you said that, it showed you recognized these qualities but did not partake of them yourself.

Now you're supposed to say how much it's changed. *World-class city* is a phrase they use in magazines these days, a great deal too much. All those ethnic restaurants, and the theatre and the boutiques. New York without the garbage and muggings, it's supposed to be. People from Toronto used to go to Buffalo for the weekends, the men to watch girlie shows and drink after-hours beer, the women to shop; they'd come back jumped-up and pissed and wearing several layers of clothes to smuggle them through Customs. Now the weekend traffic is the other way around.

I've never believed either version, the dull, the world-class. Toronto was never dull, for me. Dull isn't a word you'd use to describe such misery, and enchantment.

– Margaret Atwood
Cat's Eye

VICTOR-LÉVY BEAULIEU
In the thirties and forties.

MARGARET ATWOOD
The eighteen-forties. It's because of that they made all those regulations, because, in the beginning, Toronto was an open city and the whisky flowed like water.

VICTOR-LÉVY BEAULIEU
The Protestant church cracked down?

MARGARET ATWOOD

Yes. There were a lot of Scottish Protestants in Toronto, and workers who drink a lot aren't good for business. (Laughs.) It's part of the Protestant ethic: you work hard, you don't drink, you have a monogamous marriage. That way, you devote more time to making money.

VICTOR-LÉVY BEAULIEU

And to making money for the government. (Laughs.)

MARGARET ATWOOD

In the beginning, the temperance movement was connected to a reform movement. It went hand in hand with the movement for women's rights and universal education.

VICTOR-LÉVY BEAULIEU

Were there big temperance campaigns in Toronto as there were in Québec?

MARGARET ATWOOD

That movement went across the whole Western world, the United States, England . . . When you're not used to something and then you suddenly have a lot of it, you become dependent on it faster.

VICTOR-LÉVY BEAULIEU

But weren't the immigrants who came to Toronto mostly of English culture – English, Scottish, some Irish?

MARGARET ATWOOD

The Scots and the Irish are not of English culture. The Irish spoke Irish. And the Scots from the highlands spoke Gaelic. Those were the Scots who had been driven out by the English. There was a sort of genocide. Those people were killed like animals. The ones who came here didn't necessarily speak English. You can't speak of the English, the Scots, and the Irish as the same thing. They were enemies. You'd see on signs in the nineteenth century, "No Englishmen allowed."

VICTOR-LÉVY BEAULIEU

I'd like to talk a little more about your father. In the novels where you talk about your father, one feels very clearly the enormous influence he had on you. But some of the things you say about him give the impression that he was a man with very definite ideas. In *Cat's Eye* there's a passage about diabetics, and the father says, "Oh yes, we take care of diabetics now, they're treated and allowed to bring more diabetics into the world." He seems to think that wasn't a great advance for science or for mankind. In other scenes, you recall similar situations. Was your father a person with very strongly held philosophical and social ideas?

MARGARET ATWOOD

My father was quite an extraordinary man. Self-taught, very intelligent, with a lot of interests. As influences, I can cite two things. The first is that he was erudite. There were all kinds of books in the house. In the bush, with no movies, no television, no radio, reading books was the thing to do. I learned to read when I was very small. The second thing is that my father didn't make much distinction between sons and daughters. When we were in the woods, it wasn't a good idea to wear a skirt, because of the bugs. He would never say, "You can't do that because you're a girl." Paddling a canoe, building things, using tools, I did all that just like a boy.

VICTOR-LÉVY BEAULIEU

Which wasn't very common, because boys and girls were raised very differently in those days.

MARGARET ATWOOD

Very differently, especially in cities and towns. And I think my mother married my father to avoid becoming the little wife of a little country doctor, doing housework and organizing afternoon teas. My father chose my mother's clothes, and before she got married her sisters chose them for her. And now, it's my sister and I who do it. She hates shopping. I found it hard when I was a teenager, because I didn't have a mother who was interested in evening gowns and all that. I had to take care of that all by myself.

VICTOR-LÉVY BEAULIEU
Did your father have a good sense of humour? It seems he did, from what you write.

MARGARET ATWOOD
The whole family had a sense of humour, what they call in France an Anglo-Saxon sense of humour. In Canada, we call it Nova Scotia or Maritimes humour. A deadpan sense of humour. We tell lies just to see if they'll be believed. For example, on April 1, I came down to breakfast. Graeme, who was listening to the BBC from England, said, "What a scandal! They say that President Clinton and Princess Diana are having an affair." And I said, "That's awful! Who says that?" He said, "The *New York Times* and the *Washington Post*." I said, "Oh, that's terrible!" (Laughs.) I believed it because it was just barely credible. Don't you think so? It's possible. (Laughs.) We'd make up elaborate lies like that.

VICTOR-LÉVY BEAULIEU
And your father did that?

MARGARET ATWOOD
Not exactly lies, but lots of irony. You'll run into that kind of humour if you go to the Maritime provinces, especially Nova Scotia. It's cultural. Another form of it consists of telling stories that become more and more improbable. (Laughs.)

VICTOR-LÉVY BEAULIEU
A little like in *Cat's Eye* sometimes, when the girls start telling a story and adding more and more until it's completely over the top.

MARGARET ATWOOD
Yes. Like that.

VICTOR-LÉVY BEAULIEU
But one day, you started going to school.

A lot of the time my brother doesn't seem aware of me. He's thinking about other things, solemn things that are important. He sits at the dinner table, his right hand moving, pinching a breadcrust into pellets, staring at the wall behind my mother's head, on which there is a picture of three milkweed pods in a vase, while my father explains why the human race is doomed. This time it's because we've discovered insulin. All the diabetics aren't dying the way they used to, they're living long enough so that they're passing the diabetes on to their children. Soon, by the law of geometric progression, we'll all be diabetics, and since insulin is made from cows' stomachs the whole world will be covered with insulin-producing cows, the parts that aren't covered with human beings, who are reproducing much too rapidly for their own good anyway. The cows burp methane gas. Far too much methane gas is entering the atmosphere already, it will choke out the oxygen and perhaps cause the entire earth to become a giant greenhouse. The polar seas will melt and New York will be under six feet of water, not to mention many another coastal city. Also we have to worry about deserts, and erosion. If we don't get burped to death by the cows we'll end up like the Sahara Desert, says my father cheerfully, finishing up the meatloaf.

My father has nothing against diabetics, or cows either. He just likes following chains of thought to their logical conclusions.

– Margaret Atwood
Cat's Eye

MARGARET ATWOOD
I spent a few months in school. Up to the age of twelve, I did only one complete school year, because we were in the bush.

VICTOR-LÉVY BEAULIEU
Always in the bush. That's a great excuse!

MARGARET ATWOOD

I did my schooling, but my mother was my teacher. It was better than school, because when you finished, you could go outside and play. I found school a bit boring. You had to stay in your seat all the time, and you had to raise your hand and ask, "Ma'am, may I leave the room?"

VICTOR-LÉVY BEAULIEU

It must have been a shock when you went to school regularly the whole year.

MARGARET ATWOOD

A big shock. A psychological shock even, because in that school, there was one door for the girls and one for the boys. I don't know if that still exists, or if it existed in Québec. And discipline after the war was very military. A bell rang, you lined up, and you stayed there like little soldiers. Certain clothes were forbidden. The girls couldn't wear pants.

VICTOR-LÉVY BEAULIEU

But you had mixed classes.

MARGARET ATWOOD

Yes, but they were divided. One side for the boys, the other for the girls. They put the big boys at the back of the class and the pretty little well-brought-up girls near the teacher. (Laughs.) I had some very, very good teachers, and one who was a real monster, whom I describe. But it was the same for everyone. I learned that after I published the book. I got a lot of letters. (Laughs.)

VICTOR-LÉVY BEAULIEU

It must have been the same in Québec, in English Canada, in the West, in Europe.

MARGARET ATWOOD

There were nuns. But only in the Catholic schools.

VICTOR-LÉVY BEAULIEU

In Québec there are very few people who were not educated by nuns or

At a poetry reading, Toronto, 1960.

brothers. In those years, school was quite imposing, with all the cornets and the habits.

MARGARET ATWOOD
When you were a child, were you afraid of those authority figures with their clothes?

VICTOR-LÉVY BEAULIEU
It didn't affect me personally. I must be an exception; I always had lay teachers. Usually first grade was taught by brothers and nuns, but they were short two, and they took lay teachers. I was in one of the two classes in the whole school with lay teachers. So I missed out on the cornets and the cassocks.

At noon there's the Happy Gang, on the radio, knocking at the door.

> *Knock knock knock.*
> *Who's there?*
> *It's the Happy Gang!*
> *Well, come ON IN!*
>
> *Keep happy in the Happy Gang way,*
> *Keep healthy, hope you're feeling okay,*
> *Cause if you're happy, and healthy,*
> *The heck with being wealthy,*
> *So be happy with the Happy Gang!*

The Happy Gang fills me with anxiety. What happens to you if you aren't happy and healthy? They don't say. They themselves are always happy, or say they are; but I can't believe anyone can be always happy. So they must be lying some of the time. But when? How much of their fake-sounding laughter is really fake?

– Margaret Atwood
Cat's Eye

MARGARET ATWOOD

Do you feel you were deprived of a significant experience?

VICTOR-LÉVY BEAULIEU

No, not really. I've never felt diminished or devalued or deprived of an education that would have been better given by brothers or nuns. On the contrary, I generally didn't like them very much, because, as you know, the system was very strict. There was corporal punishment and all that.

MARGARET ATWOOD

We had corporal punishment, too. They would hit us on the hands with a piece of rubber.

VICTOR-LÉVY BEAULIEU

The little details in your books make me laugh sometimes. In *Cat's Eye*, there's an episode that comes up again and again, with the "Happy Gang" radio show. In Québec it was "Les Joyeux Troubadours." The show lasted for years and years – I think it broke all the records for longevity, including the ones in the *Guinness Book of Records*. I was really under the impression that it was a typical Québécois product that didn't exist beyond the borders of Québec. In your novels, I was surprised to learn that there was an equivalent show in English Canada and that you even learned some of their songs by heart, just as we did in Québec.

MARGARET ATWOOD

You said the show started with the three knocks, and then you heard, "*Qui est là?*" ["Who's there?"]. It was exactly the same with us. "The Happy Gang" lasted for years and years. It was on at noon. We'd listen to them while we ate.

VICTOR-LÉVY BEAULIEU

There are things in your books that are strange to a Québécois reader like myself. Like the positive stuff about the Queen of England. Because, you know, the relationship of us Québécois to British royalty is not the stuff of which myths are made, as far as we're concerned anyway. In your books, you talk about Princess Elizabeth's visit to Toronto. That visit marked you. What did it mean to you?

MARGARET ATWOOD

In *Cat's Eye*, when the queen appears, the little girl falls in the mud. (Laughs.) The queen is one of those symbolic characters that mark an era. Like the Pope or President Roosevelt. Because Princess Elizabeth stayed in London during the Blitz, she had a certain moral authority in our eyes. There's an equivalent in Québec literature, in *A Season in the Life of Emmanuel* by Marie-Claire Blais: the visit of Lady Baden-Powell, that old Englishwoman with a face like a horse, to the little Girl Guides in Québec. She, too, is a strange, symbolic figure. Do you know the Charles Pachter painting? He did a painting of the Queen of England sitting on a moose's back. "The Queen of Canada." (Laughs.) It's a bizarre image. But the very idea of a Queen of Canada is a bizarre idea. It has to be translated into a Canadian idiom.

I remember thinking when the girls were born, first one and then the other, that I should have had sons and not daughters. I didn't feel up to daughters, I didn't know how they worked. I must have been afraid of hating them. With sons I would have known what to do: frog-catching, fishing, war strategies, running around in the mud. I would have been able to teach them how to defend themselves, and what from. But the world of sons has changed; it's more likely to be the boys now with that baffled look, like a night-dweller gone blind in sunlight. "Stand up for yourself like a man," I would have said. I would have been on shifty ground.

As for the girls, my girls at any rate, they seem to have been born with some kind of protective coating, some immunity I lacked. They look you in the eye, level and measuring, they sit at the kitchen table and the air around lights up with their lucidity. They are sane, or so I like to think. My saving graces.

– Margaret Atwood
Cat's Eye

VICTOR-LÉVY BEAULIEU
Into a symbol.

MARGARET ATWOOD
Yes, a symbol. Personally, I prefer a political arrangement where the head of state is not the head of the government. In the United States, the two functions are vested in one person. That's too much. People expect the president of the United States to be morally perfect. And that doesn't happen. (Laughs.)

VICTOR-LÉVY BEAULIEU
Maybe it's illusory to hope it can happen.

MARGARET ATWOOD
There's a lot of social pressure on the American president. It would be better if those functions were separated, head of state and head of government. The head of government should just conduct the business of the country. The head of state is a symbol. Queen of England, Queen of Canada, King of Canada, King of England. (Laughs.) I prefer the chiefs of Indian tribes. It's more authentic. But of what tribes? You have the choice among at least fifty-two tribes. (Laughs.)

VICTOR-LÉVY BEAULIEU
I'd like to come back to childhood and the two novels you wrote about it. You say children are not innocent, that they're often cruel, that they're basically the same as adults, only smaller. You say it for girls as well, which is relatively new in literature. Boys are usually thought to be cruel, vengeful, basically like adults, but it's very rare for girls to be described that way in literature. In Cat's Eye, Cordelia pushes Elaine to do all kinds of things, to transgress rules, break taboos. But it's all to exert control over her. This power of one little girl over another is perhaps as basic as the power that one boy can exert over another.

MARGARET ATWOOD
I've observed little girls from a few points of view. I've been a girl, I've had

a girl, and I've taught girls. There are usually differences between girls and boys. Both are aggressive with their companions, but the boys are more open about it. They hit, they push physically. Their hierarchy is more solid and it's based on something visible. The hierarchy of girls is more fluid. I didn't know from one day to the next who was on top. It could change in very Byzantine ways. There were whisper campaigns. (Laughs.) And their aggression is more verbal, more hidden, more subtle, more machiavellian.

I've received letters from women who had experiences like that when they were girls. Usually each one had a turn. One day you're Elaine and another day you're Cordelia. The victim creates other victims, and they in turn inflict torture. I've had a lot of letters from women who felt they were Elaines in their childhood; only two admitted to being Cordelias. Why? Because we suppress the memories of the pain we inflict and we hold on to our memories of the tortures we're subjected to. (Laughs.) With one person, you're a victim; with someone else, you're the torturer.

And it's the same thing between men and women. To one man, you're *la belle dame sans merci*, and to another, you're the submissive little mouse. (Laughs.)

VICTOR-LÉVY BEAULIEU

Getting back to Elaine and Cordelia, you could say Elaine copes better than Cordelia. There's a very nice scene when Elaine falls into the water in the ravine under the bridge. She could have drowned there if she hadn't suddenly come to. That's a beautiful passage on the transition from childhood to adolescence, to adult life basically, because it's through that event that Elaine leaves her childhood world, her world that's terrorized by Cordelia, or by her image of Cordelia. She's in the water and she imagines that the water comes from the cemetery, that it's fed by the dead bodies. I think that's a pivotal scene. Confidentially, when you wrote it, how did it come to you? Did you plan it or were you, to use a religious term, in a state of grace?

MARGARET ATWOOD

I have a very topographic imagination. In Toronto, there's a ravine like that and a cemetery like that. There used to be a bridge like that over the ravine and a stream running from the cemetery. A lot of my images come from reality. They turn into something else when I write. I heard a story about that stream, that there were children always falling in.

I knew girls like Cordelia. We had all kinds of stories like that. Cordelia is a girl who's not quite normal, because she has family problems. She's the youngest in her family, and the one who is most victimized. She's transferred her situation to Elaine. It's the others who are cruel, her older sister and her father. Normal little girls play all the roles, but Cordelia transgresses the boundaries. There are children who kill other children. We see that in the papers.

VICTOR-LÉVY BEAULIEU
But it's still through that act that Elaine becomes an adolescent, that she escapes childhood.

MARGARET ATWOOD
She reverses the roles. She becomes the strong one. She experiences a kind of mental, intellectual, and psychological torture, but she also tortures Cordelia.

In the endless time when Cordelia had such power over me, I peeled the skin off my feet. I did it at night, when I was supposed to be sleeping. My feet would be cool and slightly damp, smooth, like the skin of mushrooms. I would begin with the big toes. I would bend my foot up and bite a small opening in the thickest part of the skin, on the bottom, along the outside edge. Then, with my fingernails, which I never bit because why bite something that didn't hurt, I would pull the skin off in narrow strips. I would do the same to the other big toe, then to the ball of each foot, the heel of each. I would go down as far as the blood. Nobody but me ever looked at my feet, so nobody knew I was doing it. In the mornings I would pull my socks on, over my peeled feet. It was painful to walk, but not impossible. The pain gave me something definite to think about, something immediate. It was something to hold onto.

– Margaret Atwood
Cat's Eye

VICTOR-LÉVY BEAULIEU
What books did you read when you were a child?

MARGARET ATWOOD
I read everything, including books that weren't written for children. For example, I read Orwell's *Animal Farm*, thinking it was like a story by Beatrix Potter, with little rabbits, and so on. I was horrified! It was a big shock when the horse died. I read Edgar Allan Poe because his complete works were in the school library. In those days, they thought, if there was no sex in a book, it must be suitable for children. That's how all Poe's horrors got into my head when I was nine years old. I was the type of child who would read with a flashlight under the covers. I read Melville's *Moby-Dick*. It was too much for me, but it was an introduction. It was an illustrated version. And I really liked the whales. I read a lot of history, because my father was a history buff – the complete works of Winston Churchill, the history of World War Two. Churchill wrote very well as a historian. I read a lot of books on biology, of course. At one time I wanted to become a biologist.

VICTOR-LÉVY BEAULIEU
There's a book you often mention in *Surfacing*. I've wondered if it was real or an invention: *Quebec Folk Tales*.

MARGARET ATWOOD
It was an invention. But there are books like that.

VICTOR-LÉVY BEAULIEU
Were there in your childhood?

MARGARET ATWOOD
Not when I was little, but when I was a teenager, yes. Some Québec folklore was translated before I was born. Before the war, they did a lot of that kind of thing. But the Depression and then the war put a lot of publishers out of business in Canada. New ones had to be created. That was one thing my generation was concerned about, like yours. You yourself created a publishing house.

VICTOR-LÉVY BEAULIEU

Yes, we have that in common. Everything had to be rebuilt in those years. There weren't any more publishers, at least in Québec, except for the ones that belonged to the religious orders, which obviously didn't always meet the needs of literature, whether it was Québécois or English Canadian.

MARGARET ATWOOD

It was a bigger problem for you than for us. But it was also a problem for us, because the need to censor, to control, was very strong with us, too, because of the Puritan mentality, which has its equivalent in Québec in Jansenism.

VICTOR-LÉVY BEAULIEU

In almost all your books, you talk a lot about painting and drawing. Did the passion for painting and drawing come to you in childhood or did that happen later in your life?

MARGARET ATWOOD

When it rains and you're a child and you're in your little wood cabin in the forest, you have two choices: read or draw. (Laughs.) I drew a lot when I was a child. I drew lots of comic books, and I continued to draw them as an adult, because we were the comic-book generation. In the forties, there were *Batman* and *Superman*. But they weren't my favourites. I preferred *Plastic Man*. It was more literary! (Laughs.) My brother and I would create comic books.

In those days before computers, if you were a biologist, especially a zoologist or a botanist, you had to draw your own diagrams of the insides of insects and all that. My father was good at drawing. The house was full of pencils and paper. My brother always used the red pencil. When there was nothing but a stub left of his red pencil, he would borrow mine. I preferred the silver one. I had a silver pencil and a gold pencil. I drew all kinds of things in gold and silver. It was great. I also liked the pink one.

VICTOR-LÉVY BEAULIEU

Later, did you continue to paint and draw?

MARGARET ATWOOD

Yes, I continued. I even designed my clothes – they were awful! – and learned to sew. In school, there was a compulsory home-economics class. The poor teacher tried to teach it as a science. For dinner, there had to be something brown, something white, something green, and something orange on our plates. The taste didn't matter. But the colours were very important, because of the vitamins. You can't imagine how ugly the clothes we sewed in home-economics class were! But they were very well made. (Laughs.)

That's why I designed other clothes, which weren't as well made but were more eccentric. I didn't have much spending money, so I would buy industrial cotton and dye, and I would print my designs on the cotton with a stamp. One of my designs was a reptile. I wore my skirt with the reptiles to school. I had another skirt with trilobites, a kind of fossil crustacean I found very aesthetically pleasing. What did the other kids think of my creations? I have no idea! (Laughs.)

What I'm thinking about is a picture I painted, years ago now. *Falling Women*, it was called. A lot of my paintings then began in my confusion about words.

There were no men in this painting, but it was about men, the kind who caused women to fall. I did not ascribe any intentions to these men. They were like the weather, they didn't have a mind. They merely drenched you or struck you like lightning and moved on, mindless as blizzards. Or they were like rocks, a line of sharp slippery rocks with jagged edges. You could walk with care along between the rocks, picking your steps, and if you slipped you'd fall and cut yourself, but it was no use blaming the rocks.

That must be what was meant by fallen women. Fallen women were women who had fallen onto men and hurt themselves. There was some suggestion of downward motion, against one's will and not with the will of anyone else. Fallen women were not pulled-down women or pushed women, merely fallen.

– Margaret Atwood
Cat's Eye

VICTOR-LÉVY BEAULIEU
It must have been rather unusual, a home-made skirt decorated with reptiles.

MARGARET ATWOOD
It was a skirt with a crinoline, which was the style at the time of Elvis Presley. Those skirts usually had flowers on them. On mine, there were trilobites.

VICTOR-LÉVY BEAULIEU
Compared to childhood, you don't actually talk much about adolescence in your books. Is that because it's such a transitory age?

MARGARET ATWOOD
I talked about it a little in *Cat's Eye*. The truth is, I was too young when I went to high school. If you were intelligent, you were skipped forward to the next grade. I was only twelve when some kids were sixteen. They were very stupid and were repeating their school year. I was very small, and the others were very big. You had to be sixteen to quit school. So they had to stay until they were sixteen, and they were in my class. I was surrounded by giants. Later I grew, and the very tall ones left school. Eventually I was the same age as the others. But in the beginning it was hell.

I started university in 1957, in English literature. We didn't learn much Canadian literature, or even much American literature. We started with Anglo-Saxon, and went on to Chaucer, and then to Shakespeare. And finally we got to the twentieth century and we studied a little Hemingway and Faulkner. I enjoyed it. I chose university as a career, because at that time in English Canada it was impossible to make a living as a writer. You were forced to do something else. I'd tried a few other jobs, but they were too tedious. (Laughs.) University was preferable.

VICTOR-LÉVY BEAULIEU
It seems to me that 1961 was a very important year in your life, for several reasons. First, you left Canada to go to Boston for a few years, to Cambridge [to Radcliffe], to finish your studies, and then you made it official, so to speak, that you wanted to be a writer by publishing your first book of poetry, *Double Persephone*.

But before we get to the world of poetry, I have a few questions to ask you. In 1961, you were twenty-one. If you had to describe Margaret Atwood when she was getting ready to leave Toronto for another country, how would you describe her?

MARGARET ATWOOD

A bit pretentious. It was the beatnik era. If you were a writer or had a notion to take up writing, you had to dress all in black. If you were a man, you had to wear a beard; if you were a woman, it was a bit difficult, because, according to the beatniks, the role of women was horizontal. (Laughs.) So it was sort of hard to be taken seriously. But still, we were in Canada, not the United States, and Toronto was a provincial town. You had a bit more leeway to do things. There was a lot of freedom because, as you know, there weren't very many writers in those days.

VICTOR-LÉVY BEAULIEU

Were you already inspired by writers like Kerouac, Burroughs, Ginsberg?

MARGARET ATWOOD

A little by the French existentialists, a lot by Beckett's *Waiting for Godot*, and then by Québec poets such as Anne Hébert. It was also at that age that I read Marie-Claire Blais's first novel published in English.

VICTOR-LÉVY BEAULIEU

La Belle Bête [*Mad Shadows*]?

MARGARET ATWOOD

Yes. There was a café where we read poems. There was a little circle of poets. I had writer friends, and, because we were in Canada and there weren't many writers, if you introduced yourself as a writer, they were so happy to see you that you had an almost immediate in. In a bigger country, with a bigger population and great writers, it would have been difficult.

VICTOR-LÉVY BEAULIEU

What was the café called?

MARGARET ATWOOD

The Bohemian Embassy. Some people thought it was actually the embassy of the country of Bohemia. They even applied for visas. The building was very old. You went up a narrow staircase, and it was very dark, and very smoky. We would listen to jazz and folk music. There were candles stuck in Chianti bottles. Then I moved to Boston and discovered other things.

VICTOR-LÉVY BEAULIEU

When you got to Cambridge, was your dream still the one you had when you got your degree in Toronto: to write the great Canadian novel?

MARGARET ATWOOD

In Cambridge I was taken for an American because I had a Nova Scotia accent. At Harvard, you had to be serious too, but in different clothes. No black this time. You had to wear tweed. (Laughs.) My poor roommate, who was from North Carolina, had a lot of problems because of her accent. Everybody would say to her, "Oh, that's so cute! Say it again!" She asked me to teach her Canadian. She tried to learn, but without success, because she couldn't distinguish between the words *pin* and *pen*, and pronounced the word *oil* "ohl." Major linguistic studies were carried out in our little apartment. We had a lot of fun and we've remained friends.

Once in a while, I would talk about Canada. People there were totally ignorant about this country. There were a few myths that were prevalent. They would ask seriously if I lived in an igloo, with a dog team. After a while, like any Nova Scotian, I began to lie: "Yes, quite a large igloo, and I have fifteen very fine dogs." "Really? Is that so?" "Yes." "Is it very cold?" "Yes, all the time. It snows a lot, even during the summer."

VICTOR-LÉVY BEAULIEU

And yet Boston's not very far away. When you arrived in Boston, were you familiar with American literature?

MARGARET ATWOOD

Yes, American literature was my minor. My major was English literature. You had to take five exams there, four on English literature and one on

American literature. I'd studied less American literature in Toronto, so I tried to make up for that deficiency. You had to know the literature from the seventeenth century to the present. Including the Puritans and their sermons. And the literature of the eighteenth century, including texts from the time of the Revolution. The beginning of the nineteenth century – Washington Irving, James Fenimore Cooper . . . And then the great Romantics, whom I like a lot, like Hawthorne, Poe, Melville, Whitman . . .

VICTOR-LÉVY BEAULIEU
Emerson?

MARGARET ATWOOD
Emerson, yes. All the Transcendentalists, including Thoreau. I visited Walden Pond. I saw the traces of the little cabin he built there. It was very small. It's sort of the land of my ancestors, because among them were those Puritans of the seventeenth century – including a witch – and also, in the eighteenth century, Webster, who wrote the first true American dictionary. Webster was my grandmother's maiden name. So he was a direct ancestor. The lawyer Daniel Webster was a collateral relative.

VICTOR-LÉVY BEAULIEU
Daniel Webster had an interesting life. He spent years travelling all over North America, and everywhere he went, he wrote down the words he heard.

MARGARET ATWOOD
It was Noah who wrote the dictionary. I have a few ancestors who were obsessed.

VICTOR-LÉVY BEAULIEU
A bit fanatical?

MARGARET ATWOOD
Yes, a bit crazy. And the Atwood ancestors were not exactly pirates, but they were privateers; that is, licensed pirates.

I am sitting on the
edge of the impartial
bed, I have been turned to crystal, you enter

bringing love in the form of
a cardboard box (empty)
a pocket (empty)
some hands (also empty)

Be careful I say but
how can you
    the empty
thing comes out of your hands, it
fills the room slowly, it is
a pressure, a lack of
pressure
    Like a deep sea
creature with glass bones and wafer
eyes drawn
to the surface, I break

open, the pieces of me
shine briefly in your empty hands

– Margaret Atwood
untitled, *Power Politics*

VICTOR-LÉVY BEAULIEU
So there were freebooters in your family?

MARGARET ATWOOD
Yes. It's very good for a writer to have a few ancestors like that. (Laughs.)
The witch is absolutely necessary, and you have to have a few pirates.
Because writers are pirates. They steal. It has to be said.

VICTOR-LÉVY BEAULIEU

As William Faulkner said, they're thieves. You can't be a writer if you don't steal. Well, that's about enough about American literature. But while you were still in Boston, you must have had quite a lot of contact with English-Canadian literature too, even if only through the university.

MARGARET ATWOOD

It was impossible to study Canadian literature at that time – either in Toronto or in Boston. At the University of Western Ontario, there was a professor teaching Canadian literature. But in general, it was looked down on. I think the same was true for Québec literature in Québec; real literature was French literature, and Québec literature was considered a non-literature. It was the same in Australia and New Zealand. It's a post-colonial attitude: what matters is the literature of the great powers.

VICTOR-LÉVY BEAULIEU

But Canadian literature already existed. Were there any authors you liked?

MARGARET ATWOOD

I read a lot of Canadian literature on my own. At that time, I was writing for little magazines, literary journals. I published some poems. I had friends who were writers. But in those days you couldn't hope to earn a living by writing. So you had to think of something else. The easiest thing was for me to become a teacher. There were a lot of jobs in the universities. It was a time of expansion. That's no longer the case.

It was particularly interesting for me to study American literature, because they had had exactly the same problems we had. After the Revolution, a lot of people wondered where the great American writers were, and the great painters. "Why don't we have a literature of our own?" And poor Melville came along. The anglophiles said his *Moby-Dick* was barbaric, and the young Americans said it was too European. And that great book disappeared for almost sixty years. Melville was very disappointed and very depressed. He'd tried to write the great American novel and he'd done it, but it wasn't recognized because of that colonial mentality.

VICTOR-LÉVY BEAULIEU
It was almost by chance, a few years after his death, that someone read it and decided it was brilliant, that it had to be reissued. *Moby-Dick* could have spent another thirty or fifty years in the limbo of that colonial prejudice.

MARGARET ATWOOD
In the twenties and thirties, the creation of an American studies program in a university like Harvard gave rise to a lot of opposition in the administration. In the sixties, English Canada experienced the same problems and resistance. "Is there a Canadian literature?" "No, it doesn't exist." "Yes, it exists, but it's inferior. Why would anyone read it?"

VICTOR-LÉVY BEAULIEU
They said it was a regional literature, of no consequence.

MARGARET ATWOOD
Yes, secondary. If you wanted to read something really good, you had to read the English, or at the very least the Americans.

VICTOR-LÉVY BEAULIEU
In Québec, you had to read the French, the Europeans. But before, you were talking about Anne Hébert and Marie-Claire Blais, whom you read when you were twenty-one.

MARGARET ATWOOD
Yes, because I didn't feel that post-colonial distaste for Canadian literature. I preferred to read Canadian literature, for intellectual reasons but also for practical reasons: if I wanted to get my own books published, where and with whom would I do it? Reading authors published in Canada helped me get to know the publishers and what kinds of books they published. Irving Layton had started to write, Leonard Cohen had started – not to sing but to write poems. We were a little younger than they, so we weren't completely without models.

VICTOR-LÉVY BEAULIEU
And Gabrielle Roy?

MARGARET ATWOOD
Gabrielle Roy was on my French course in school. I studied *La petite poule d'eau* [*Where Nests the Water Hen*] word by word.

VICTOR-LÉVY BEAULIEU
You read it in translation?

MARGARET ATWOOD
No, in French. It was a French course. I studied French for five years in high school and four years in university. We had language labs with micro-phones. My teacher was a Polish woman. So I learned French with a Polish accent. And in university, I had the formidable Mlle. Rièse. She was a Swiss lady, a friend of Nathalie Sarraute. So I studied English literature and some French and philosophy.

VICTOR-LÉVY BEAULIEU
What did Canada represent to you at the time you went to Boston?

MARGARET ATWOOD
When you're in your country, you don't think about it much. But when you travel for the first time, it forces you to think about it, especially when you're in a place that superficially resembles your own country. Boston is not that far from Toronto. I had to think and make comparisons. I had Canadian friends there, but also friends from the South, Faulkner's South, and from the West. It was the people who didn't belong to the Establish-ment there who were willing to make friends. You could talk to them. The Americans knew a lot about their country, but not about others'. So history, for them, was sort of a grey fog. (Laughs.)

    In Canada, it was just the opposite. We knew a lot about other coun-tries, but almost nothing about our own country. There was no such thing as Canadian studies, so we had to find things out for ourselves. All that has changed, I think.

VICTOR-LÉVY BEAULIEU

In Québec, the publishers were controlled by the religious communities. Of course, in school we studied books written by priests. That's how we read Félix-Antoine Savard, for example – because he was a priest. That's how we could read the first Félix Leclerc books, because he was published by a publishing house that belonged to a religious order. I don't know about Ontario, but in Québec the Department of Public Instruction (the Ministry of Education hadn't been created yet) was controlled by religious communities. Every year they bought books by Québec authors like Félix Leclerc and also all the priests who wrote, and distributed them in schools as prizes at the end of the year. There were such charming books as *La perle au fond du gouffre* [The pearl at the bottom of the abyss], which was written by a nice little missionary, but once in a while you'd stumble across a Gabrielle Roy, a Félix Leclerc, or a Léo-Paul Desrosiers, which gave us a glimpse of our own literature. I don't know if this system existed in English Canada during the same period.

MARGARET ATWOOD

Puritanism was rampant in the high schools. A large part of Canadian literature was written in the twentieth century, and, as you know, there's sex in it. There weren't a lot of novels from the nineteenth century – without sex – available. All there were were those twentieth-century novels – with sex. But if you were teaching high school and you taught something with sex in it, the parents would make a fuss, they'd get all excited, and so would the students. *Hamlet* was censored. (Laughs.) It still happens today with some fundamentalist religious sects. They're supposed to read a novel by Margaret Laurence – "Oh no! I don't want my children reading that filth, that smut!"

VICTOR-LÉVY BEAULIEU

Have any of your books been censored in the schools?

MARGARET ATWOOD

Oh yes! *The Handmaid's Tale*. But I don't write for children. The students say, "We're not children." So it's always a fight between the students, the parents, the teachers, the authorities, and here it's sex that causes the problem. With others, it's religion.

VICTOR-LÉVY BEAULIEU
In Québec also, sex was censored in books. *Le Cassé* [*Broke City*] by Jacques Renaud was censored. I had a book that was censored, *La nuitte de Malcomm Hudd* [The night of Malcomm Hudd]. I even got a letter from a lady whose daughter was reading *La nuitte de Malcomm Hudd*, who told me I should have my face washed with vitriol for having written such things. She reminded me of a verse from the Gospel: "It were better for him that a millstone were hanged about his neck, and he be cast into the sea, than that he should offend one of these little ones." And to top it off, she Scotch-taped a beautiful little plastic crucifix to the bottom of the letter and wrote: "Woe to him who is touched by scandal." That was in the sixties.

MARGARET ATWOOD
We have to quote another excerpt from the Gospel: "The wind bloweth where it listeth."

VICTOR-LÉVY BEAULIEU
I don't know if it's the same in English Canada, but that happens less in Québec now, for one simple reason: Québec literature is taught less and less in the schools, colleges, and universities.

MARGARET ATWOOD
Why?

VICTOR-LÉVY BEAULIEU
Because of changes in the teaching of French. Readings have become optional, so that students read less and less literature.

MARGARET ATWOOD
And watch more and more television.

VICTOR-LÉVY BEAULIEU
Yes. (Laughs.)

Charles Pachter

Montréal, 1966

MARGARET ATWOOD

I think that's a worldwide problem. That's what they say. But when you go to a bookstore and see all the books that are sold, you realize that literature is not dying out at all.

VICTOR-LÉVY BEAULIEU

It's distribution that's the problem. Again this morning, in the *Globe and Mail*, there was an interview with a bookseller talking about that. He says it's worse now than it was twenty years ago, that while it's easy to find the bestsellers, all the books that are published in smaller numbers are no longer available or are very hard to get in Toronto bookstores.

MARGARET ATWOOD

Yes, that's been a problem in the last ten or fifteen years. But when a big tree falls in the forest, the young trees grow. There's still a market for new, experimental literature. But it's true that now it's more difficult to get it distributed. It's got worse here, and in the States too.

VICTOR-LÉVY BEAULIEU

The life expectancy of a book, even a bestseller, in the States is quite short.

MARGARET ATWOOD

They say it takes six weeks for it to get established. But you have another factor, the price clubs. They buy a few books in bulk and sell a lot of copies at low prices. This changes the bestseller lists. It's not a good thing for literature. It used to be that if you sold a certain number of copies, you would be on those lists. Now it's harder. It would be cheaper for the small bookstores – not the chains – to get their supply of books from price clubs than from the publishers.

VICTOR-LÉVY BEAULIEU

So in 1961, you officially became a writer with the publication of *Double Persephone*. Why poetry, you who dreamed of writing the great Canadian novel?

1

You walk towards me
carrying a new death
which is mine and no-one else's;
You face is silver
and flat, scaled like a fish

The death you bring me
is curved, it is the shape
of doorknobs, moons
glass paperweights

Inside it, snow and lethal
flakes of gold fall endlessly
over an ornamental scene,
a man and a woman, hands joined and running

2

Nothing I can do will slow you
down, nothing
will make you arrive any sooner

You are serious, a gift-bearer,
you set one foot
in front of the other

through the weeks and months, across
the rocks, up from
the pits and starless
deep nights of the sea

towards firm ground and safety.

– Margaret Atwood
"He is last seen," *Power Politics*

MARGARET ATWOOD

I began with the three kinds of writing that I still do now, poetry, fiction, and essays. But in 1961, in English Canada, it was easier to publish poetry. There were only five publishing houses and only five literary magazines, and it was very difficult to publish, especially novels. Why? Because novels were long. Longer than poetry. They required more paper and cost more, and it was thought that there was no readership for novels. It was simpler if you had a co-publisher, a publishing house in the United States or England. Paradoxically, it was said that Canadian literature didn't exist, that Canadian identity didn't exist, but when you wrote a novel, the Americans and the British said, "This is too Canadian for us."

It was also easier to publish poetry because you could produce it yourself with a small hand press. And that's what I did with *Double Persephone*. We set the poems letter by letter, and we printed two hundred copies. I sold them myself, visiting booksellers and asking them to take four or five copies. It cost fifty cents. Recently, I saw that slim volume of seven poems in a rare-book catalogue, evaluated at eighteen hundred dollars. I only have one copy left. Too bad! I made the cover myself, and used rubber cement to bind the pages. (Laughs.) That wasn't a great idea!

The snake winds through your head
into the temple which stands on a hill
and is not much visited now.

Toppled stones clutter the paving
where the blue snake swims towards you,
dry in the dry air,
blue as a vein or a fading bruise.
It looks at you from the side of its head
as snakes do. It flickers.

What does it know
that it needs to tell you?
What do you need to be told?

You are surprised to hear it speak.
It has the voice of a flute
when you first blow into it,
long and breathless; it has an old voice,
like the blue stars, like the unborn,
the voice of things beginning and ceasing.

As you listen, you grow heavier.
It asks you why you are here,
and you can't answer.

It begins to glow,
it's almost transparent now,
you can see the spine
with its many pairs of delicate ribs
unrolling like a feather

This has gone far enough,
you think, and turn away.
It isn't what you came for.

Behind you the snake dissolves
and flows into the rock.

On the plain below you is a river
you know you must follow home.

– Margaret Atwood
"The Blue Snake," *Snake Poems*

VICTOR-LÉVY BEAULIEU

Poetry has always fascinated me, probably because I've never been able to write it myself. The first time I saw you was at the East Lansing campus of the University of Michigan at a conference on North American literatures. I had been invited to it, with Marie-Claire Blais, as a Québec writer, and you as an English-Canadian writer. That was in 1984. You read some of your poems. I was in the hall listening to you. There was a lot I didn't understand because at that time my English was even worse than it is now. But your voice touched me. I found it warm, resonant. It spoke, as I recall, of grandmothers, dolls, and – I think – a bus trip. After your reading, I would have liked to find myself near you, as I said in a piece I wrote, just to brush against your skin. I thought it must be as warm and resonant as your voice. It was magical. To me, poetry is magic. You must have some views about that. What is it that attracts you about poetry? Is it the magical, almost sacred, quality?

MARGARET ATWOOD

Now that's a hard question. All I know is that poetry is written very differently. It takes will-power to write a novel, and you have to work for hours, regularly, and concentrate. And you have to think of things like the novel's structure. With poetry, on the other hand, you have to remain free, to create an empty space, and the poem enters it, not through your will. It's a kind of magic, a kind of conjuring. The magician draws an empty circle, enters the empty circle, and conjures. That has something in common with writing poetry.

Poets are very annoying to other people because they do absolutely nothing. (Laughs.) Everyone asks, "Why aren't you doing anything?" And the poet answers, "I'm writing." I started with poetry, but also with the other forms, when I was in high school. But at that time I hadn't read any poetry written in the twentieth century. They only taught poems from the eighteenth and nineteenth centuries. When I read twentieth-century poetry for the first time, I was overwhelmed. I didn't understand a word of it. I read T.S. Eliot at seventeen. I said, "This is terrible! What can *I* do?" But I kept going.

VICTOR-LÉVY BEAULIEU

And which of the twentieth-century poems that you read enlightened or interested you?

MARGARET ATWOOD

A lot of poets of the generation preceding mine, and, among the best of them, some women. For example, P.K. Page, Anne Wilkinson, Jay Macpherson, Margaret Avison. I read all those poets in university. And also Anne Hébert, who was translated by F.R. Scott – but I read her in French. And after that I continued with other poets, from the United States. I have to mention Sylvia Plath, who was a great poet.

VICTOR-LÉVY BEAULIEU
Why do you say, "I have to mention?"

MARGARET ATWOOD
I have to mention her because Sylvia Plath committed suicide in the sixties. It was thought that, if you were a woman poet, you had to commit suicide to be taken seriously. People asked me, "But when will you commit suicide?" (Laughs.) That created problems for us, the living ones!

VICTOR-LÉVY BEAULIEU
I can imagine!

MARGARET ATWOOD
But fortunately, you could be a novelist and stay alive.

VICTOR-LÉVY BEAULIEU
It seems to me that what you have written revolves around three major themes. The first, for me, is mythology. You speak in your poetry of Proteus, Frankenstein, Orpheus and Eurydice, and, in *Morning in the Burned House*, Daphne, Helen of Troy, and Cressida. I'd like to know what importance you place on mythology, which after all is a human creation. Is it to give a context to things, especially man-woman relationships? It seems to me that's the meaning of the poem called "Daphne and Laura and So Forth," which ends with the words, "He was running, / he was asking something, / he wanted something or other." I'd like you to talk about mythology in relation to your poetry.

MARGARET ATWOOD
When I was young, I was fascinated by Greek, Roman, and Egyptian history. And I still have a very strong interest in archaeology. I love visiting ruins,

reading books on archaeology, and going to museums with statues of the ancient gods. There are four great collections of the stories of our culture: the Greeks and Romans; Christianity; folk tales and fairy tales, like the French fairy tales and the Grimm brothers' fairy tales; and for North Americans, Native American mythology. And these motifs have begun to enter into the common language of symbols. I read a lot about mythology when I was young. Myths are part of my literary imagination.

As you know, poets and novelists use such figures as a kind of mask. You yourself have just written *Le carnet de l'écrivain Faust* [The notebook of the writer Faust]. Faust is a mythological figure. When you have a story that everyone knows, you can use that story and reinterpret it. We read the book to find out what new meaning is being attached to the story. Many women characters in Greek mythology are being reinterpreted – for example, Medea, who killed her children. From one point of view, this mythical character is very bad. But from another point of view, she can be reinterpreted as a feminist metaphor. So what meaning do you give to ancient history?

You know the writer Robert Graves, who wrote *The White Goddess*? Graves said, if you're a woman poet, you have to kill your lover, not once, but once a year! (Laughs.) But if you're a poet and you don't want to kill your lover, what can you do? It was disturbing for me when I was twenty years old to read a book like that. Fortunately, you don't have to believe every story Graves tells.

In restaurants we argue
over which of us will pay for your funeral

though the real question is
whether or not I will make you immortal.

At the moment only I
can do it and so

I raise the magic fork
over the plate of beef fried rice

and plunge it into your heart.
There is a faint pop, a sizzle

and through your own split head
you rise up glowing;
the ceiling opens
a voice sings Love Is A Many

Splendoured Thing
you hang suspended above the city

in blue tights and a red cape,
your eyes flashing in unison.

The other diners regard you
some with awe, some only with boredom:

they cannot decide if you are a new weapon
or only a new advertisement.

As for me, I continue eating;
I liked you better the way you were,
but you were always ambitious.

– Margaret Atwood
"They eat out," *Power Politics*

VICTOR-LÉVY BEAULIEU

I certainly hope not! (Laughs.) What also strikes me in your poems – this is a second theme – is what I would call the search for Canadian female origins. For example, you did a series of poems called *Five Poems for Grandmothers* in 1978 and, especially, *The Journals of Susanna Moodie*, which covers three periods in the life of what we could call a composite woman, since it takes place from 1832 to 1969. For me, these texts constitute the mythology of the founding mother of Canada. I think that was a great and beautiful moment of writing in your life. I would like you to tell me how the idea for those poems came to you, how they were created, and what inspired them.

MARGARET ATWOOD
Susanna Moodie is a true history, but a rather strange one. I read Susanna Moodie in one of our houses. We had the book when I was small.

VICTOR-LÉVY BEAULIEU
Was she a writer herself?

MARGARET ATWOOD
Yes. She wrote a book called *Roughing It in the Bush*, about her trials and tribulations. She was a high-society Englishwoman who came to America with her husband, who was also upper-class but who didn't have much money and who, I must say, wasn't very practical. They wanted to have a pretty farm with an orchard, a few cows . . . They'd read the advertisements of the time. As usual, the ads were full of lies. They arrived here in the eighteen-thirties, and the piece of land they were given was mostly swampland. They had to cut down trees and build a house. They weren't workers. It was very cold, and there were a lot of blackflies. It was a nightmare. And Susanna Moodie wrote a book about her experiences. She wanted to warn other English people not to come to Canada.

VICTOR-LÉVY BEAULIEU
It was hell for her.

MARGARET ATWOOD
For the Irish, the Scots, poor people, it wasn't so bad. But for a grand lady, it was too tough. I read Susanna Moodie's account when I was young, and then forgot it completely. But when I was twenty-six, I dreamed I'd written an opera about Susanna Moodie. It's very strange, because I don't know how to write music. I went to the library and found the book and reread it. After a while, I began writing those poems. At first there were only seven. Then the other poems came. It's really the story of Susanna Moodie, which is quite the opposite of my own experience, because I grew up in the bush.

It's life that's a nightmare for me, not the bush. They're sort of a reverse of myself, a mirror image.

VICTOR-LÉVY BEAULIEU
When the book came out in English Canada, it got good reviews, and it was very well received by the public.

MARGARET ATWOOD
Yes, that's true.

VICTOR-LÉVY BEAULIEU
The third theme of your poetry is more intimate: little things from every-day life, a memory, a dream, some objects of wood or stone, an ordinary morning, a visit to Toronto with friends. How do you choose those moments? They're mostly transient moments – why one moment rather than another, one subject rather than another? Do they just come to you?

MARGARET ATWOOD
As I said, you wait for poems. It's not the ego that chooses the subject. It's the poetry that makes the choice. I don't want to appear mysterious, but that's the truth. Ask any poet, they'll tell you the same thing: you wait for the poems. If you have a poem written, you can work on it, rearrange it, put in punctuation . . . I write in my head. When I'm looking out the window and doing absolutely nothing, I'm writing. You write a poem with a pen. But the first experience is an experience of the ear. You listen to the poem. Then you write.

VICTOR-LÉVY BEAULIEU
We couldn't leave the world of your poetry without saying something about *Snake Poems*. This suite of poems was published in French, and I read it in French and in English, because I'm fascinated first by snakes, but perhaps even more by snake women. Of all the animals – and you say this in the poem – the snake is the only one that doesn't sing. It's not human, in some sense. Which leads you to say that the snake is a great subject for poetry.

They are allowed to inherit
the sidewalks involved as palmlines, bricks
exhausted and soft, the deep
lawnsmells, orchards whorled
to the land's contours, the inflected weather

only to be told they are too poor
to keep it up, or someone
has noticed and wants to kill them; or the towns
pass laws which declare them obsolete.

I see them coming
up from the hold smelling of vomit,
infested, emaciated, their skins grey
with travel; as they step on shore

the old countries recede, become
perfect, thumbnail castles preserved
like gallstones in a glass bottle, the
towns dwindle upon the hillsides
in a light paperweight-clear.

They carry their carpetbags and trunks
with clothes, dishes, the family pictures;
they think they will make an order
like the old one, sow miniature orchards,
carve children and flocks out of wood

but always they are too poor, the sky
is flat, the green fruit shrivels
in the prairie sun, wood is for burning,
and if they go back, the towns

in time have crumbled, their tongues
stumble among awkward teeth, their ears

are filled with the sound of breaking glass.
I wish I could forget them
and so forget myself:

my mind is a wide pink map
across which move year after year
arrows and dotted lines, further and further,
people in railway cars

their heads stuck out of the windows
at stations, drinking milk or singing,
their features hidden with beards or shawls
day and night riding across an ocean of unknown
land to an unknown land.

> – Margaret Atwood
> "The Immigrants," *The Journals of Susanna Moodie*

MARGARET ATWOOD

For poetry and also because a lot of people are afraid of snakes. But not me.
I grew up with snakes. In northern Canada, in northern Québec, there are
no poisonous snakes. All the snakes are very nice. The snake is an ancestral
symbol of wisdom. Many divinities were associated with snakes. The god
of health has two snakes; you see them on pharmacists' signs. It's also well
known that the most prevalent paranoia is the fear of snakes. Cats come
second, and then spiders. The snake is also the symbol of eternity and
renewal. The poet Shelley used the snake.

VICTOR-LÉVY BEAULIEU

But Judaism made it a bad creature. For example, in the Garden of Eden,
Eve is said to have smashed in its head.

MARGARET ATWOOD

That's scandalous . . . it's a rumour that's absolutely false! (Laughs.)

VICTOR-LÉVY BEAULIEU
What is the key to your suite of poems, the conclusion, the reason why they were written, or the symbolism?

MARGARET ATWOOD
The reason why. You're always looking for the reason why. It's impossible to find the exact reason. In astrology, Scorpios are represented by three symbols: the eagle, the snake, and the scorpion. The snake is the evolved Scorpio. The most evolved of all is the eagle. My poems are an examination of snakes from all sorts of points of view, even from the point of view of a meal, because you can eat snake. I've done it. As in the poems.

VICTOR-LÉVY BEAULIEU
Is it good?

MARGARET ATWOOD
It's like chicken, but fatter and with a lot of bones. You have to be careful.

VICTOR-LÉVY BEAULIEU
But you also say that the snake is a red snowball. That seemed surprising to me. I wondered why.

MARGARET ATWOOD
Poets work with correspondences and associations. That poem is about the myth of Adam and Eve. The snake offers the fruit of knowledge of good and evil. Traditionally, that fruit is an apple. The apple is red and round. The heart is red and round. The poem says that the snake offers death in the shape of an apple and in the shape of a heart, a heart torn from the body. The red snowball, the blood snowball, is death. The apple is the torn-out heart. The apple is a symbol of death, and the shape of that apple is a blood-red snowball. Why snow? Because it's cold. It's death. Why red? It can all be explained.

VICTOR-LÉVY BEAULIEU
Getting back to your biography, you finished your degree in Boston in 1963, and you came back to Canada.

I can't believe I'm on this road again, twisting along past the lake where the white birches are dying, the disease is spreading up from the south, and I notice they now have sea-planes for hire. But this is still near the city limits; we didn't go through, it's swelled enough to have a bypass, that's success.

I never thought of it as a city but as the last or first outpost depending on which way we were going, an accumulation of sheds and boxes and one main street with a movie theatre, the itz, the oyal, red R burnt out, and two restaurants which served identical grey hamburger steaks plastered with mud gravy and canned peas, watery and pallid as fisheyes, and french fries bleary with lard. Order a poached egg, my mother said, you can tell if it's fresh by the edges.

– Margaret Atwood
Surfacing

MARGARET ATWOOD
For the first time.

VICTOR-LÉVY BEAULIEU
You spent a year in Toronto, then you went to Vancouver.

MARGARET ATWOOD
Yes, as a very junior professor.

VICTOR-LÉVY BEAULIEU
From Vancouver, you could see Canada through the other end of the lens, so to speak. Did that change the vision you had of Canada since leaving Toronto and going to Boston?

MARGARET ATWOOD
It was my first trip from Toronto to the West Coast. I went by train because I wanted to see the countryside. Have you ever taken that train trip?

VICTOR-LÉVY BEAULIEU
Not yet.

MARGARET ATWOOD
It's huge. Enormous. You leave Toronto in the evening, you keep going, you keep going, you go into forest, you cross the Great Lakes. You get up in the morning, and you're still in the forest. You keep going. Finally, you get to the Prairies. The train goes faster because the land is flat. You get to the Rocky Mountains. This is the third day. You start climbing through the Rockies, you keep going, you keep going, and in the morning you get up, and you're still in the Rockies! It takes a very long time, and they're very impressive, even more impressive for me because, when I caught my first glimpse of the Rockies in the distance, my suitcase fell on my head. So they made a big impression. The Rockies – thud!

I had a great time out West. I lived in a small apartment. Vancouver was a very small city, without the big buildings there are now. I had an absolutely fantastic view of the Pacific and Vancouver Island, and Mount Baker on the other side. I didn't have a lot of money, or much furniture. I wrote on a card table, on my typewriter. I wrote a lot because I lived alone. I could stay up all night. When I had a family, I had to go to bed earlier. But back then I stayed up, drank coffee, and wrote. I wrote a collection of poems and a novel. Those were the first two books I published. I had written a novel before that, but it wasn't published.

VICTOR-LÉVY BEAULIEU
Did you keep the manuscript?

MARGARET ATWOOD
Yes. For a young writer of twenty-two, it was good, but I have no desire now to see it come out as a book.

VICTOR-LÉVY BEAULIEU
After Vancouver, in 1967, you moved to Montréal.

MARGARET ATWOOD
After another stay in Boston, yes.

VICTOR-LÉVY BEAULIEU
Why Montréal? What brought you there, even if only for a year?

MARGARET ATWOOD
I had found work at Sir George Williams University [now Concordia]. I wanted to live in Montréal to improve my French by speaking with francophones. But I didn't have any francophone friends then, and there were two different worlds. Entering the francophone world was difficult if you were an anglophone, a stranger, with no friends. I was also working like a dog. I taught a lot of classes and I had piles of assignments to correct.

VICTOR-LÉVY BEAULIEU
You were teaching literature?

MARGARET ATWOOD
English Victorian literature and American literature – your heroes, Melville *et al.* Someone gave me a button that said, "Moby Dick is not a social disease." (Laughs.)

VICTOR-LÉVY BEAULIEU
So, during that year, you weren't able to talk with a lot of francophones in Montréal.

MARGARET ATWOOD
I had francophone students, but they insisted on speaking English with me. I don't know why! (Laughs.) But I was able to practise in the stores, like Ogilvy's. It was very good for my confidence. When I spoke French in Ogilvy's, the saleslady would say, "I don't speak French. Mabel, come here." (Laughs.)

VICTOR-LÉVY BEAULIEU
How did you find the situation in Montréal in 1967?

MARGARET ATWOOD
It was Expo year, so everyone was pretty happy. It was before the events of 1970. People were friendly, with the exception of an old nun who hit my

poor husband with an umbrella. My husband was an American from Montana. He didn't speak a word of French. He was attacked by an old nun! (Laughs.) And he was Catholic, so it wasn't fair!

VICTOR-LÉVY BEAULIEU
So you were in Montréal when General de Gaulle, on the balcony of City Hall . . .

It's a room, with bed, dressing table surmounted by mirror, night table plus lamp and telephone, linoleum-patterned drapes covering the windows which in their turn cover the night and a drop of ten stories to molten lights and metal parts, hall opening on bathroom which includes a sink and two taps, hot and cold, closed door. Outside the door is another hall and a line of similar closed doors. It is all correct, all in place though slightly dented around the edges. I've been trying to sleep in the bed, with no success. I'm going back and forth across the floor, raising from the carpet an airport smell of upholstery cleaner. Earlier there was a tray with steak rinds and shreds of old salad on it, but I set it out in the hall a long time ago.

From time to time I open the windows and the room is inundated with traffic noise as though it is part of a city-sized motor; then I close the windows and the room heats again, internal combustion engine. Sometimes I go into the bathroom and turn the taps on and off, taking drinks of water and sleeping pills, it gives me the illusion of action.

– Margaret Atwood
"Under Glass," *Dancing Girls*

MARGARET ATWOOD
It was after that. We'd gone to Alberta, because it was my husband's turn to have a job. He thought Alberta would be like Montana. It wasn't, and we spent two very difficult years there. There was an attitude in the West against people from the East, especially if you were a young writer who had

published a few books. There was a lot of resentment. People were constantly saying, "So, you're from the East. Your books only got good reviews because you were at Harvard." And "Why don't you get your hair cut?" (Laughs.) All that has changed since, but I still believe it's more difficult to be a young writer, especially a young woman writer, than an older writer. People are afraid of young writers.

She married Joe Bates in May at the end of our second year, and at first I thought it was an ideal match. Joe was then a graduate student, almost seven years older than she was, a tall shaggy man with a slight stoop and a protective attitude towards Clara. Their worship of each other before the wedding was sometimes ridiculously idealistic; one kept expecting Joe to spread his overcoat on mud puddles or drop to his knees to kiss Clara's rubber boots. The babies had been unplanned: Clara greeted her first pregnancy with astonishment that such a thing could happen to her, and her second with dismay; now, during her third, she had subsided into a grim but inert fatalism. Her metaphors for her children included barnacles encrusting a ship and limpets clinging to a rock.

– Margaret Atwood
The Edible Woman

VICTOR-LÉVY BEAULIEU
What do you think that comes from?

MARGARET ATWOOD
They're afraid of young people in general, because they're the unknown, they're energy, they're the generation that follows yours and takes its place. I think that's natural. The feminist movement was just beginning then. So there was triple pressure: I was from the East, a woman writer – maybe a feminist, who knew? – and a young writer. It was no paradise. The attitude was completely different from Vancouver. But writers can use all experiences, good and bad, for something.

VICTOR-LÉVY BEAULIEU
That attitude you talk about, isn't it the same attitude that brought the Reform Party into being?

MARGARET ATWOOD
Not exactly. I didn't experience it as political – it was just an attitude that was unwelcoming.

VICTOR-LÉVY BEAULIEU
They considered you an outsider.

MARGARET ATWOOD
An outsider, even though they themselves had been outsiders from the East two or three years before. (Laughs.) The West is a land of immigrants. It's similar in the United States, outside New York. There's a resentment against the centre. That's also the case in Nova Scotia. I'm more accepted there because I have family there.

Now everything has changed in Alberta among people who read. Because, for writers, the world isn't divided into regions or nationalities. The first division for us is between readers and non-readers. (Laughs.) After that, you can talk about other things. Alberta has a big new pool of readers.

VICTOR-LÉVY BEAULIEU
In comparison with the rest of Canada?

MARGARET ATWOOD
Yes. Bigger than a lot of other places in Canada. I think it's because the winters are so long and they have to stay home.

VICTOR-LÉVY BEAULIEU
I'm sure you're right, because I had a friend who was a teacher in Alberta who wrote me quite often, "Send me books, please! Send me books." He found the winters very long.

MARGARET ATWOOD

There are bookstores there now, and if an author gives a lecture, it's always full. I was there before the oil boom.

VICTOR-LÉVY BEAULIEU

Which completely changed the whole landscape of the West.

MARGARET ATWOOD

It also changed people's mentality. I had some very funny experiences there. I gave my first interviews in Edmonton, and I did my first book signing in a store. It was in the men's underwear department at the Hudson's Bay Company.

VICTOR-LÉVY BEAULIEU

Why? Did they want to know what was underneath the surface?

MARGARET ATWOOD

I was sitting at a table with my books. These poor men would come to buy their underwear and they'd find a young woman with a book called *The Edible Woman*. I sold two copies very quickly. It was funny and horrible at the same time.

I also gave interviews. I was asked, "So, Mrs. Atwood, when do you find time to write, with the housework and the cooking to do?" And one poor man who wasn't very attractive asked, "Do men like you?" I asked, "Which men?"

VICTOR-LÉVY BEAULIEU

You were talking about *The Edible Woman*, your first published novel, which came out in 1969. A first novel is very important, if not for the public, at least for the author. I remember the first one I had published in Montréal, almost at the same time as you, in 1968. I'd written it young, a little like you – at eighteen. It was finally published five years later. It's really special the first time you see the words you've written multiplying in the form of books that are everywhere in the bookstores. It was for me, anyway. How was it for you, that first experience of writing and being published?

Because you discover a lot of things when you write your first book. You meet a publisher, and often it's quite special. I believe that in your case it was a bit strange, your first meeting with your publisher – or the man who would become your publisher.

MARGARET ATWOOD
That was Jack McClelland. In 1966, I sent my novel to his publishing house, and they lost it. They'd written to tell me my manuscript was accepted. But after that, nothing. I was finishing my studies at Harvard and doing my exams. I began writing letters to ask what was happening with my novel. No answer. It was very disconcerting. Who had that manuscript anyway? No one knew.

Then I won the Governor General's Award for *Circle Game*, and Jack McClelland read an article about it in a newspaper. Not knowing that I had sent him that manuscript, that he had the manuscript, although it was mislaid, he wrote me a letter saying: "I want to read your novel." (Laughs.) I answered, "You've had that manuscript for two years." Dismay. He telephoned me: "I want to buy you a drink." So I met him in a little café. He drank five Bloody Marys and I drank one. Then he said, "We would like to publish your novel." I replied, "Have you read it?" He answered, "No, but I'm going to do so right away." I think poor Jack McClelland published my novel out of guilt.

VICTOR-LÉVY BEAULIEU
I believe *The Edible Woman* was very well received, both in Canada and elsewhere.

MARGARET ATWOOD
Yes and no. It was at the very beginning of the feminist movement. In Canada, there were some critics who said, "This is feminism." Others, who didn't know much about feminism, said, "This is a novel written by a young woman a bit lacking in maturity." But I was lucky, because it was published in the United States and in England. And it was in England that it was best received. Why, I don't know. Perhaps because it was a sort of bizarre social comedy, and the English like bizarre stuff.

VICTOR-LÉVY BEAULIEU

The idea of that novel, which tells the story of a woman who finally decides to become anorexic to avenge the fact that women are treated as objects, came to you in a funny way, didn't it?

MARGARET ATWOOD

Yes, but that was before anorexia was known. I knew nothing about the disease. There was something symbolic for me that involved cannibalism more than anorexia. It was sort of a poetic arrangement, with objects, symbols. It was about the consumer society. This woman worked for a market-research company. I did that myself in Toronto. It's almost an exact description. I found it very interesting. We did all sorts of weird surveys.

VICTOR-LÉVY BEAULIEU

What did you do surveys on? Consumer products that were being put on the market?

Watching him operating on the steak like that, carving a straight slice and then dividing it into neat cubes, made her think of the diagram of the planned cow at the front of one of her cookbooks: the cow with lines on it and labels to show you from which part of the cow all the different cuts were taken. What they were eating now was from some part of the back, she thought: cut on the dotted line. She could see rows of butchers somewhere in a large room, a butcher school, sitting at tables, clothed in spotless white, each with a pair of kindergarten scissors, cutting out steaks and ribs and roasts from the stacks of brown-paper cow-shapes before them. The cow in the book, she recalled, was drawn with eyes and horns and an udder. It stood there quite naturally, not at all disturbed by the peculiar markings painted on its hide. Maybe with lots of careful research they'll eventually be able to breed them, she thought, so that they're born already ruled and measured.

– Margaret Atwood
The Edible Woman

Toronto, 1970.

MARGARET ATWOOD

I wrote the questionnaires. The questions were prepared by psychologists, but the psychologists couldn't write simple questions. In a survey, the questions have to be simple. The people asking them have to understand them, and so do the people answering them. I separated the psychologists' questions into different parts and tested them. And we tested the products ourselves. We tested Pop Tarts. The first time, they all exploded in the toaster. They had to add more cement and more glue. And replace several toasters. (Laughs.) We also tested bran flakes with raisins. There was always someone who returned a box saying, "I found a dead fly in my cereal."

I know I was all right on Friday when I got up; if anything I was feeling more stolid than usual. When I went out to the kitchen to get breakfast Ainsley was there, moping: she said she had been to a bad party the night before. She swore there had been nothing but dentistry students, which depressed her so much she had consoled herself by getting drunk.

"You have no idea how soggy it is," she said, "having to go through twenty conversations about the insides of people's mouths. The most reaction I got out of them was when I described an abscess I once had. They positively drooled. And most men look at something besides your *teeth*, for god's sake."

She had a hangover, which put me in a cheerful mood – it made me feel so healthy – and I poured her a glass of tomato juice and briskly fixed her an alka-seltzer, listening and making sympathetic noises while she complained.

"As if I didn't get enough of that at work," she said. Ainsley has a job as a tester of defective electric toothbrushes for an electric toothbrush company: a temporary job. What she is waiting for is an opening in one of those little art galleries, even though they don't pay well: she wants to meet the artists.

– Margaret Atwood
The Edible Woman

VICTOR-LÉVY BEAULIEU
You used that experience in *The Edible Woman*.

MARGARET ATWOOD
It was too weird. I had to put it in a novel. It was before the advent of micro-computers and modern technology. It was almost medieval.

I still have friends from those days. I was going through a personal hell, but outside that personal hell I had a lot of fun.

VICTOR-LÉVY BEAULIEU
The Edible Woman could be described as a dazzling début in the world of literature, because since then you've been writing nonstop.

MARGARET ATWOOD
I've been writing nonstop since I was sixteen. It was only being published that was missing.

VICTOR-LÉVY BEAULIEU
So, since then you've always been published. For example, in 1972, *Surfacing* – which we've already talked a bit about – in which you introduced all the themes you would subsequently explore further: childhood, relationships between men and women, the more complex relationships between women, and the relationship between the urban world and the country – the wide-open spaces, the forest, the rural world, the world of animals and of water. You use all these themes in quite different forms and genres. For example, in *Bodily Harm*, the journalist, who has been operated on for breast cancer and flees to the Caribbean, finds herself once more in a strange, unfamiliar world that she doesn't control, and she has to relearn how to live and function in a solitude that's new to her and that's double: the solitude of being, first, an outsider and, then, a woman whose lover has left her. In *Lady Oracle*, Joanne Foster is an important poet who's robbed of life by her rather neurotic past. It's women's experience of sex, with a constant subtext of mutilation – potential, feared, dreamed of, or fantasized. It's there in other books, too, but more subtly, I would say. As in *Dancing Girls*, which is not a novel but a collection of stories.

Like poetry, short stories fascinate me, no doubt because I could never really write them. What attracts you to the short story? Because you write stories that are very "touchy," that take the reader into a very intense, very concentrated, world. You write poetry, you write novels, but why the short story?

MARGARET ATWOOD

Strangely enough, Canada is one of only two countries in the world where a collection of short stories can become a bestseller. We've got writers like Alice Munro and Mavis Gallant. The other country is Wales. I asked why and I was told, "No one here can earn their living by writing, so we don't have time to write novels." In Canada, it began with a CBC-Radio program produced by Robert Weaver in the sixties ["Anthology"]. Taking part in that program was the only way to earn money by writing, and they broadcast poems and short stories.

I went to university before there were courses in writing. I've never taken such a course. No one ever told me, "You're a poet, you have to write poems," or "You're a novelist, you have to write only novels," or "You're a short-story writer." So I stayed open to all the forms. Except theatre. I've never written a play.

The other wives, too, wanted their husbands to live up to their own fantasy lives, which except for the costumes weren't that different from my own. They didn't put it in quite these terms, but I could tell from their expectations. They wanted their men to be strong, lustful, passionate and exciting, with hard rapacious mouths, but also tender and worshipful. They wanted men in mysterious cloaks who would rescue them from balconies, but they also wanted meaningful in-depth relationships and total openness. (The Scarlet Pimpernel, I would tell them silently, does not have time for meaningful in-depth relationships.) They wanted multiple orgasms, they wanted the earth to move, but they also wanted help with the dishes.
                                                    – Margaret Atwood
                                                    Lady Oracle

VICTOR-LÉVY BEAULIEU
You've never even tried to write one?

MARGARET ATWOOD
I've written for television. But that's something else, because with a camera you have a lot of freedom. You can go anywhere, you can show things and faces close up. In the theatre, you have only actors, very limited space, and very restrictive conditions, and you have to know the theatre, I think, to work with the actors and directors. Otherwise, you write plays like Tennyson's. They're so bad that they're not really plays. I've read plays by nineteenth-century poets, and I've developed a fear of doing what they did. The theatre is very, very special. You work in a team, like in film.

VICTOR-LÉVY BEAULIEU
With set designers, costume designers . . .

MARGARET ATWOOD
You have to have access to that kind of milieu. You have to know the people. I've read in some of the introductions you've written to plays: "I thought of So-and-so in this role. I wrote this role for him. We worked together. Someone else made suggestions. I followed them." In the theatre, you exchange ideas.

VICTOR-LÉVY BEAULIEU
Yes. I feel that writing for the theatre or for television, unlike novels or short stories, is like writing a piece of music. When you write for television, there are seventy people who read your score, and not everyone has the same reaction. There are differences, disagreements. When you write for the theatre, you're also writing a piece of music, but the people who are important are the actors. It's obviously an advantage if you know the actors you're writing for. It goes much more quickly, because you hear their voices when you're writing. You know how an actor works, how he breathes, where he puts pauses, silences. So at the same time it's easier to write and it's also more stimulating, because it's real teamwork, working together. You write a play, you go to rehearsals, everyone gives their opinion. The lighting director says, "According to such-and-such symbolism in the text, I would use

such-and-such a colour." It's fascinating. But it's a lot of work. There are a lot of production meetings. There are writers who are incapable of doing this; they're scared, because of basic differences in the writing. When you write a text, either a short story or a novel, you're alone with yourself while you're writing. It's rare for a publisher to come knocking on your door and say, "I have to have the novel right away." That's part of the freedom of writing.

The short story is even more special because it's compressed in time. I like short stories a lot. When I read them, I have the impression of a life condensed into ten or fifteen pages. When I read Borges, I found it fabulous how in eight or ten pages he could tell not just a story but a whole life, a character. I thought it would be amazing if you could do something that concentrated and that powerful in a novel. I don't know if you have the same impression as I do about that. I've read your short stories: for example, "The Grave of the Famous Poet." I was very impressed, because there's so little plot. It's all a matter of atmosphere. You find yourself on a kind of island with two characters. They visit the grave of the poet and a ruined castle. You don't really know who the poet is that they're talking about. You're drawn into the atmosphere of a couple in the process of breaking up for reasons you're not really aware of. It's all done in subtle touches, it takes place in fifteen pages, and when you get to the end you know just about everything you need to about the characters. I wonder how a person can manage in so few pages to create a universe like that, to render it in that way. That's beyond me. I'm not capable of writing that kind of thing.

MARGARET ATWOOD

There are examples in Québec, like Jacques Ferron, one of your heroes. It so happens I worked on the translation of some texts by Ferron. And there were a lot of short-story writers in American literature in the nineteenth century; I grew up with Poe, for example. And I also like Stevenson a lot.

VICTOR-LÉVY BEAULIEU

Did you read Stephen Leacock, either when you were young or later?

MARGARET ATWOOD

Yes. He was a humorist. But there were also authors who wrote animal stories that a lot of children of my generation read. There was Charles [G.D.]

Roberts, and Ernest Thompson Seton, who wrote a lot of stories about wild animals I was familiar with. These were tragic stories, because wild animals never die in their beds. (Laughs.) It was always war and murder for those poor animals. I read the stories when I was very young, and I cried. They used to give those books to children for Christmas. So I spent a lot of Christmases crying over those poor animals that were dropping like flies.

Stomach full of blood, head full of blood, burning red, she can feel it at last, this rage that has been going on for a long time, energy, words swarming behind her eyes like spring bees. Something is hungry, something is coiling itself. A long song coils and uncoils itself just in front of the windshield, where the red snow is falling, bringing everything to life. They park the virtuous car and she is led by the two young men into the auditorium, grey cinderblock, where a gathering of polite faces waits to hear the word. Hands will clap, things will be said about her, nothing astonishing, she is supposed to be good for them, they must open their mouths and take her in, like vitamins, like bland medicine. No. No sweet identity, she will clench herself against it. She will step across the stage, words coiled, she will open her mouth and the room will explode in blood.

– Margaret Atwood
"Lives of the Poets," *Dancing Girls*

VICTOR-LÉVY BEAULIEU

I spent all last night with you. I lay in bed rereading some of your poetry. In my dreams, I found myself again on the East Lansing campus of the University of Michigan in 1984, when I saw you and heard you for the first time. And again it was warm, resonant, and magical. To give our listeners an idea of it, I would like to ask you to play a game and make my dream a reality. Would you read one of your poems?

MARGARET ATWOOD

In French or in English?

VICTOR-LÉVY BEAULIEU
In English, perhaps, since that's how I heard you the first time.

MARGARET ATWOOD
An old poem or a recent poem?

VICTOR-LÉVY BEAULIEU
Your choice.

MARGARET ATWOOD
Something very short. (Laughs.) And very simple. "The Moment." "The moment when, after many years / of hard work and a long voyage / you stand in the centre of your room, / house, half-acre, square mile, island, country, / knowing at last how you got there, / and say, *I own this*, / is the same moment the trees unloose / their soft arms from around you, / the birds take back their language, / the cliffs fissure and collapse, / the air moves back from you like a wave / and you can't breathe. / *No*, they whisper. *You own nothing. / You were a visitor, time after time / climbing the hill, planting the flag, proclaiming. / We never belonged to you. / You never found us. / It was always the other way round.*"

VICTOR-LÉVY BEAULIEU
In 1985 you published *The Handmaid's Tale*, which made you one of our major contemporary writers internationally. *The Handmaid's Tale* could be considered the first part of a trilogy that would also include *Cat's Eye* and, in 1993, *The Robber Bride*. Those three novels are so important in your work, and they speak very strongly to me as a male reader. They evoke all sorts of images for me.

Let's start with *The Handmaid's Tale*. For people who haven't read it yet, it takes place after a military *coup d'état*, in what has become the Republic of Gilead. Because of the falling birth rate, women are conscripted by the rulers and treated as breeding animals. They live monastic lives, in a hierarchy symbolized by the colour of their costume. The narrator, Offred, is at the bottom of the pecking order as a Handmaid. Her colour is scarlet, as in Hawthorne's *The Scarlet Letter*. In the Hawthorne novel, scarlet symbolizes sin, or prostitution, or sexual freedom. What symbolic value does red have in your novel? Is it the same?

MARGARET ATWOOD

Red has a lot of meanings in Western culture. It's the colour of Mary Magdalene, the great sinner of the church of sinners, and it goes without saying that it represents sexuality. But it's also the colour of blood and, as such, the colour of sacrifice. And it was also the colour worn by prisoners-of-war in Canada. Why red? Because it snowed a lot, and it was easy to spot the prisoners against the snow when they escaped. It's also the colour of the Red Cross and the colour for wet nurses. And of course I'd read *The Scarlet Letter*.

The first government of the United States was a fundamentalist government. The United States was founded by seventeenth-century Puritans. It wasn't a democracy then, but a very strict theocracy, especially with respect to sex. Countries continue the way they began; they rearrange the symbols and the structures, but something remains of their origins. And the presidents of the United States have continued to quote the first theocrats, who referred to their colony as "a city upon a hill," and "a light to all nations." Reagan, for instance, repeated these early Puritan references to the Bible. The United States, beginning with the Puritans, considered itself an example not only to its own people but to the whole world. And that has continued. (Laughs.) It's a utopia/dystopia. And all utopias/dystopias are responses to certain questions asked by society. I asked myself, if you wanted to seize power in the United States, how would you go about it? Not through communism. Not through Marxism. Not through democracy, because that would be a contradiction. But if you proclaimed, as the Republicans now do, "The will of God is with us, follow us" – that's what theocracy did. And it's also a form of tyranny, because when you join politics and religion, you have tyranny.

VICTOR-LÉVY BEAULIEU
Fanaticism.

MARGARET ATWOOD
It becomes impossible to disagree with the system without being accused of blasphemy.

VICTOR-LÉVY BEAULIEU

And American fanaticism has its origins in Puritanism. The witch hunts, all that.

MARGARET ATWOOD

Yes. Especially in the northeastern states.

VICTOR-LÉVY BEAULIEU

In an appendix to *The Handmaid's Tale*, you provide "Historical Notes." There we learn that the Republic of Gilead was built on the ruins of Bangor, Maine, which had in the sixties and seventies been a stronghold of feminism. All the women intellectuals and artists lived in sisterhood. I suppose you drew on that era to write your novel. What have you kept from that whole movement?

MARGARET ATWOOD

The centre of Gilead is Boston, or Cambridge, which was also the centre of Puritanism in the United States. Bangor, Maine, is a city – this is only in the novel – used to escape from the system, because it's located farther north. In difficult periods, a lot of people tried to flee to Canada from the United States, and vice versa. There were constant escapes in both directions. Canada was the end of the underground railroad during the period of slavery in the United States. And draft-dodgers took refuge here during the Vietnam War.

VICTOR-LÉVY BEAULIEU

Likewise, a lot of artists and intellectuals from Québec or English Canada emigrated to Bangor or around there, supposedly to create a freer society. Were you familiar with that movement?

MARGARET ATWOOD

No. But I know that after the 1837 Rebellion a lot of people from Toronto and Ontario fled to the United States.

VICTOR-LÉVY BEAULIEU

I'd like to go back to *The Handmaid's Tale*. In that book, Offred navigates between two worlds. That's how the novel is structured. At night, she dreams, thinks about her past, and remembers the Old World. During the day, she's forced to live in the New World that has been imposed on her. In the Old World, women had freedom and pleasure in being together and having friendships. It was a struggle, but one that took place in relative harmony. But don't you think that the world before the catastrophe, before the *coup d'état* that brought in this totalitarian power, is a little idyllic as recounted by Offred, considering what goes on in society today? It seems to me that her view of the past is a little rosy, not nearly as dark as some feminists saw it.

There's time to spare. This is one of the things I wasn't prepared for – the amount of unfilled time, the long parentheses of nothing. Time as white sound. If only I could embroider. Weave, knit, something to do with my hands. I want a cigarette. I remember walking in art galleries, through the nineteenth century: the obsession they had then with harems. Dozens of paintings of harems, fat women lolling on divans, turbans on their heads or velvet caps, being fanned with peacock tails, a eunuch in the background standing guard. Studies of sedentary flesh, painted by men who'd never been there. These pictures were supposed to be erotic, and I thought they were, at the time; but I see now what they were really about. They were paintings about suspended animation; about waiting, about objects not in use. They were paintings about boredom.

– Margaret Atwood
The Handmaid's Tale

MARGARET ATWOOD

No, because totalitarian governments like that always come out of difficult conditions. When you have very hard conditions, you propose solutions. If you're a dictator, those solutions always involve a loss of freedom – but they are solutions. Like Hitler. "Conditions are very tough. Here's the solution. But you have to do exactly as I say." The period before the catastrophe was a period of freedom, yes, but also a period of difficult conditions, even for women. There were a lot of rapes, a lot of criminality, unstable economic conditions, a lot of pornography – and some feminists even in our time have tried to outlaw pornography. And that's a debate that's still going on. If you defend pornography, you defend freedom. But you always have to choose between freedom and certain very difficult conditions, including the loss of freedom imposed by dictatorships. We're all in search of a balance between the two.

VICTOR-LÉVY BEAULIEU

In prison, Offred comes to miss the time when the most important things, as she says, were precisely the ones that seemed the least important – for example, being Luke's wife, being a mother, enjoying the little pleasures, leading an almost suburban life. Obviously, in her situation, as a virtual prisoner, all those little moments of her previous life seem magical to her and she's nostalgic for them. She feels this way because she's deprived of almost everything, particularly her sensuality. It seems to me that Offred rediscovers her sensuality thanks to the Commander, who invites her into his office. That's a beautiful scene in the novel. At first they're happy just to play Scrabble, like children, and then to read some passages from a book, because books are forbidden in the new republic. Then they go on to necking, as if they were teenagers. It's as if the character went from a state of regression, from childhood to adolescence, then to that love – no, not love, because love too is forbidden there, but to intimacy, and to defiance, because of the fact that Offred is with a man she has no right to be with. They are transgressing a taboo, a new taboo of this new society. That to me is the essence of the whole novel. Every society is based on taboos. A society desires something and, to obtain that thing, it prevents some other thing from happening. That's what we call a taboo. I would like you to talk about taboos in *The Handmaid's Tale*, and the importance you place on breaking taboos. And the difficulty her new situation represents for a woman like Offred.

MARGARET ATWOOD

One thing at a time! (Laughs.) First, taboos. This novel is closely based on history and reality. The details are all real. That is to say, there have been times when men did things exactly that way. The rules of dress. The kidnapped children – in Argentina, for example. And during the war, the Germans stole blond Polish children to raise them as good Aryans. This concern is very, very old.

VICTOR-LÉVY BEAULIEU
And the experience in Romania.

MARGARET ATWOOD
And slavery in the United States. Slaves were forbidden to read. And the education of women, for centuries – either reading in general was forbidden, or the reading of certain things. Reading the Bible was forbidden for centuries, not only to women but to all lay persons. There are all sorts of false justifications.

Take birth control in Romania, for example. When you have a dictatorship, it tries to control everything, even love, even reproduction. Absolutely everything. To regulate reproduction, they try to control the activities of women, to decide who will have the power to reproduce and when. In the novel, extreme pollution has made people sterile. This is a contemporary problem. Fertility, especially among men, is on the decline because of all the chemicals we eat and breathe. Utopias and dystopias always address the societies of their time. But with a taboo comes the desire to transgress that taboo, because humans by definition are transgressive creatures. I think this is because we have two eyes, two hands, two lobes of the brain. A statement is made and it's impossible for us not to think the opposite. (Laughs.) So naturally taboos are accompanied by transgressions. My novel is also based on my reading of accounts by people in concentration camps during the war. It is to the prisoner's advantage that the structure of oppression is made up of corruptible people. Otherwise, the prison environment will be extremely strict and the chances of survival very poor.

VICTOR-LÉVY BEAULIEU
The atmosphere the novel describes is absolutely inhuman, intolerable. That total absence of pleasure, of desire. It's as if people were murdering themselves day after day. And with no safety valve, things can only explode.

My presence here is illegal. It's forbidden for us to be alone with the Commanders. We are for breeding purposes: we aren't concubines, geisha girls, courtesans. On the contrary: everything possible has been done to remove us from that category. There is supposed to be nothing entertaining about us, no room is to be permitted for the flowering of secret lusts; no special favours are to be wheedled, by them or us, there are to be no toeholds for love. We are two-legged wombs, that's all: sacred vessels, ambulatory chalices.

So why does he want to see me, at night, alone?

If I'm caught, it's to Serena's tender mercies I'll be delivered. He isn't supposed to meddle in such household discipline, that's women's business. After that, reclassification. I could become an Unwoman.

But to refuse to see him could be worse. There's no doubt about who holds the real power.

– Margaret Atwood
The Handmaid's Tale

MARGARET ATWOOD

A true dictatorship is a pyramid. The people that hold the power have all the pleasures. They believe in their value, but reserve them exclusively for themselves. That explains the very strict rules concerning sex. There's a secret house in the novel, where women play the forbidden roles. But only the men in power have access to it, not the others. In this type of structure, men don't have all the power and women none – in a true dictatorship most men also lack power. They too are very regimented, very controlled. The story in my novel is told by a woman, but a man without power talking about the same society would describe the same suffering, the same absence of pleasure.

VICTOR-LÉVY BEAULIEU

In the Soviet gulag described by Solzhenitsyn, men have no more pleasure or desire than women do in the world you describe, because there, too, the power was controlled by the few, who appropriated all privileges, including sexuality, reading, money.

MARGARET ATWOOD

In the West today we live in a kind of pyramid. At the bottom of the pyramid are the poor, who have very little. The middle of the pyramid is bigger than it once was, and at the top those who hold the power are more numerous than they were. But it's still a pyramid.

VICTOR-LÉVY BEAULIEU

But in our pyramid, you can still move from one level to another. It's still possible to move either towards the top or towards the bottom. Movement is possible. Whereas in the totalitarian societies you're describing . . .

MARGARET ATWOOD

In the society I described in the novel, all I did was apply what the funda-mentalists say they will do when they hold the power. They've said they would do all those things – keep women in the home doing the housework and having children. It's their dream!

VICTOR-LÉVY BEAULIEU

There's a character who I think is very important in *The Handmaid's Tale*, and that's Lydia, who is the narrator's aunt and the "fairy godmother" of feminism before the catastrophe. But when the new totalitarian society is established in the republic, Aunt Lydia, surprisingly, goes over to the enemy. It's she who chairs the meetings where women are put on trial for breaking the new laws made for the benefit of the men. Did you mean to show through the character of Lydia that there's an unconscious or poten-tial traitor within every feminist?

MARGARET ATWOOD

No. That character is based on the history of imperialisms. For example, the British in India raised an army of Indians to control the rest of the Indians. All good imperialists have done this kind of thing. So, if you want to control women, you have to grant some women a tiny bit more power so that they'll control the others. It's not a question of her ideology changing, but you have a situation where those in control say: "You've got all these problems. We have the solution. We'll take care of everything."

VICTOR-LÉVY BEAULIEU

The end of *The Handmaid's Tale* is a bit elusive – like several other of your novels. Although the characters have gone through their situation, things are still unresolved. You don't really know where they're going. This is the case of the narrator in *Surfacing*, who, after her quest for her father in the North and her discovery of him drowned with his camera around his neck, remains in a state of indecision. You don't know where she'll go or what she'll do or what will become of her. There are no clues. It's the same thing in *The Handmaid's Tale*. At the end of the book, Offred, because she has broken the laws, gets into a van and disappears, but we don't know if she's going to her death, like a lot of her friends who were hanged by the dictatorship, or to freedom, maybe in Canada, a possibility that is alluded to. I would have liked to know if Offred finally falls into the hands of the executioners, or if she escapes. Did you have a specific purpose in leaving me, the reader, in doubt, or did it just come out that way?

MARGARET ATWOOD

I think that's characteristic of the writers of our time. I've noticed that you do the same thing at the end of your novels.

VICTOR-LÉVY BEAULIEU

I didn't want you to remind me of it!

MARGARET ATWOOD

It's very difficult now to end a novel. It used to be, particularly in nineteenth-century novels about women, that you could end a novel with a wedding. But that isn't credible any more, because everyone knows that marriage isn't paradise and, besides, it's only a beginning. So, if you want to end purely and simply with an event, you have to do it with a death. But I'm an optimist; I don't kill my heroines. Maybe I'll start! (Laughs.) But it's also like history. In history, you've got events and you've got characters, and from time to time those characters disappear. In a way, I created a historical character.

VICTOR-LÉVY BEAULIEU

The Handmaid's Tale is considered one of the great literary successes of the eighties in Canada, the United States, and Britain. What does that represent in sales? Do you know?

MARGARET ATWOOD

Oh my goodness, I'd have to add it up. [Pause.] About two million, six hundred thousand, in English. But there was a film made from it. A serious film. That sells more copies of a novel.

As I'm standing up I hear the black van. I hear it before I see it; blended with the twilight, it appears out of its own sound like a solidification, a clotting of the night. It turns into the driveway, stops. I can just make out the white eye, the two wings. The paint must be phosphorescent. Two men detach themselves from the shape of it, come up the front steps, ring the bell. I hear the bell toll, ding-dong, like the ghost of a cosmetics woman, down in the hall.

Worse is coming, then.

I've been wasting my time. I should have taken things into my own hands while I had the chance. I should have stolen a knife from the kitchen, found some way to the sewing scissors. There were the garden shears, the knitting needles; the world is full of weapons if you're looking for them. I should have paid attention.

But it's too late to think about that now, already their feet are on the dusty-rose carpeting of the stairs; a heavy muted tread, pulse in the forehead. My back's to the window.

– Margaret Atwood
The Handmaid's Tale

VICTOR-LÉVY BEAULIEU

The Handmaid's Tale was adapted for the screen by Harold Pinter, and the film directed by Volker Schlöndorff. How did that come about?

MARGARET ATWOOD

We had the choice between a director from the East Coast and one from the West Coast. We opted for the director from the East Coast, because he was the one that had the idea of getting Harold Pinter. With that kind of subject there's a danger of making an exploitation film, really weird, with whips, and so on. There's a risk of falling into pornography. I felt we had to avoid that. Even then, after the film was made, some of the advertising had a pornographic aspect. But the film company doesn't control the advertising in every country; the distributor does.

VICTOR-LÉVY BEAULIEU
You knew Harold Pinter?

MARGARET ATWOOD
Not before the film. But I knew his plays. He started out as a playwright when I was a student. So I saw a lot of his plays.

VICTOR-LÉVY BEAULIEU
What was your relationship with him like?

MARGARET ATWOOD
I prefer to leave everything to do with the film to the filmmakers. I was a consultant, because I'm the expert on that period of history. (Laughs.)

VICTOR-LÉVY BEAULIEU
Did you get along well with Pinter?

MARGARET ATWOOD
Yes, quite well.

VICTOR-LÉVY BEAULIEU
And how many months did it take him to write the screenplay?

MARGARET ATWOOD
Many months. Usually it takes at least a year to write a script and revise it. And it was a very, very difficult film to make, because it's a tough subject for the people with the money. It's not a cop movie. They tried to add a bit of that, but still . . . And the philosophy of the plot is difficult. It's controversial and there's a danger of conflict.

VICTOR-LÉVY BEAULIEU
And how did it go with Schlöndorff? Did you know him before?

MARGARET ATWOOD
No. I work in my little room. I never go out. (Laughs.)

VICTOR-LÉVY BEAULIEU
During production, did you meet with Schlöndorff?

MARGARET ATWOOD
Yes. And I visited the set. I said hello to Faye Dunaway, and to Natasha Richardson, who played Offred. I saw the house. But I was only there one day, because it's stressful for the actors when the author is there.

VICTOR-LÉVY BEAULIEU
Why? Does it give them stage fright?

MARGARET ATWOOD
They're anxious. "Am I doing what the author wants?" And authors have a reputation for hating films based on their works.

VICTOR-LÉVY BEAULIEU
Yes. So when you saw the film, what did you think of it?

MARGARET ATWOOD
They avoided pornography. (Laughs.) It's a very strong, disturbing film. But the ending was changed. It's more optimistic than the book. The end of the film shows the woman in a van, very visible from the helicopters.

VICTOR-LÉVY BEAULIEU
Did this first experience with Pinter and Schlöndorff make you want to write for the movies?

MARGARET ATWOOD
I beg your pardon. It wasn't my first experience.

VICTOR-LÉVY BEAULIEU
There'd been a play, I think, long before, on the same subject.

MARGARET ATWOOD
Let me explain. (Laughs.) I wrote my first screenplay, for *The Edible Woman*, in 1971 with Tony Richardson, in France. The film wasn't made, but writing the screenplay was very interesting. Afterwards, I continued script-writing with a few pieces for television. I wrote a screenplay of *Surfacing*, which was filmed [in 1981], but not using my script. The director was Claude Jutra. I think poor Claude was already becoming sick, but no one knew it. I met a man that had been there during the filming and I asked him if he'd noticed any signs. He said, "Yes, but we thought maybe he was taking drugs or something like that." I think that affected the film.

VICTOR-LÉVY BEAULIEU
Was that movie made for television?

Karen's mother was sitting in a rocking chair beside the window, looking exhausted. Her linen outfit was all creased. She had her shoes off and was fanning herself with her hat, but when the pig came into the room she gave a slight scream.

"It's okay, she's house-broken," said the grandmother.

"That is the limit," said Karen's mother, in a tight, furious voice.

"Cleaner than most people," said the grandmother. "Smarter, too. Anyways, this is my house. You can do what you like in yours. I didn't ask you to come here and I won't ask you to leave, but while you're here you can take things as you find them."

She scratched the pig behind the ears and gave it a slap on the rump, and it grunted gently and squinted up at her and then went over and flopped down sideways on the afghan. Karen's mother burst into tears and scrambled out of her chair, and headed out of the room in her stocking feet, with her white gloves crushed to her eyes. Karen's grandmother laughed.

– Margaret Atwood
The Robber Bride

Graeme Gibson

Alliston, 1976

MARGARET ATWOOD

No, it was made for the theatres. After that, I wrote some scripts for television and for the movies. But now I don't write scripts, because it's tedious and I'm too old. (Laughs.)

VICTOR-LÉVY BEAULIEU

Is it that it's tedious, or that they take too long to write?

MARGARET ATWOOD

Film is kind of summer camp for adults. You're with a group. If you like the group, it's very pleasant; otherwise, it's a nightmare. You have a lot of interaction with all sorts of people. Anyway, the script is only the beginning, because after that all sorts of other factors come into play. With movies, you're not the controlling factor. You're simply the very disposable writer. They can throw all your favourite scenes – what you think is the best part of the work – in the garbage.

VICTOR-LÉVY BEAULIEU

That must be frustrating.

MARGARET ATWOOD

If you're a megalomaniac, it is. And I think novelists are basically megalomaniacs. They want to control everything. It was very interesting to work that way, but I have no desire to do it any more.

VICTOR-LÉVY BEAULIEU

We've already discussed *Cat's Eye*, which I feel is your best novel. To me it's your masterpiece. You've made a definitive statement about childhood. But *Cat's Eye* isn't just a great novel on childhood and relationships between girls. A big part of it is about relationships between women, and between women and men. Elaine is a painter, and she comes back to Toronto for the opening of an exhibition of her paintings. This gives her a chance to look at her life as an artist and, especially, as a woman – which hasn't been totally happy. Right at the beginning, Elaine says she feels useless, that everything she does is of no value in her eyes. Why does Elaine say that?

MARGARET ATWOOD

She's an artist. All artists feel that from time to time.

VICTOR-LÉVY BEAULIEU

Elaine has had two men in her life. The Hungarian Josef, who's also an artist but who works in film, leaves Toronto to try his luck in the United States, because he says Toronto has no *joie de vivre* or soul. In a way, Josef introduces Elaine to life and to culture. Then John comes into the picture, and Elaine thinks, "Two men are better than one. I tell myself I'm in love with both and I avoid having to choose." John is a painter. What he offers Elaine is escape, pleasure, disorder, and discord. For him, there are two kinds of women, intelligent ones and stupid ones. Basically, aside from painting, John isn't good for much. He's not a great lover or a great father, and he almost never has anything to say. To me, he's just a bore. Why did Elaine live with him and have a child with him? Could it be that within the artist is a woman who's kind of sentimental?

MARGARET ATWOOD

Why? Fidelity was obligatory in the fifties and sixties, before feminism. You're too young to remember those days, Victor-Lévy. It was normal then for women to think their situation was abnormal if they were not married. What choice did they have? There weren't many women artists, because it was also normal to look down on women, especially if they were artists. So what choice did Elaine have? To live alone or to live with a man – and what man, a dentist maybe? If you lived with another artist, you were inevitably despised, as a woman and as a woman artist. In that respect the novel is very faithful to the time it describes. Now there are a lot of other choices. And men have changed. But in the early sixties, during the Beatnik period, it was fashionable to consider men the creators and women toys, supporting players. If you talk to women painters, you hear stories like that. The question is not why she didn't choose the perfect man. Does such a thing exist? Perhaps it's no longer so, but in those days a man didn't consider himself a man if he wasn't what he might consider assertive, what others might consider abusive. See, for instance, Donleavy's *Ginger Man*, or even Kerouac's attitudes towards women. You were a man or a mouse. If you were a man, you necessarily had to oppress women.

VICTOR-LÉVY BEAULIEU

At the end of the book, Elaine, instead of rebelling against men, throwing her lover out or taking another lover, or becoming a lesbian even, just remains apathetic. Why?

MARGARET ATWOOD

At the end of the novel, Elaine has been married for several years, to a third man who isn't part of the story. But at the beginning, you know she's married. She has two daughters. She lives in Vancouver. She has a normal life. But inside, she's still depressed, because she hasn't resolved certain things in her past.

VICTOR-LÉVY BEAULIEU

That's what I was going to say. When the novel ends, her story isn't resolved. She's dealt with a number of things, especially after her suicide attempt, but she's still not out of the woods.

MARGARET ATWOOD

The resolution of that novel is connected to her relationship with Cordelia, not to her relationships with men.

VICTOR-LÉVY BEAULIEU

It's like what happens in *The Robber Bride*, which came after *Cat's Eye*. That book aroused some controversy in feminist and other quarters. For those who haven't read it yet, let's say that it tells the story of three women who are victims of a fourth woman. One after the other, Zenia steals the husbands of Tony, Charis, and Roz. All three women have had other men in their lives, but far in the past. For one of them, her father was a womanizer and mostly absent; for another, men are represented by a perverted uncle who abused her when she was little. Tony, Charis, and Roz grew up, got married, had children, had lovers. But their husbands and their lovers are no Rudolph Valentinos or Sylvester Stallones. They're weak, sentimental, a bit mediocre – or let's say ordinary – with a macho streak that leads them to succumb to Zenia's advances without really even meaning to. They're too cowardly to refuse and not brave enough to really say yes. They make it into something of little consequence. The three women, on the other hand, end up with a deadly hatred for Zenia, who they see as a double agent with a completely Byzantine concept of pleasure. I find Zenia fascinating. I find her an absolutely wonderful character. I'd like you to talk a bit about her. When you were writing the novel, what exactly did Zenia represent to you?

Zenia has stolen something from him, the one thing he always kept safe before, from all women, even from Roz. Call it his soul. She slipped it out of his breast pocket when he wasn't looking, easy as rolling a drunk, and looked at it, and bit it to see if it was genuine, and sneered at it for being so small after all, and then tossed it away, because she's the kind of woman who wants what she doesn't have and gets what she wants and then despises what she gets.

What is her secret? How does she do it? Where does it come from, her undeniable power over men? How does she latch hold of them, break their stride, trip them up, and then so easily turn them inside out? It must be something very simple and obvious. She tells them they're unique, then reveals to them that they're not. She opens her cloak with the secret pockets and shows them how the magic trick is worked, and that it is after all nothing more than a trick. Only by that time they refuse to see; they think the Water of Youth is real, even though she empties the bottle and fills it again from the tap, right before their very eyes. They want to believe.

– Margaret Atwood
The Robber Bride

MARGARET ATWOOD

Zenia is the return of the *femme fatale*. And the *femme fatale* is an arche-type that has endured for a very, very long time and that has been impor-tant, for men but also for women, because the *femme fatale* has power. And if you're a nice, good, innocent woman who tries to do everything you're supposed to, you don't have power. Power is always power for evil and for good. You have the choice. But without power, there is no active role. The character of Zenia is exaggerated, because she's seen only through the eyes of others. And there are two kinds of people in life you exaggerate: people you love and people you hate. Those three women feel a kind of love-hate for Zenia. They begin with friendship, then Zenia betrays all three of them in different ways, and they end up hating her. But Zenia remains an object of fascination. She's a mythic figure, a deity who plays all kinds of tricks, like Mercury or characters in American Indian legends. She's a sort of juggler, a magician, and she's a big liar. She gives three versions of her life, and each one is false, but we don't know it. With a liar like that, you never know whether she's telling the truth. I was very interested in this figure who plays tricks, because, in mythology, she's also the messenger of the gods. Zenia has messages to give to those three women. She's a kind of teacher. You're not the same after an encounter with Zenia; she changes your life. And from the point of view of writing, figures like these are absolutely necessary. Without a god who plays tricks, you don't have a novel, you don't have a story, you don't have unexpected events or elements of chance.

VICTOR-LÉVY BEAULIEU
You don't have myth.

MARGARET ATWOOD
That's right.

VICTOR-LÉVY BEAULIEU
In *The Robber Bride*, Tony is an expert on the study of war. What do you see as the relationship between war and feminism?

MARGARET ATWOOD
The four women in the novel were born just before or during the war. All their parents, especially the fathers, were killed or damaged or traumatized by the war. That was the experience of that generation. We all know people who went to war. Our lives were changed by it, even with respect to food. Tony places that war in the very broad perspective of war in general. What is war but the story of theft? You heard the news from Chechnya? The soldiers would come into your house and take what they wanted. And if you objected, *bang!* they'd kill you. It's piracy. You must have read about all those paintings stolen first by the Germans and then by the Russians. Now there's a lot of discussion as to who those stolen paintings really belong to.

Zenia is also a goddess of war. She takes what she wants. She's a kind of soldier, a pirate. She has no respect for the rules; she always breaks them.

VICTOR-LÉVY BEAULIEU
But there's another type of character who's a mystic and who ends up committing suicide. It was surely on purpose that you made Charis a mystic.

MARGARET ATWOOD
Have you spoken to any New Age mystics?

VICTOR-LÉVY BEAULIEU
Not that much, I must admit.

MARGARET ATWOOD
These New Age mystics are looking for ways to make life more pleasant, more bearable. But if your life is already pleasant and bearable, you don't need them. A Zenia knocks on your door and you open it and she says, "Hello, I'm Zenia. I would like to come into your life and completely destroy it." You answer, "No, thank you, goodbye," and you close the door. Those three women have a weakness in their character. Without this opening, Zenia would not have been able to get in. I had to construct each character so that there was a door in her character that opened up and let Zenia in.

But ping-pong is a diversion. Tony's real game is off in a corner, beside the tiny refrigerator they keep down there for ice-water and West's beer. It's a large sand-table, bought at a daycare-centre garage sale some years ago, but it isn't full of sand. Instead it contains a three-dimensional map of Europe and the Mediterranean, made of hardened flour-and-salt paste, with the mountain ranges in relief and the major bodies of water done in blue Plasticine. Tony has been able to use this map over and over, adding and subtracting canals, removing marshes, altering coastlines, building and unbuilding roads and bridges and towns and cities, diverting rivers, as occasion has demanded. Right now it's set up for the tenth century: the day of Otto the Red's fateful battle, to be exact.

For the armies and the populations, Tony doesn't use pins or flags, not primarily. Instead she uses kitchen spices, a different one for each tribe or ethnic grouping: cloves for the Germanic tribes, red peppercorns for the Vikings, green peppercorns for the Saracens, white ones for the Slavs. The Celts are coriander seeds, the Anglo-Saxons are dill. Chocolate sprinkles, cardamom seeds, four kinds of lentils, and little silver balls indicate the Magyars, the Greeks, the North African kingdoms, and the Egyptians. For each major king, chief, emperor, or pope, there's a Monopoly man; areas in which each has sovereignty, actual or nominal, are marked by lengths of cut-up plastic swizzle stick, in matching colours, stuck into squares of gum eraser.

It's a complex system, but she prefers it to more schematic representations or to ones that show the armies and the strongholds only. With it she can depict interbreeding and hybridization, through conquest or through the slave trade, because populations are not in fact homogeneous blocks, but mixtures.

— Margaret Atwood
The Robber Bride

VICTOR-LÉVY BEAULIEU

You can see that flaw in Tony and in Charis, but with Roz it's a bit different. She's a rich businesswoman and she doesn't function as Charis and Tony do. It's true she works in a world that's still completely dominated by men, because men still hold the economic power. I was intrigued and fascinated by the relationships of a working woman with a man's problems in a world of women, the connections between the world of business and that of women as such. How exactly does Roz see them?

MARGARET ATWOOD

Why does Roz let Zenia into her life? Roz also has her weaknesses, in her past and also in her present, because she has a husband who's a skirt-chaser. In England they say, "He has problems keeping it in his pants"! (Laughs.) Roz is quite aggressive. Zenia presents a challenge, a problem that Roz thinks she alone can solve. Zenia also presents a temptation to each of these women. For Tony it's intellectual, for Charis it's spiritual, for Roz it's more practical. And Zenia tailors her lies to each of them.

VICTOR-LÉVY BEAULIEU
In literature written by women so far, at least in what I've read, there's little mention of hostility between women. Their solidarity is emphasized. What's new in *The Robber Bride* is how that solidarity disintegrates whenever Zenia shows up.

MARGARET ATWOOD
Oh, but think about it! The three women have a lot of solidarity. They help each other. But there are pirates among women as there are among men. The idea that women are angels, that they're not mean, is very nineteenth-century: women are either angels or devils. Women are human beings, therefore a mixture. It's just as inappropriate to talk about "Woman" with a capital *W* as about "Man" with a capital *M*. You're Victor-Lévy, I hope, not "Man"!

VICTOR-LÉVY BEAULIEU
I hope so too!

MARGARET ATWOOD
Zenia is not the universal woman. She has a personality that can be described, she isn't representative of all women.

VICTOR-LÉVY BEAULIEU
Tony and Roz would like to eliminate Zenia; they even consider murdering her. At one point we know they're ready to do it and take responsibility for it. And surprise! Zenia is found dead. She's fallen into a fountain from the balcony of her hotel room. We don't know if she died of an overdose or if someone killed her.

MARGARET ATWOOD
There are six possibilities. You pick!

VICTOR-LÉVY BEAULIEU

Instead of choosing one, I'll ask you a question. Is there a limit that a woman – author or character – can't go beyond? Murder? In a novel written by a man, the guy would probably kill the woman. It's part of male logic. But here, they plot to commit a murder, they almost plan it, they prepare to carry it out, and surprise! the murder has already occurred, or the suicide – we don't know which. I would like to hear what you have to say on that difference.

MARGARET ATWOOD

Each of the three women thinks she wants to, and can, commit murder. But when the time comes, I don't think they're capable of it. Each one had time to carry out the plot. Each one thinks the other two committed the murder, and tries to protect her friends.

VICTOR-LÉVY BEAULIEU

It could also have been Roz's son. As I recall, Zenia found him quite attractive.

MARGARET ATWOOD

There are other possibilities as well. But it's not up to me to decide for you.

VICTOR-LÉVY BEAULIEU

You wanted to write an interactive novel?

MARGARET ATWOOD

All novels are. Reading is the most interactive medium there is. They used electrodes to measure electrical activity in the brain while people watched a movie, read, and watched television. Television, almost nothing. Radio, more. Movies, more still. But it's during reading that the brain is the most electrified. Why? Because the reader has to imagine the music, the setting, the costumes . . .

VICTOR-LÉVY BEAULIEU

The imagery is your own when you read.

MARGARET ATWOOD

The words propose, and the reader's imagination disposes. Radio is very interactive. Before the age of television, a lot of children were terrified by radio. Like the program "Inner Sanctum," which was horror stories. You'd listen to the little noises, the door opening, the footsteps approaching.

VICTOR-LÉVY BEAULIEU
And the sound of chains!

MARGARET ATWOOD
Yes. And your heart would start beating quickly. After it, the children all went to sleep with their heads under the covers. It was terrifying, especially when you were alone at home.

My back is on the sand, my head rests against the rock, innocent as plankton; my hair spreads out, moving and fluid in the water. The earth rotates, holding my body down to it as it holds the moon; the sun pounds in the sky, red flames and rays pulsing from it, searing away the wrong form that encases me, dry rain soaking through me, warming the blood egg I carry. I dip my head beneath the water, washing my eyes.

Inshore a loon; it lowers its head, then lifts it again and calls. It sees me but it ignores me, accepts me as part of the land.

When I am clean I come up out of the lake, leaving my false body floated on the surface, a cloth decoy; it jiggles in the waves I make, nudges gently against the dock.

— Margaret Atwood
Surfacing

VICTOR-LÉVY BEAULIEU
Let's go back to the ending of *The Robber Bride*. I really like the last scene. You wrote:

"'Okay,' she says to Charis, and Charis thrusts both arms and both hands and the flower vase straight out from her body, over the railing, and there is a sharp crack, and the vase splits in two. Charis gives a little shriek and pulls her hands back as if they've been burned. She looks at them: there's a slight blue tinge, a flickering. The pieces of the vase splash into the water, and Zenia trails off in a wavering drift, like smoke.

"'Holy Moly!' says Roz. 'What did that?'

"'I think she hit it on the railing,' says Tony.

"'No,' says Charis in a hushed voice. 'It cracked by itself. It was her. Entities can cause things like that, they can affect physical objects; they do it to get your attention.'

"Nothing Roz or Tony is likely to say will change her mind, so they say nothing. Charis herself is oddly comforted. It pleases her that Zenia would attend her own scattering. It's a token of her continuation. Zenia will now be free, to be reborn for another chance at life. Maybe she will be more fortunate next time."

That's the scene when they throw Zenia's ashes into the waters of Lake Ontario, and you have them wonder how to go about it: do they throw just the ashes, or do they break the vase the ashes are in?

You're fascinated by water. You talk about it in all your novels. *Surfacing* ends with a water scene that's similar, but at the same time very different. In *Cat's Eye*, the little girl falls into the water at the bottom of a ravine. When I read *The Robber Bride*, I wondered: Why did you have them throw Zenia's ashes into the water and why remove them from the vase and scatter them?

MARGARET ATWOOD

The water was my idea, and it's also a reality. The northern part of North America is a landscape of water. When you look at the map, you see a lot of water. There are three archetypal deaths in this landscape: you freeze, you get eaten by a bear, or you drown. The death of a character should be archetypal. Zenia was a kind of siren, and the element of sirens is water. Why scatter her ashes like that? That's a little obscure. Have you seen a lot of vampire movies?

VICTOR-LÉVY BEAULIEU

Not that many, no. They scare me.

MARGARET ATWOOD

But you have to! (Laughs.) At the end of a lot of vampire movies, the vampire is burned and its ashes are scattered. In a Christopher Lee movie, you know that, after a certain amount of time, the ashes of the vampire will come back together and form the vampire again. That's the image I wanted to create. Zenia, too, is a vampire. A siren and a vampire. I wanted her that way also because of ghost stories. There are a lot of them in English and English-Canadian literature. I've talked to some Québécois about this, and they tell me they don't have a lot of ghosts, and nor does France. Maybe they were all killed during the French Revolution! One of the qualities of ghosts is that they can break things. Charis thinks it's Zenia who breaks the vase containing the ashes. The others think Charis accidentally threw the vase against the boat. The possibility remains that the ghost of Zenia is living among us. Zenia is an archetype, and archetypes are eternal. Everything can be explained. No mysteries! I have to say, too, that Lake Ontario is now so poisoned that all the fish in it are blind. Poisoned water for Zenia, the vessel of poison.

VICTOR-LÉVY BEAULIEU

Will she return once her ashes are reassembled?

MARGARET ATWOOD

One hopes so. I've received a lot of letters asking me if Zenia has disappeared for good or if she's going to come back.

VICTOR-LÉVY BEAULIEU

To what do you attribute this question? To the fact that people were fascinated by the character?

MARGARET ATWOOD

I propose to write a sequel, *Son of Zenia*. (Laughs.) I've been asked for another story about Zenia. It's like that with some characters. Readers want to know more about them.

VICTOR-LÉVY BEAULIEU

You finished *The Robber Bride* a while ago. I know you've been working on something else since. When I finish a book and publish it, I'm always astonished by people I meet or by journalists who ask, "Are you working on another novel?"

MARGARET ATWOOD
It's just to make conversation.

VICTOR-LÉVY BEAULIEU
No doubt. But it seems obvious to me that, since I'm a writer, I'm always working on a new book, however long it takes me to finish it. You must get asked the same question. What are you working on now?

MARGARET ATWOOD
I'm at page two hundred and twenty-five of another novel. The only thing I can say is that the action of this novel is set before the middle of the nineteenth century. I never give details of what I'm working on. I'm superstitious.

VICTOR-LÉVY BEAULIEU
Does the story take place in Canada?

MARGARET ATWOOD
Yes, but it wasn't yet Canada at the time. It was pre-Canada. Prehistory.

VICTOR-LÉVY BEAULIEU
Was it better then?

MARGARET ATWOOD
From the point of view of the sanitary conditions, no. (Laughs.) From the point of view of diseases, people died like flies in epidemics. But you'll see when I'm finished.

VICTOR-LÉVY BEAULIEU
In the meantime, can I at least know how you write?

MARGARET ATWOOD
Usually on pads of yellow paper, with a black pen that glides easily. And I

make a lot of notations. I write a lot of pages. After it's well under way, I sometimes continue on the computer. And I write from nine in the morning till one in the afternoon. After that, I'm free. I require a certain number of pages from myself each day. In the beginning, I wait and think a lot, I don't write. But when I start writing, I do it very, very quickly. When I get to the end, there's a lot to redo, to rearrange, because, when you start, you don't know exactly what it will be. So it's sometimes necessary to redo the beginning.

VICTOR-LÉVY BEAULIEU

I think it's important for you to find the right beginning.

MARGARET ATWOOD

I've started several novels that I didn't finish because I started out on the wrong track with them. You have to place yourself, think, reflect. But you know all that. It's true for most writers, I think.

VICTOR-LÉVY BEAULIEU

Yes, but there are some who work very differently. Some write the first sentence and go all the way to the end almost without stopping, without crossing anything out. [The French writer] Le Clézio claims to write this way. Other writers amass piles of notes beforehand. Their descriptions of characters almost make up a bible. Hubert Aquin would first conceive the structure of his novel, laying it all out and preparing it, and then he would bring his characters into the structure, so to speak. There are different ways of working. Writers find their novels as they write. What do you start from when you write a novel? A situation? A character?

MARGARET ATWOOD

Usually from a situation, from a voice. I hear this voice, and I imagine situations with different characters. With the novel I'm working on, I'd been thinking about the subject for twenty years and looking for the way to do it. I finally found it. I tried a few other paths without success. But for me, that's normal. I thought about *Cat's Eye* for twenty-five years before starting it.

VICTOR-LÉVY BEAULIEU

Does carrying a book in yourself like that for two, five, ten years before writing it affect your relationships with the rest of the world, your husband, your children?

MARGARET ATWOOD

When you write, you lead a double life, yours and that of the characters you're creating. Sometimes you're distracted. Fortunately, my husband is also a writer, and he understands. Besides, he's more forgetful than I am.

VICTOR-LÉVY BEAULIEU

You're a writer who's famous all over the world. What effect does that have on you?

MARGARET ATWOOD

It's not exactly like being Elizabeth Taylor. You can be a famous novelist more privately. There are no mobs waiting at my door, trying to tear off pieces of my clothing. It's not like being Madonna. You get a lot of letters, and you answer them. I have to say, too, that in Canada you're not allowed to get too much of a swelled head. If you do, someone will burst it for you. (Laughs.)

VICTOR-LÉVY BEAULIEU

Your works have been translated into more than thirty languages. There must be some constraints attached to this literary glory. I'm thinking, for example, of relationships with a large number of publishers, invitations to conferences, promotional activities. You're forced to really manage your books and your time. I wonder how you're able to do it all while still writing, and writing as intensely as you do.

MARGARET ATWOOD

I arrange my time in blocks: one little block for all that, and the rest for writing. Fortunately, I have a very good assistant, who works wonders for me. I look after the writing, and she takes care of an astonishing number of other things. Otherwise, it would be unbearable. There are only twenty-four hours in a day, unfortunately. I've tried to change that, but without success. (Laughs.)

VICTOR-LÉVY BEAULIEU

In 1972, you published *Survival*, a guide to Canadian literature. It seems to me that that book is an essential part of your work. In *Survival*, you demonstrate not only the existence, the necessity, and the originality of Canadian literature, but also its importance. When that book was published, there was very little discussion or teaching, and in fact hardly any distribution, of Canadian literature in Canada. Hence the title of the book. What was your purpose when you wrote that book?

MARGARET ATWOOD

I was working with a very small publishing house, House of Anansi. Anansi is the name of an African god, a juggler who plays tricks. I think it's also the case in Québec that young writers have to go to small publishers to get their first books published. In order to survive financially, Anansi had published a series of guides, including one on the law, which showed how to write your own contracts, and one on venereal disease. With my colleague Dennis Lee, I proposed to do a little guide, sort of a VD guide to Canadian literature. That didn't exist then. There were two or three books written by professors and read by professors, but, for the general public, there was absolutely nothing – nothing systematic anyway. The writers had begun to become known – Lee, Leonard Cohen, Mordecai Richler, Margaret Laurence – but there was still almost no criticism. The post-colonial attitude was: "No, Canadian literature does not exist. It's a secondary literature, not important." So I proposed this guide of about a hundred pages. But with Dennis Lee involved the project got bigger. The purpose was to establish, one, that Canadian literature existed, and two, that it was different from English and American literature. The content and the approach were different, since it is logical to assume that, if a country is different, its literature will be, too. We thought we would sell two or three thousand copies, but it was a huge success. It sold a hundred thousand copies. The general public in Canada had been unaware that there was a Canadian literature; their teachers had told them there was nothing except for Stephen Leacock. This was a big discovery, and it gave rise to a lot of interest. On the one hand, the book was praised, and on the other, it was violently attacked. So there was a huge controversy. It was inevitable: I'm a Scorpio.

VICTOR-LÉVY BEAULIEU
Why was it attacked?

MARGARET ATWOOD
The detractors asked, "Why did she write a book on something that doesn't exist?" "Why write about a secondary, unimportant literature?" My approach was also controversial. Everything was attacked, the central theme of survival, even the photograph on the back cover.

VICTOR-LÉVY BEAULIEU
But the theme of survival was clearly demonstrated. In a country the size of Canada, with its wide-open spaces, its cold temperatures, and its small population, it was natural in the beginning that people thought first of survival. You can't think of anything else when you don't know whether you're going to eat the next morning, whether you're going to freeze, whether you're going to be able to cross this vast expanse of water. And people attacked you for that?

MARGARET ATWOOD
For that and other things. I also think the academics didn't like me trespassing on their turf.

VICTOR-LÉVY BEAULIEU
But those academics weren't teaching Canadian literature to their students.

MARGARET ATWOOD
A few were. Others didn't want that literature to be taught. In the sixties there was sort of a vacuum in the universities. The student population had grown very, very quickly. So a lot of professors were imported from England and the United States. The universities were full of people who either were not of Canadian origin, or who were but had a post-colonial mentality: "Yes, I'm Canadian, but I studied at Oxford and I know what's

what." But I gave a series of lectures at Oxford three years ago.* They let me choose what I talked about. I decided to look at Canadian subjects, especially the literature of the North, which has all the things the English really love: cannibalism, Indians, the Franklin expedition that was lost in the Arctic.

Our country is large in extent, small in population, which accounts for our fear of empty spaces, and also our need for them. Much of it is covered in water, which accounts for our interest in reflections, sudden vanishings, the dissolution of one thing into another. Much of it however is rock, which accounts for our belief in Fate.

In summer we lie about in the blazing sun, almost naked, covering our skins with fat and attempting to turn red. But when the sun is low in the sky and faint, even at noon, the water we are so fond of changes to something hard and white and cold and covers up the ground. Then we cocoon ourselves, become lethargic, and spend much of our time hiding in crevices. Our mouths shrink and we say little.

Before this happens, the leaves on many of our trees turn blood-red or lurid yellow, much brighter and more exotic than the interminable green of jungles. We find this change beautiful. "Come and see the leaves," we say, and jump into our moving vehicles and drive up and down past the forests of sanguinary trees, pressing our eyes to the glass.

We are a nation of metamorphs.

Anything red compels us.

– Margaret Atwood
"Homelanding," *Good Bones*

---

* These lectures were later published as *Strange Things: The Malevolent North in Canadian Literature.*

VICTOR-LÉVY BEAULIEU
And how did it go?

MARGARET ATWOOD
Very, very well, but it was sort of funny. There's no point in a Canadian talking to the English about Shakespeare and Milton. They already get a lot of that from their own.

VICTOR-LÉVY BEAULIEU
You also give Québec literature a place in *Survival*. You talk about Gabrielle Roy, Roger Lemelin, Anne Hébert, and Marie-Claire Blais, among others. But it seems to me that, in 1972, you had difficulty, not in understanding Québec literature – I think you understood it well – but in imagining its future. It seemed easy for you to talk about English-Canadian literature and to predict that it would gain recognition in the relatively near future. For Québec literature, on the other hand, your predictions were a bit more vague. Am I mistaken?

MARGARET ATWOOD
I had to choose works that English-speaking readers could obtain in translation. There were only a few. I noted some similarities, but also some differences. The big difference was that, in Québec literature, you find a lot more novels in which the narrator says, "Burn the house down and start over." It was noticeable, even at that time.

I ended *Survival* with the question "Have we survived?" That question is still very current. I wrote the book almost twenty-five years ago, and since then our economic domination by the United States is even greater. The Canadian government is dismantling all its structures for supporting the arts, social programs, the health-care system, care of the elderly, and so on. The question of Québec's separation also has a potential impact on this. Canada will be transformed into several little countries, including the country of Ontario. We already have our own beer, Upper Canada Ale. Maybe there will be a little kingdom of Alberta, with King Preston Manning. Who knows? Maybe people will want to join the United States, and the United States will say, "No, thanks. Newfoundland? No, thanks." Notice that this doesn't stop Newfoundland from being very popular from a literary point of view. *The Shipping News*, a novel by [E.] Annie Proulx – who has lived in Québec – is about Newfoundland. Proulx is American, and her novel, which is very popular and very well written, won the Pulitzer Prize.

VICTOR-LÉVY BEAULIEU
When free trade with the United States was being discussed, was it out of concern for the survival of Canada that English-Canadian intellectuals – with a few exceptions – opposed it?

MARGARET ATWOOD
Yes, we were against free trade.

VICTOR-LÉVY BEAULIEU
As opposed to Québec, where few intellectuals were against it.

MARGARET ATWOOD
Have they changed their minds?

VICTOR-LÉVY BEAULIEU
For the most part, I don't think so. But in Toronto, in English Canada, what threat does free trade represent, in particular for culture?

MARGARET ATWOOD
There's a clause in the free-trade agreement that stipulates that, if the government of Canada grants money for the arts or education exclusively to Canadians, the United States can take reprisals in any industry. For example, if Canada adopted a film policy that called for a certain percentage of Canadian films in theatres, the United States could attack the fishing industry. The results of this clause are already evident. The Canada Council and a lot of other programs are being dismantled because the Canadian government is now afraid to fund the arts.

VICTOR-LÉVY BEAULIEU
Isn't the same thing happening in the book industry in English Canada with the establishment of the big bookstore chains in major centres like Toronto?

MARGARET ATWOOD

Yes, that has begun. Right now, Harbourfront, which is the biggest English-language writers' festival in the world, is in the process of disappearing because of neglect by the government.[*]

VICTOR-LÉVY BEAULIEU

You're talking about the federal government?

MARGARET ATWOOD

Yes. The Ontario government has a good track record.[**] But the federal government, in spite of all the studies showing that the arts generate major economic spinoffs for society, has simply turned its back. It refuses to understand, because of free trade.

VICTOR-LÉVY BEAULIEU

How do you answer people who say – and this is the government's position – that this isn't a big problem in English Canada, since an author can always get published in New York or Boston and there will always be a potential market south of the border?

MARGARET ATWOOD

Actually, relatively few Canadian writers are published in the States. There's a problem of first publication for young artists and writers. I admit it's not a problem for me.

VICTOR-LÉVY BEAULIEU

Because you publish first with a Canadian publisher and then in the United States.

MARGARET ATWOOD

I can do what I want. But I'm very old. For young people, the problem is access to publication. They're usually published by small publishers, whose

---

[*] Saved to date, but still underfunded. (Margaret Atwood)

[**] Since the election of the Harris Tories, not any more. (Margaret Atwood)

Andrew MacNaughton

At the time of the publication of *Alias Grace*, Toronto, 1996.

books are generally sold in the independent bookstores. If that network disappears, the young writers will be cut out.

VICTOR-LÉVY BEAULIEU
There won't be anywhere where young writers can publish and be sold, is that it?

I planned my death carefully; unlike my life, which meandered along from one thing to another, despite my feeble attempts to control it. My life had a tendency to spread, to get flabby, to scroll and festoon like the frame of a baroque mirror, which came from following the line of least resistance. I wanted my death, by contrast, to be neat and simple, understated, even a little severe, like a Quaker church or the basic black dress with a single strand of pearls much praised by fashion magazines when I was fifteen. No trumpets, no megaphones, no spangles, no loose ends, this time. The trick was to disappear without a trace, leaving behind me the shadow of a corpse, a shadow everyone would mistake for solid reality. At first I thought I'd managed it.

– Margaret Atwood
Lady Oracle

MARGARET ATWOOD
Yes. If you look at the statistics, you'll see that almost 85 per cent of young writers publish their first works with small literary publishers. It's become very difficult for a young author to get a start with the big publishers. It used to be easier. The situation is similar in the United States.

VICTOR-LÉVY BEAULIEU
Why is that?

MARGARET ATWOOD
In the United States, the big bookstore chains dominate the market, and they want to have books they can sell a lot of copies of. So they favour either

authors who are already known or sensationalistic subject matter. This mass market includes detective novels, romance books for women (how to find love, and so on), how-to books (how to make your funeral arrangements or insulate your windows).

VICTOR-LÉVY BEAULIEU
Yes, a whole paraliterature, in fact.

MARGARET ATWOOD
Poetry and literary works by young authors are a challenge to sell to the mass market, because they're unknown quantities. There are some publishers who even present books they're considering publishing to the chains, and, if the chains say no thank you, the authors could lose their chance for a publishing contract.

VICTOR-LÉVY BEAULIEU
The book just doesn't get published.

MARGARET ATWOOD
That's where the dominance of the big bookstore chains is taking us.

VICTOR-LÉVY BEAULIEU
In Ontario now, are there small houses that publish poetry and novels by young writers and that kind of stuff?

MARGARET ATWOOD
Not hundreds, but some. I began in 1960, and at the time there were five literary magazines in English Canada and five publishers in all, big and small. The field has grown since then, but its growth has slowed down since the seventies. Now that the Ontario government has slashed its budget, I'm afraid a lot of the small publishers will go under.

VICTOR-LÉVY BEAULIEU
And with free trade, the situation could become even worse. I've been in bookstores in Toronto. A few years ago, you'd see "price in the United States

$29.95," let's say, and "price in Canada $39.95." There was a difference in the prices. But since free trade, I think, the prices have evened out.

MARGARET ATWOOD
The dollar fell. Now it looks cheaper to buy an American book.

VICTOR-LÉVY BEAULIEU
If the big chains get established, especially in English Canada, isn't there a danger that the rules of the game in publishing and distribution will change? They buy in large quantities, and are therefore able to sell at lower prices. There's no way the small Canadian publishers can stay competitive.

MARGARET ATWOOD
Yes. That's the problem.

VICTOR-LÉVY BEAULIEU
Isn't there a danger of free trade having the same effect on Canadian culture in general in the long term? On film, for example?

MARGARET ATWOOD
I'm not a politician or an astrologer. I don't know. English-Canadian films have always had problems, because distribution is controlled by the Americans. This has been a problem for forty years. And yet cinematography was practically invented by Canadians. *Nanook of the North* was the first major documentary film. But everything in that field is more and more controlled by Hollywood. If you try to change that, you have to deal with Jack Valenti, the representative of the Hollywood organization. He'll make all kinds of threats, and he has the ear of the United States government.

VICTOR-LÉVY BEAULIEU
Which protects their interests.

MARGARET ATWOOD
Absolutely. All the more so since entertainment is the only export the United States makes money on.

VICTOR-LÉVY BEAULIEU

To change the subject, Quebecers will be voting in a referendum on sovereignty this year [1995]. The government of Québec is going to ask a question something like: "Are you in favour of the sovereignty of Québec, with
economic and political union with English Canada?" How does this question that Québec could ask its people in the coming year strike you as an
English Canadian?

MARGARET ATWOOD

As a former writer of surveys, I must say that the answer depends on the
question. Also, we know that, when you have a series of questions, the answer
to question three changes if you make it number one. It's very easy to
manipulate surveys. I think the problem is knowing exactly what the question is, what is being proposed. Right now, I don't think even the Québec
government knows exactly what it wants to propose to the people of
Québec. When it comes time for the referendum, the question will have to
be absolutely clear; it will have to be clear what is being asked, what the
words mean. If I were a Quebecer, I would want to know exactly what
structure was being proposed. If I say yes, what am I saying yes to? If I say
no, what am I saying no to? It's impossible to predict the results of the
changes that are being proposed. Even renovating your house leads to
unforeseen results. I do a lot of gardening. If I plant something in one place,
that has unexpected consequences for another plant nearby. But the future
is full of risks for everyone. We're going through a period of great change.
You're proposing to become sovereign, but sovereign over what? We're all
in the hands of the business world. And money can travel around the world
with a telephone call. Even governments don't have as much power as they
once did.

VICTOR-LÉVY BEAULIEU

They're no longer in control.

MARGARET ATWOOD

So the question is, where do you really have powers you can exercise? It's all
very well to be an exporter; you can only export if another country wants
to buy from you.

VICTOR-LÉVY BEAULIEU

Supposing Québec says yes to a clear question in the referendum on sovereignty, how do you think English Canada would react? How would you
react?

MARGARET ATWOOD

That's the future! I really don't know. Would I need a visa to enter Québec?
There would be lots of opportunities for smuggling! (Laughs.) Would
Québec create an army? Would it attack Labrador? Who knows? It would
depend on the climate of the time.

VICTOR-LÉVY BEAULIEU

And God knows that's changed in the past three years, if only with the
Reform Party, the Bloc Québécois, and the near disappearance of the
Conservative Party.

MARGARET ATWOOD

Everything changed with one election, and everything could change again
with another. We've seen the almost complete disappearance of the Conservatives, who had the biggest majority since Adam and Eve. Loyalty to
parties hardly exists any more. Everyone votes according to their immediate interest. We're seeing a proliferation of small pressure groups – envi-
ronmentalists, business . . . They have a lot of influence. It was the pressure
groups that changed the vote on free trade here. They spent four million
dollars to influence public opinion in its favour in the two weeks preceding
the vote. The result was the undermining of the universality of social programs. The Liberals have taken the torch from the Conservatives – and
their principles.

VICTOR-LÉVY BEAULIEU

While Canadian society is being dismantled from the top, and social programs are being weakened, you can't say the rest of the world is doing that
well either. What's happening in Québec and Canada is part of contemporary world history. You travel a lot, and you have correspondents all over
the world. How do you foresee the future for this world, which I find quite
schizophrenic, with all its terrorism and religious fanaticism?

MARGARET ATWOOD

The fall of the Berlin Wall changed everything. But a lot of what you see in the U.S. is still dictated by ideology. For example, in 1845 to 1847, the potato blight caused a terrible famine in Ireland. The mentality of the British government at the time was a capitalist mentality in favour of free trade and market forces. And the god of market forces forbade intervention on the pretext that market forces should prevail. Out of a population of about eight million Irish, a million died, because the British government chose not to act. The consequences of this refusal are still evident today. It convinced the Irish once and for all that the British government did not have their interests at heart. And it will end up costing the British a lot more than it would have cost them to take action. Market forces are not a god, but an idol. Whenever political authorities start killing people or letting them die in the name of market forces, they're sacrificing to an idol. That's my sermon for today. (Laughs.)

VICTOR-LÉVY BEAULIEU

Isn't the same thing happening pretty much everywhere in the world today?

MARGARET ATWOOD

Not exactly. In Europe, for example, you have Germany, France, Scandinavia, capitalist economies that don't share this extreme ideology and that are preserving their social structure. They'd rather spend money on that than risk a massive rise in unemployment, poverty, ignorance, and violence. Here we're going back to the mid-nineteenth century, with the very rich on one side and the very poor on the other. The gap gets bigger year by year.

So now it's my turn to ask you what you think will happen with the referendum.

VICTOR-LÉVY BEAULIEU

Everything will depend on the question asked. I agree with you that things have to be clear. Ask the people of Québec if they're in favour of sovereignty or not, period, and once they've voted on sovereignty . . .

MARGARET ATWOOD

Why not use the word *independence?*

VICTOR-LÉVY BEAULIEU

Personally, I'm an *indépendantiste*; I don't hide it. I'd be perfectly in agreement if they simply asked the people of Québec, "Are you in favour of the independence of Québec, yes or no?" Period.

MARGARET ATWOOD

That's simple.

VICTOR-LÉVY BEAULIEU

It's simple and it says it all. Whereas the word *sovereignty* can have several meanings. It could be regional sovereignty, it could be cultural sovereignty, it could be sovereignty over anything. But with *independence*, I quite agree with you, things are clear. I would be in agreement with asking that question. Obviously, if the question is clear, there are two possibilities: the majority of Quebecers say yes or the majority say no. If the majority say no, that really doesn't change anything with regard to the problems Canada is going through as a society, because those problems are there and have already been identified. Solutions have to be found for them anyway. If the people of Québec say yes to independence, that will force everyone to negotiate the nature of that independence.

MARGARET ATWOOD

And if the government says, "We aren't obliged to negotiate anything"?

VICTOR-LÉVY BEAULIEU

The central government?

MARGARET ATWOOD

Yes.

VICTOR-LÉVY BEAULIEU

That doesn't scare me, because I'm one of those people who think that it's up to a collectivity to decide its future. It's first of all the collectivity's choice. If it decides that its future lies in independence, I don't see how another society can say, "No, we won't grant you independence." When a society demands its independence, when it wants it and decides to obtain it, that independence is not a favour given by the neighbouring country or the country it was part of.

MARGARET ATWOOD
What will you do with regard to the native people?

VICTOR-LÉVY BEAULIEU
To me, the native people of Québec aren't much of a problem . . .

MARGARET ATWOOD
But it poses a problem for them.

VICTOR-LÉVY BEAULIEU
For them, yes, I know. In the history of Canada, the native peoples have always benefited from having two levels of government, federal and provincial. For reasons of language in most cases, and also of strategy, the federal government was more profitable for them than the provincial governments. This is as much the case in Ontario and the West as it is in Québec. With the demands of native peoples all over the world, not just in Canada, obviously their eyes got bigger, and so did their stomachs, I would say, and they were put in a peculiar situation: on one hand being treated as third-class citizens, on the other hand being granted privileges. The whole issue became distorted.

MARGARET ATWOOD
The natives claim that almost a third of the territory of present-day Québec belongs to them. They also state that, if Québec separates, they'll separate from Québec. Isn't that a problem for you?

VICTOR-LÉVY BEAULIEU
No, not at all. I don't think the problem of the natives in Québec is a serious problem that would put Québec independence in jeopardy. Some native groups claim up to 85 per cent of the territory of Québec belongs to them. That's an unrealistic expectation.

MARGARET ATWOOD
But do you believe that the native peoples have a society of their own?

VICTOR-LÉVY BEAULIEU

I do believe that. The native peoples of Québec – the ones I know best – are societies that are very different from each other. The society of the Pointe-Bleue Montagnais, for example, is not at all the same kind of society as that of the Mohawks of Kahnawake.

MARGARET ATWOOD

I meant societies in the plural.

VICTOR-LÉVY BEAULIEU

In Québec, there are many aboriginal societies, and their objectives are very different. The Cree of northern Québec don't think at all the same way as the Mohawks of the Montréal area. They have a hard time agreeing on their demands even among themselves. Still, in the past two years, the natives have understood a certain number of things. They see clearly that it's rather illogical to claim possession of 85 per cent of a territory they haven't occupied for years.

MARGARET ATWOOD

But if they say, "Yes, Québec can separate, but we also want to separate from Québec," would you answer yes?

VICTOR-LÉVY BEAULIEU

That's not what the native peoples of Québec are demanding. What they want is a certain amount of territory, which, personally, I'm quite prepared to grant them. They're demanding autonomy in managing their affairs, which I'm quite willing to grant them – which the Québec government, even the Liberal government, was willing to do. When you look at it from Québec, the native problem is very different from the image you may have in Toronto or the Canadian West. I find that what I know of the native peoples in Québec is not at all the same as what I sometimes read about those in the United States or English Canada.

MARGARET ATWOOD

But you say they're not part of your proposed country. Do they remain part of Québec or not? Part of the territory and part of the government?

VICTOR-LÉVY BEAULIEU
To me it's obvious that they remain part of the territory.

MARGARET ATWOOD
But what if they don't want to?

VICTOR-LÉVY BEAULIEU
Well, then we'll see. (Laughs.)

MARGARET ATWOOD
It's always a majority-minority problem. The Indians of Québec are unquestionably a minority that's older than the Québécois and the Anglos here, with their own languages and cultures. Québec is a minority in Canada. The Anglo-Québecers are a minority in Québec. In a democracy, the majority has the control. How fair is that?

VICTOR-LÉVY BEAULIEU
There are majorities that control by means of ethnocide and genocide.

MARGARET ATWOOD
Have you read de Tocqueville on "the tyranny of the majority"?

VICTOR-LÉVY BEAULIEU
Yes. But there are other majorities in the world that don't act that way at all.

MARGARET ATWOOD
We're all in the hands of the majority now. The majority of the market. The majority of money. With this endemic idolatry of market forces, the market controls even politicians.

VICTOR-LÉVY BEAULIEU
Let me ask you a question. From the English-Canadian point of view – or simply from your own – what would the ideal Canada be like?

MARGARET ATWOOD
Mine isn't the Canadian point of view. I have my own point of view. We're not at the negotiating table. I'm not the prime minister. Too bad! (Laughs.)

Marian was sitting at the kitchen table, disconsolately eating a jar of peanut butter and turning over the pages of her largest cookbook. The day after the filet, she had been unable to eat a pork chop, and since then, for several weeks, she had been making experiments. She had discovered that not only were things too obviously cut from the Planned Cow inedible for her, but that the Planned Pig and the Planned Sheep were similarly forbidden. Whatever it was that had been making these decisions, not her mind certainly, rejected anything that had an indication of bone or tendon or fibre. Things that had been ground up and re-shaped, hot-dogs and hamburgers for instance, or lamb patties or pork sausages, were all right as long as she didn't look at them too closely.

– Margaret Atwood
The Edible Woman

VICTOR-LÉVY BEAULIEU
Give it a try, just to see.

MARGARET ATWOOD
Okay. First you cut along the border with scissors and you let the United States float away down near South America. That's the ideal Canada. (Laughs.) During the war the Australians said of the Americans: "They're overpaid, oversexed, and over here." (Laughs.) They're one of the biggest markets for my books – I'm controlled by the market too. Our histories are closely connected and the citizens of the two countries travel back and forth a lot. It's not personal. It's the pressure from the U.S. government, which wants to control everything.

I'm very suspicious of ideals. I've studied utopias. Every time a utopia, a perfect society, is created, the result is a dystopia. The trouble is, in a utopia all the citizens have to agree with you. And when they don't, what do you do? Cut off their heads? Lock them up in concentration camps? The twentieth century has had an abundance of utopias that ended up in total horror. The Nazis. And the Soviets. In a utopia, the society is made up of ants, each one equivalent to the next. Humanity is not like that. In our world, where the problems are now so huge, our governments are very little indeed. Up against environmental problems, skyrocketing populations, new uncontrollable diseases, we're just minor players. We can make our little arrangements, but the really big problems loom over us all.

VICTOR-LÉVY BEAULIEU
It's mind-boggling. And yet both governments, Québec and Canadian, in their last elections, were talking about a full-employment policy.

MARGARET ATWOOD
Blah-blah-blah. Good luck!

VICTOR-LÉVY BEAULIEU
Isn't the basic problem that it takes fewer and fewer people for our society to produce what people need? So the real question is: what do you do with the people you don't need for production?

MARGARET ATWOOD
We all become artists.

VICTOR-LÉVY BEAULIEU
That might be a solution, but it's a bit utopian!

MARGARET ATWOOD
Everyone knows that artists get sustenance from their work. They don't need food. (Laughs.)

VICTOR-LÉVY BEAULIEU
It seems to me that women have never faced so many problems as they do at this point in history. It seems everything conservative in men is joining forces against them. This is true of the Muslim fundamentalists, as it is of the Catholic church, which is very fundamentalist, if only in John Paul II's position against abortion, birth control, and women truly taking part in society. With the rise of all these right-wing forces against women, isn't there a danger that we'll find ourselves in the world you described in *The Handmaid's Tale*?

MARGARET ATWOOD

It's an extension of the attitude towards women in the nineteenth century. It comes back century after century. Why are men so afraid of women? What is it about women that's so terrifying to men? Maybe it's not exactly women they're afraid of. Maybe it's an ancestral terror connected to being a man, to finding out if you're a real man or not. I believe that's a question men ask themselves a lot. That kind of question isn't very important for women. We know we're women. It's unavoidable. (Laughs.) But the poor men are so busy with hierarchies of men, real men, maybe men, and non-men, and they use women as a measuring stick: I'm a man because I'm not a woman. It bothers men when women are like them. I find the brutal refusal of abortion quite simply immoral. The world's population is increasing so fast that we're forced to make a choice: control the number of births or face plague, famine, and war, with all their consequences. Birth control is the most moral option. But that wasn't exactly the question you were asking.

I knew she'd died when the ashtray broke. It cracked right across. It was the one she gave me. I knew she was right there! It was her way of letting me know.

Glorious scenes, *Glorious* scenes! Nobody made scenes like hers. Vulgar as all-get-out. Of course, she would always apologize after-wards. She needn't have done. Not to me.

What I miss is what she'd say. What she would have said. That's the difference: you have to put everything into the past conditional. *Bereft*, you might call it. Not her word, though – too po-faced. *That* was her word.

I went over there, did a little weeding. It's fading though, what she looked like exactly. I can remember her tone of voice, but not her voice. It's funny the way you keep on talking to people. It's as if they could hear.

– Margaret Atwood
"Death Scenes," *Good Bones*

VICTOR-LÉVY BEAULIEU

That answers it. (Laughs.) To change the subject . . . one doesn't really write if one doesn't have accounts to settle with death. The theme of death is everywhere in your work – in your novels, your stories, your poetry. In *Power Politics* you write, "Returning from the dead / used to be something I did well / I began asking why / I began forgetting how." And also, "growing older, of course you'll die / but not yet, you'll outlive / even my distortions of you." In *Good Bones*, which was recently published in a French translation, you speak of the angel of suicide. In another very beautiful work entitled "Homelanding," you write, "Some of our visitors, especially the young ones, have never heard of death and are bewildered. They think that death is simply one more of our illusions, our mirror tricks; they cannot under-stand why, with so much food and music, the people are so sad. But you will understand. You too must have death among you. I can see it in your eyes." And in *Surfacing*, you write: "They think I should be filled with death, I should be in mourning. But nothing has died, everything is alive, everything is waiting to become alive." Would you care to talk about your relationship with death?

MARGARET ATWOOD

Death is universal and inescapable. If you've discovered the secret of immortality, please share it! A word taken out of its context loses its meaning. I think all writers speak of death. It's one of the great themes of lit-erature, along with love, war, nature – and what else? Meals, perhaps. There are a lot of meals in my writing. Meals are more precise than deaths. It's too general a question, I think. How do we speak of non-life? We find ourselves without references. And if no one died, what would happen? The Jehovah's Witnesses believe in a heaven on earth, with families and children, and no death. I talk to them sometimes. I've asked them what will happen when the earth is full. They don't have the answer to that. Nor does John Paul II.

VICTOR-LÉVY BEAULIEU

Of all the books one writes, there's always one book for which the writer has a special affection. Perhaps it's for the particular time when the book was written, I don't know. For me, it's my first novel. I was obsessed by it even after it was written, so much so that I've written two different versions of it since. Of everything you've written, is there one book for which you have a special affection?

MARGARET ATWOOD

That's a question I never answer, because I have a superstition that it's forbidden to choose one book over another. If you do that, the Muse will be angry with you. Your books are gifts from the Muse, and it's forbidden to scorn any one of them.

VICTOR-LÉVY BEAULIEU

But the choice could be one of affection rather than scorn.

MARGARET ATWOOD

If you have more than one child, you're forbidden to have a favourite.

VICTOR-LÉVY BEAULIEU

We've come to the end of this first part of our conversation. I've spent four days in Toronto with you and talked to you about your work. I was very conscious, when I arrived, of being a bit like the sailor Herman Melville talks about. You sail on the surface of the water, but you don't penetrate its depths; you can go all the way around the world, but its depths elude you. However, it has been a beautiful voyage and I thank you for making it possible. In a few days, we'll see each other again, in Trois-Pistoles, for the rest of our conversation. Let me ask you one last question. How do you see this trip to the far reaches of Québec, so to speak – practically to the Gaspé, which means "the end of the known world" in an Indian language?

MARGARET ATWOOD

It's not unknown territory to me. It's the country of my childhood. I travelled all over Québec when I was younger. But I'm sure everything has changed. So I'll be seeing a lot of new things and having a lot of new experiences. I'm older than you, Victor-Lévy, but I'm not as old as all that. I still enjoy fresh and extraordinary experiences. That's what I hope for from my upcoming trip to Trois-Pistoles.

Gilles Gaudreau

Victor-Lévy Beaulieu in front of his home in Trois-Pistoles, 1985.

Trois-Pistoles

MARGARET ATWOOD
Victor-Lévy Beaulieu, you were born in September 1945, right at the end of the Second World War. Do you think the war affected you?

VICTOR-LÉVY BEAULIEU
I was born on September 2, 1945, the day of the Japanese surrender. Obviously I have no memories of the war. When I was small, they used to talk about it at home. My father wasn't in the war, for medical reasons. Some of my uncles were, but most of them evaded conscription; they hid in the woods so they wouldn't have to join the army. That's more the image of the war that's stayed with me.

On the other hand, I also remember the descriptions they gave us in school, in grades one, two, three, and four. Québec was a very religious society. I remember the teacher asking the little guys in the class, "What would you do if the Germans came here and forced you to trample on the crucifix and smash it and spit on it, and told you that, if you refused, they'd dig a hole and bury you up to your neck and leave you there to die?" I remember that I answered – and I think I was the only one in the class – that I would trample on the crucifix rather than be buried in the hole. My parents would tell how at night in the lower St. Lawrence all the lights were turned off in the houses to keep the German submarines patrolling the Gulf from seeing the coastline and being able to land. My family was poor, and my parents told how, during the war, there was rationing of butter, milk, bread, and everything. But I don't think the war deeply affected the region, or my family either.

And that old Hugo whom I revere, he too was once fourteen years old. In a school notebook, on April 16, 1816, he wrote, "I will be Chateaubriand or nothing." Which in his language meant, "I will be the genius of the century, or I will be nothing." I was more modest at that age and had less faith in life. And the eternal litany over and over. We didn't have money. I would have to leave school soon, and drag my carcass into a crummy little bank on Carré Saint-Louis between two or three fools who made fun of me because I scribbled miserable poems on the backs of deposit slips and naively asked myself who I was. Today I read Jack Kerouac, and this sentence in particular, so totally despairing, so real when I think what we were, lost in the big city, unable to forget the past, the land we had left, the memories of miseries, sicknesses, and long winters: "I'm stupid too. Even a cretin. Maybe only French Canadian, who knows?"

– Victor-Lévy Beaulieu
Pour saluer Victor Hugo [In tribute to Victor Hugo]

MARGARET ATWOOD
I was born in 1939, at the beginning of the war. It was a time of anxiety and depression. You were born at a time of victory, celebration, and hope. So my second question is whether you think that had an influence on your writing and your political views?

VICTOR-LÉVY BEAULIEU
It certainly did. The postwar period, in Québec as in English Canada, was a time of prosperity. People had more money; the war industries had produced wealth, and that wealth was used to build houses, expand farms,

construct factories. There was an economic boom after the war, and even my parents and my distant relatives benefited from it. But there's another aspect to it. Families in Québec were big; there were thirteen children in our house. The limited acreage wasn't enough to support so many people. Only the eldest son could stay on the farm. The others had to take their little bundles and go somewhere else. So a lot of people moved to the big cities, to Québec City and Montréal, where most of the war industry was. They went to work in the factories, and after the war they stayed there.

This exodus meant that people who stayed in the country considered themselves poor and in a sense deprived. Drained of its new blood, the country suddenly became old. The young men who came back from Europe were no longer interested in the country either. On the battlefields, they had met soldiers from other countries and discovered a freedom of thought that didn't exist here. All that ferment contributed to the desertion and impoverishment of the countryside in Québec. That's partly what made my father decide to move to the city. The city was attractive because of money, because of TV – which had just arrived – and all the modern technology. The uprooted farmers found life a little easier there. That's why so many fled the misery of the rocky little back-country farms, where children were a good and abundant source of manpower but were a burden as soon as they became adults. So the war was experienced, I think, in two ways in Québec: the enrichment of the city and the impoverishment of the country. And that's how I came to Montréal. Because of the economic boom brought about by the war.

MARGARET ATWOOD
Good answer!

VICTOR-LÉVY BEAULIEU
It was a good question.

MARGARET ATWOOD
Here's another question, one that's a little more personal. You were the sixth child of a family of thirteen. What was it like to live in such a big family? I'm curious. Did the older ones help take care of the younger ones? Did you wear hand-me-down clothes, as my mother and her sisters did?

VICTOR-LÉVY BEAULIEU

Yes. The oldest one broke the clothes in, and the younger ones kept on wearing them, passing them on until they were threadbare.

I feel now that, being the sixth of thirteen, I was in a privileged position. My older brothers were supposed to take care of us. But at their age, they wanted to play outside with their friends, not watch us. That allowed me to go unnoticed in the family. My older brothers reached adolescence during the postwar boom, in a society that was opening up in every way and offering access to information as never before, if only through television. My parents and my grandparents were very austere people, very strict, for whom Catholicism was everything and life had to follow the precepts of religion. My brothers had to fight to loosen that overly rigid framework. But when I came along, seven years after my eldest brother, it was already a generation later. Besides that, my father had gone away to work before we moved to Montréal. So he wasn't at home very often. My mother had to take care of the thirteen children, and the result was that she had to give us a little freedom, because otherwise it would have been unbearable in the house. Being the sixth allowed me to gain my independence quite early and to be left alone.

MARGARET ATWOOD

You've anticipated one of my questions. But I'll add another one, about your mother. That interests me a lot. When you were all around the table, did she impose rules on you?

VICTOR-LÉVY BEAULIEU

Yes. And there was more than that. I'm left-handed, and, at that time in Québec, you weren't allowed to write with your left hand. My mother was very strict. She had no choice – she didn't have time to ask each of us what was wrong. Rather it was: you sit down and you don't say a word. I couldn't manage to write with my right hand, which created all kinds of problems for me. In the evening, we'd do our homework on the big kitchen table, and my mother would supervise us. At school they'd told my mother that it wasn't good for me to write with my left hand. So my mother watched me to make sure I wrote with my right hand. And since I was incapable of doing that, I would wait. Fortunately, my mother always had something to do in the house – dishes, washing, sewing – she also made our clothes. So when she went away from the table, I would take advantage of the opportunity to write what I had to, very, very quickly, and when she came back I'd pretend to be writing with my right hand. I was scolded in school and I was scolded at home. I became rather rebellious because of it. Until my father got fed up and took me to school one morning to see the head brother. He told the head brother, "I think he's left-handed and he'll be left-handed for the rest of his life. I don't want to hear any more about it." So I was finally able to write with my left hand. But in school, they put me in the last row at the back of the class so I wouldn't bother anyone; and at home, I would sit at end of the table so I wouldn't hit anyone with my left elbow. I imagine that contributes to making you understand that you're different from other people. You couldn't play baseball if you were left-handed, because there were only gloves for right-handed people. And you couldn't play hockey. You couldn't play this and you couldn't play that. So you found yourself somewhat excluded. That led you to form your own opinions, to keep to yourself a bit, to be self-reliant.

MARGARET ATWOOD

And all that comes from being a leftist?

VICTOR-LÉVY BEAULIEU

Left-handed, *gaucher*. That's completely different from a leftist, *gauchiste*. (Laughs.) For a child who knows that every night he's going to be scolded and rapped on the knuckles with a ruler because he writes with one hand rather than the other, the mother-son relationship takes on a completely different meaning than usual. His mother becomes someone difficult, hard, not lovable in the deepest sense of the word. When you've experienced that in your childhood, it takes you some time to get over it.

MARGARET ATWOOD

Do you know the story of Dr. Jekyll and Mr. Hyde, by Stevenson? Do you think writers in general, and you in particular because of those two hands, have dual personalities?

VICTOR-LÉVY BEAULIEU

To write, to live in the skin of characters you invent, requires more than a dual personality. It requires a multiplication of personalities. Any writer, including you, unconsciously exploits at least two aspects of the self, the good side and the bad side. To write, you have to have that to start with. I don't think people who are one-dimensional make writers who are interesting to read or filmmakers who are interesting to watch. If Fellini had been a one-dimensional person, I don't think I would have found his films very interesting. If Marcel Proust had been like that, I might never even have read him. It's an important part of a writer.

MARGARET ATWOOD
You started with a lead on the rest of us. The left hand is the hidden personality, the personality that mustn't be revealed. The right hand is the personality of the appearances you have to show to others.

The Old Man slept in his easy-chair. (Dribble was running down his chin. His foot had a tic: every ten seconds his skinny leg shook violently under his trousers.) "It hurts," thought the woman. "It hurts in my stomach. Maybe that's what death is." She wiped her hands and put them on her stomach. She thought of a religious ceremony and saw a man in black touching her stomach. She saw a priest kneeling before her. Running his fingers over her, he was saying: "That's death in your stomach, Milienne honey. You needn't get excited. Death is long sometimes, it wants to live before ending." She put her hands back in the water. Thinking about death didn't frighten her. No elephant's ears came to mind like when she listened to songs on the radio. There was a kind of peace, as if death were already present in the gestures she made: in the water that squirted from the milk bottle when she stuffed the old dishrag through its neck, and in the sun that came through the window, making a column of light where the golden specks of dust were swarming. Suddenly her stomach hurt her very much. Tears came to her eyes.

– Victor-Lévy Beaulieu
The Grand-Fathers [*Les grands-pères*],
translated by Marc Plourde

VICTOR-LÉVY BEAULIEU

That's true. In school, the teacher saw something malevolent in the fact that I wrote with my left hand. She said, "Take your pencil in your right hand. Squeeze it hard in your hand. Does it get hot? It doesn't get hot, does it? Now take it in your left hand and do the same thing. It gets hot, doesn't it?" When you're six years old and the teacher says that to you, you answer yes. Then she adds, "You see, it's not good, is it?" History tells us that left-handed people were once forbidden to stay in certain cities. The Hebrews taught left-handed children to use a slingshot. In battle they would put them in the front lines against the enemy troops, who, all being right-handed, were not expecting stones to come from the left. That gave them an advantage. It's even said that Goliath was killed by David because David was left-handed and Goliath didn't expect a stone to come from the wrong side. In the Middle Ages, if you were thought to be a witch and you were also left-handed, you were burned at the stake in every case. A sinister aspect was always associated with the left. When you're a child, you're impressionable. When they tell you about the flames of hell, images come to you, terrible images. When I was eighteen, I had polio. I had it on the left side. I could have done as many others did and written with my right hand, but I didn't have a knack for it. I thought that perhaps I had chosen the malevolent side of things.

MARGARET ATWOOD

Marked by the Devil.

VICTOR-LÉVY BEAULIEU

Who's a much more interesting character.

MARGARET ATWOOD

Yes, I know.

VICTOR-LÉVY BEAULIEU

Without the Devil, God is very monotonous.

MARGARET ATWOOD

You grew up in Saint-Paul-de-la-Croix and Trois-Pistoles, small towns in rural Québec, at a time when things were very tightly controlled by the church and by Maurice Duplessis and his ilk. Did you feel cut off from the major cultural centres? Did you have any idea that those centres existed? Maybe you felt protected, far away from them?

VICTOR-LÉVY BEAULIEU

I spent my childhood and part of my teens in Trois-Pistoles, Saint-Paul-de-la-Croix, and Saint-Jean-de-Dieu. I must say that in those days rural society was not as disorganized as it later became, and as it often still is. In 1950, in rural society, there was a cultural life. In almost all the villages in Québec, such as Trois-Pistoles, there was a local newspaper and there were local writers and people who published books, wrote songs, performed in shows. There was even a theatre in Trois-Pistoles. It was called the parish hall, but they did theatre there. My father did theatre and so did my uncles.

This homogeneous society was self-sufficient. You could be satisfied with what it had to offer. For generations of Québécois in small villages, foreign territory was the next village. In Trois-Pistoles, it was Saint-Éloi, Île-Verte, or Rimouski, before it was Montréal. Montréal was very far away, and so was Québec City. With a few exceptions, no one ever went there. Often, people didn't know anything about the city. No one would even go there to visit relatives, who in some cases had been living there for thirty years, fifty years.

Rural society was still very much circumscribed by political power – Duplessis – and religious power – the clergy that controlled everything from A to Z, from birth to death. This form of bureaucracy appears more repressive than that of today. Today's democracy, as much of a caricature as it is, is less painful to live in than the system of Duplessis and the nuns, brothers, and clergy who controlled everything. But living in the country had the advantage of distancing you from all that in your everyday life. You took care of the animals, the ploughing, the crops. You had a lot of freedom on your own land. That's why I can't say I had an unhappy childhood. Quite the contrary.

MARGARET ATWOOD

You've said your family was very devoted to music and that everyone played an instrument. I've noticed that music is very important in your plays. What was your instrument?

VICTOR-LÉVY BEAULIEU

Here again, I'm a bit of an exception in my family. I have absolutely no talent for music. I've tried and tried to learn even a few tunes on the piano, or the harmonica, which is practically the national instrument of any self-respecting Québécois. But I was never able to learn. It's true that everyone in my family had a good ear. My maternal grandmother played the violin the old-fashioned way, holding it not on the shoulder but right over the heart. That fascinated me. I wondered what it must be like to play with the violin right over your heart. From the sound of it, it must have been something quite special. My paternal grandmother played the accordion and the piano. My uncles and aunts were all musicians. Before the sixties families were large, and because of the isolation in winter, you had to entertain yourself. Since we didn't have access to radio or television or movies, people would get together and they'd all play music. Except for incompetents like me, of course.

Rituals were always accompanied by music. In traditional Québec families in the old days, ritual was very important. When I wrote my television series "L'Héritage" [The legacy], I remembered some of those rituals and put them in it. For example, in my family, our father would sit at a specific place at the table, so that he could watch all the comings and goings. One old tradition that I vaguely recalled was that if a boy was courting a girl and the girl came to the house, she didn't have the right to eat at the family table until they were married. Every big Québec family had a little table, and the future daughter-in-law or son-in-law had to eat there. I had a scene in "L'Héritage" where that happened, and everyone said, "Oh no, that couldn't be, that's impossible! Come on!" In an old document drawn up right here in Trois-Pistoles, it was written in black and white that the father gave everything on his farm to his son, specifying, "The son will never make his father eat at the little table." I imagine the father stipulated this because he was afraid his son would do to him what he must have done to the son by making his young lady eat at the little table.

There were rituals that accompanied the passage to adolescence, marriage, the birth of children, and death. These rituals enabled the society to remain united and to mark the events of life, both the good and the bad. My childhood was full of big celebrations, like the feast of Corpus Christi and the Procession. We'd leave from the church in Trois-Pistoles and go down to the Fatima shore, which you've seen, where there are still little statues of Our Lady of Fatima. We'd go there in a procession, with songs, music, a brass band. It was the big celebration of the year, and afterwards we'd go back to the church. Those are images that remain etched in our minds. When I took part in big celebrations in Montréal, there wasn't any of the playfulness there was in those big celebrations of my childhood. Saint-Jean-Baptiste Day, the floats – all that shaping of life had a meaning that has been forgotten or put aside today in our bureaucratic society. That's too bad.

MARGARET ATWOOD

Do you remember any songs from your childhood?

VICTOR-LÉVY BEAULIEU

Yes, some.

MARGARET ATWOOD

Could you sing a little song for us?

VICTOR-LÉVY BEAULIEU

No, I'm no better at singing than at playing music. The only memory that has been given to me is for words and events. Yes, I remember some songs that my uncles sang. I won't sing, but I'll recite a verse for you: "The devil left hell and went around with his cart collecting his own. You, baker who bakes bad bread, get in, get into my cart. You, shoemaker who makes bad shoes, get in, get into my cart." It's one of the first songs I heard, as a child. It's always stayed in my head. One of my uncles sang it very well, with mouth music. There were lots of songs like that. Everything was material for songs. They say that in France everything ends with a song; in Québec, everything started with a song. There were songs before, during, and after every event. People would also sometimes amuse themselves by altering them. One of the most incredible things I've ever heard in my life was a parody of the "Tantum Ergo" sung at mass. Someone had done a terrible parody of that, which he sang at family gatherings, and everyone laughed and had a lot of fun listening to it. There again, it goes back to rituals. It was a way of taking the ritual and turning it upside down and making it say exactly the opposite. It was healthy in such a closed society to take the lid off once in a while and let off a little steam.

MARGARET ATWOOD
It seems to me you have a good ear.

VICTOR-LÉVY BEAULIEU
For music? I'm not so sure. When I listen to a piece of music I understand the structure and it seems easy to reproduce. You know that, if there are two beats there, there will be three that follow. A good musician will manage to twist it in another direction; when you expect three beats, he'll give you four. That's easy enough to understand. But when you come to play, just exposing yourself makes you lose the structure you've identified. Your memory is more visual than auditory. You see the music but you no longer hear it. So you can't play it.

MARGARET ATWOOD
Did your family do other artistic things? Did they put on plays? Do you have any painters in the family?

VICTOR-LÉVY BEAULIEU
In my family, besides musicians, there are amateur actors. They put on plays in parish halls.

MARGARET ATWOOD
What about knitting? That's also an art.

VICTOR-LÉVY BEAULIEU
All the women knitted and did needlepoint. Maybe not because they liked it that much, but because they had to do it. In my family we played music and put on shows. Very few people wrote, but a lot painted.

MARGARET ATWOOD
Naïve paintings?

VICTOR-LÉVY BEAULIEU
My godmother painted on glass. It was fashionable at one time, in Québec anyway.

MARGARET ATWOOD
And it's coming back. I saw an exhibition of paintings on glass in New York, done by Hungarian women.

VICTOR-LÉVY BEAULIEU
Was it interesting?

MARGARET ATWOOD
I found it very interesting. It was very naïve painting, but very powerful.

VICTOR-LÉVY BEAULIEU
In my family, those who didn't paint, do theatre, or play music, made do with jigsaw puzzles. My grandmother had boarders. We would go to her house on Sundays and there were always five or six boarders there. One of them did huge puzzles, things with ten thousand pieces. I once went into his room and was amazed to see that the walls were covered with jigsaw puzzles all the way up to the ceiling. He would do them and paste them on cardboard, and stick them up.

MARGARET ATWOOD
I did puzzles at one time in my life. It can become an obsession.

VICTOR-LÉVY BEAULIEU
When my daughters were young, here in Trois-Pistoles, we did at least one every summer. On rainy days, you get up in the morning, you go to put in a piece or two, and you end up spending the whole morning at it.

MARGARET ATWOOD
It's a little bit like writing, I think. You're looking for the missing piece.

VICTOR-LÉVY BEAULIEU
And there's always one missing. But at least with a jigsaw puzzle, at a

certain point you can say it's finished. You're done with it. But with writing . . .

MARGARET ATWOOD
It's exactly like when you publish books.

VICTOR-LÉVY BEAULIEU
Except that when you publish a book, you've generally started another, so that it doesn't make any difference that it's published, because emotionally you're already involved in another book, you're working on something else. The one you've just published is already far away. With a puzzle, the emotional investment isn't as great. (Laughs.)

MARGARET ATWOOD
Did anyone in your family garden? That's also a form of artistic expression.

VICTOR-LÉVY BEAULIEU
Gardening, yes. My grandparents had two kinds of gardens. There was a vegetable garden, but often, for one of my grandmothers at any rate, there was a flower garden too, because, among her beets and her carrots, she planted a lot of flowers. So that when you went into her garden in the summer, there were so many flowers that you didn't know there were beets and carrots. My other grandmother surrounded everything with raspberry bushes. She claimed that fruits and vegetables, like people, had to adapt to good or poor conditions. It was clever. All she'd do was make a little hole in the ground and put in the seeds. She never weeded. It always amazed us that, at the end of the summer, she had fruits and vegetables that were as nice as anyone's. She'd say you had to let nature do its job, and that, if the soil was poor, there was no point in enriching it, you just had to plant things that required poor soil, and that for other species, you had to go where the soil was rich. Her garden was very special. She could have rose bushes fifty feet from the house, and then all of a sudden she could have a little patch of cabbages two hundred feet away, because there the soil was black and they grew well, and then she could have pumpkins somewhere else. So the effect was sort of anarchic, but at the same time very pleasing.

MARGARET ATWOOD
Are there other writers in your family? I had an aunt who wrote little stories for the Sunday paper.

VICTOR-LÉVY BEAULIEU
No. In my family, as far as I know at any rate, no one was tempted by writing. Some of my aunts kept diaries, and my mother kept a diary for twenty years.

MARGARET ATWOOD
Did you have books in the house? Newspapers?

VICTOR-LÉVY BEAULIEU
At that time in the country, and this is true later as well, the books you had in the house were the ones given at school as prizes at the end of the year by the old Department of Public Instruction, which was the fore-runner of the Ministry of Education. That department was controlled by religious orders, who published Québec authors like Félix Leclerc. At the end of the year, the Council for Public Instruction would meet and buy books, which would be distributed to the most deserving students in the schools. Those were the books that came into our home. That's how I read Gabrielle Roy, Félix Leclerc, and other Québec authors of twenty, thirty, forty years ago. Besides that, my father had given my mother *L'encyclopédie de la jeunesse* [The young people's encyclopedia] and *Pays et Nations* [Countries and nations], in sixteen or twenty volumes from Grolier, as a wedding present. Those were the first books I read when I was young. The encyclopedia had condensed versions of stories like Lewis Carroll's *Alice in Wonderland* or "Scipio Africanus" or "The Geese That Saved Rome." And they were all illustrated. Those were the very first stories I read in my life.

MARGARET ATWOOD
At what age?

VICTOR-LÉVY BEAULIEU
As soon as I started reading, which was at about six or seven years old.

MARGARET ATWOOD

Did you learn to read in school, or did your older brothers and sisters teach you?

VICTOR-LÉVY BEAULIEU

I'm sure that, coming from a big family, I arrived in school already knowing how to read a little. I knew the alphabet, I knew how to say the little sentences children used to read then. I still remember the first text they taught in grade one, which started with "Tell me, Jean, who tore the first page out of this picture book?" I learned it before I started school. And besides *L'encyclopédie de la jeunesse* and *Pays et Nations*, there were some religious books in our home. It was part of the cultural heritage of Québec.

Among them was a martyrology, with all the saints, virgins, popes, and missionaries who had been martyred by those horrible barbarians who wouldn't accept them. It was full of sadomasochistic illustrations. There was one in particular that upset me whenever I looked at it. It was the one about the martyrdom of St. Andrew, who gave his name to the St. Andrew's cross, because he was crucified with his head down and his feet and legs extended in the shape of an X, instead of the usual way. That gave me nightmares. That martyrology was in a drawer in my parents' dresser. We weren't allowed to read it, because it wasn't meant for children. So, when my parents weren't there, I would go into their room and take out the martyrology and read it and look at the pictures. Those weren't the kind of pictures you saw on the walls in our house!

MARGARET ATWOOD

Did you want to become a martyr?

VICTOR-LÉVY BEAULIEU

No, not really.

MARGARET ATWOOD

Or to martyr others?

VICTOR-LÉVY BEAULIEU

Not really that either. I wasn't really into that kind of thing. My parents would certainly have liked me to become, not a martyr, but a missionary or priest. That was also in the tradition in Québec. Usually in big families, one of the sons had to become a priest. He was the only one that was sent to study at the seminary. A family without a priest wasn't a good Catholic family. But in my family, you see, there were thirteen children, and not one became a priest, not one became a brother or a nun. I remember, when we lived in the country, my parents tried with my eldest brother. It didn't work. Then they tried with the second one, who they also sent to the seminary. Since they were poor, one of my aunts paid the tuition. It didn't work with him either. The third brother didn't go to the seminary, because he wasn't interested in studying. After a while, they got to me, the fifth son in the family.

Early one morning when I was bringing the cows in to the stable for milking, my father came up behind me and put his hand on my shoulder and said, "Wouldn't you like to be like Father Labelle some day?" Father Labelle was a Québec priest who settled the Laurentian region. I wasn't at all interested. And the most frightening thing that happened in my childhood was in the middle of one summer when the priest from the village of Saint-Jean-de-Dieu and the Christian Brothers came to our house. The priest was supposedly there for his parish visit. All of a sudden, one of the brothers looked at the boys all lined up. Another brother came into the house carrying a cassock, and he also looked at us. Then he pointed at one of us and said, "This cassock would look good on you. Try it on. You'd make a good brother." Each one of us was afraid the brother would pick him.

MARGARET ATWOOD
Well, you could have said, "But I'm marked by the Devil. I'm left-handed."

VICTOR-LÉVY BEAULIEU
No doubt. But the fact remains that there were a lot of boys just on our road who studied in the seminary because of that.

MARGARET ATWOOD
Charles Pachter, whom you met in Toronto, had a grandmother who told him when he was five years old, "If you look a nun in the eye, your teeth will fall out of your mouth." He did it, and lo and behold, his teeth fell out. (Laughs.)

So we moved in May. Even though for that whole week, the weather had been relatively good, we could still see hard, dirty snow in the ruts. And the birds weren't singing. I have to say that we were leaving Trois-Pistoles, the St. Lawrence, Île aux Basques, and the Fatima shore for Saint-Jean-de-Dieu, a tiny little nothing of a village fifteen miles inland, where the land was rocky and bare. Dirty snow and silent birds topped it off nicely. But Papa Toothpaste was in a good mood. He'd always liked moving. In eighteen years, he'd done it fifteen times. With every kid, just about. And it was always for the last time and it was always to stay. Mama Toothpaste had finally resigned herself to it. Especially since this year we were moving closer to her family and her few childhood friends. But still it was a terrible blow for Mama Toothpaste when, just past the covered bridge over the Boisbouscache, the old truck stopped in front of our new house. A heap of ill-fitting boards, big pieces of cardboard covering the windows, and no toilet in the old house, which creaked with the least gust of wind, no paint on the walls, not even any bedrooms. With his characteristic genius for moving, Papa Toothpaste divided the attic into two sections with a partition of boards, and putting the girls on one side and the boys on the other, he shouted, his face dripping with sweat, "Don't stand on ceremony. We're not in Trois-Pistoles any more."

– Victor-Lévy Beaulieu
Race de monde [What kind of creatures]

VICTOR-LÉVY BEAULIEU

Imagine if he'd looked somewhere else! (Laughs.) In fact, there was a whole religious mythology that was prevalent then in Québec. But my family avoided it, even though on my father's side there were a lot of priests and nuns and a lot of missionaries. When I was little, those missionaries, usually White Fathers who were back from Africa or China or South America, would come to my grandfather's place in the summer. We would spend the evening listening to them talk about Papua New Guinea, Nyasaland, and China. It was fascinating to listen to them. That was the only news we got of the rest of the world. To my mind, that aspect of the religion had a very liberating side.

MARGARET ATWOOD
You could travel.

VICTOR-LÉVY BEAULIEU
Those missionaries were impressive, with their long white robes, a huge crucifix hanging from their belt, their big white beards. We got more than a class in political science or geopolitics from them; we got a picture of the world that we never would have got otherwise. If you were a Québécois missionary in Africa, the work wasn't at all the same as if you were an American, British, or French missionary, because, under the cover of religion, they were protecting their colonial empires. The Québécois didn't have any empire to protect, so they went into those countries with a much greater openness towards the people. For many young Québécois, the missionaries' stories were their first window on the world.

MARGARET ATWOOD
There were no kindergartens during the last war, so I started school at the age of six. At what age did you start school, and did you like it at first?

VICTOR-LÉVY BEAULIEU
Like almost all kids in Québec at that time, I started at six.

MARGARET ATWOOD
Was it a big shock?

VICTOR-LÉVY BEAULIEU
Yes. I didn't like it at all. There was a tradition that, when little boys started school, they had to know two things: how to tie their shoelaces in a nice bow and how to tie a necktie.

MARGARET ATWOOD
That's not easy!

VICTOR-LÉVY BEAULIEU

It's very complicated, and what's more, my parents taught me to do it right-handed. But a person who's left-handed doesn't tie knots and bows the same way as right-handed people. Even today, my daughters, when they see me tie my shoelaces, ask how I can tie them like that, because it's upside down. Obviously, not being allowed to be left-handed made me hate school. But it gave me an advantage in a way. It taught me to work fast and to grasp things quickly, because at school, just like at home, I did my work as quickly as I could, when the teacher, or my mother, wasn't paying attention.

I hated the way we were taught, and teachers in general. I was quite lucky though, compared to most Québécois my age that I know, who were taught by nuns and brothers. Thanks to a combination of circumstances, I was never taught by a priest or a nun. When I was in grade one, a brother got sick and was replaced by a woman teacher, what we used to call a schoolmistress. And in grades two and three, the same thing happened. Then when we moved to Saint-Jean-de-Dieu, in the country, we also had a schoolmistress.

MARGARET ATWOOD

Was it you who made the brothers sick?

VICTOR-LÉVY BEAULIEU

I wish I could say it was! In Saint-Jean-de-Dieu, in the local country school, there were maybe fifteen children altogether, from grades one to seven, and there was only one schoolmistress to teach all those grades. The first one we had in Saint-Jean-de-Dieu was barely seventeen years old. She was younger than certain students who had repeated their fourth, fifth, and sixth grades. That teacher had a very hard time. Teachers in country schools would live in a small apartment in the school. We kids would smoke cedar cigarettes. We'd crush dried cedar bark and roll it in paper, and smoke that in school. The poor teacher didn't last the whole school year. We were happy, because we had only the equivalent of about five months of school altogether that year.

The next year was quite different. The authorities considered our little part of the country rather resistant to education. So they sent us a cantankerous old schoolmarm. On her first day in the school, she came in and sat down at her desk and started to bawl us out, saying, "You won't do like last year, you won't work the way you did last –" and right in the middle, her dentures fell out on the floor. We all started laughing, and after that we never did take her very seriously. So I can say that, from grade one to grade seven, which was when we left the country, I was never really in school. In the fall, in September and October, we had to dig up the potatoes. After that, we had to harvest the grain. During those two or three months, our attendance was pretty sporadic. And then in the early spring, we had to do the ploughing, then the seeding. I remember we had so little interest in school that we built a camp behind the school, in the woods, and we spent our days there. The schoolmistress would run after us with her long wooden ruler. She would jump over fences and look everywhere for us, and not find us. So I've always thought of school in terms of rebellion and playing hooky.

MARGARET ATWOOD
But you had fun?

VICTOR-LÉVY BEAULIEU
My brothers and I had a lot of fun, yes. Things were different when we came to Montréal.

MARGARET ATWOOD
The fun ended with the move to Montréal? You went to high school in Montréal North. Did the whole family come to Montréal?

VICTOR-LÉVY BEAULIEU
Yes. It was in 1958. I was thirteen. Before Montréal North, we lived in Rivière-des-Prairies. There were still dairy farms there. The tip of the island was farmland. There were also a few cottages there, where people from the city would spend their summer holidays. For us, coming from the country, it wasn't as bad as if we'd moved right downtown in a working-class neighbourhood. I went to a school – this had to be a sign from heaven – named after [St.] Dominic Savio.

Paul Laverdure

At Pius IX secondary school, Montréal North, 1961.

MARGARET ATWOOD
Was it a big school?

VICTOR-LÉVY BEAULIEU
No, it was a small elementary and high school. I hadn't finished grade seven when I arrived there, and I didn't understand much of anything. I found it even more boring than in the country. I would spend my afternoons in class crying. I was completely depressed and desperate. One time – I don't know how I did this, because I was quite shy, like all country people who come to the city – but I stood up and walked out of the classroom and went to see the principal, and I said, "I'm sick of being in grade seven. I want to be in grade eight." I'll never know if the principal did this to make fun of me, but he said, "Okay, I'll try you in grade eight for a month. If it doesn't work, you go back to grade seven. If you do all right, you stay in grade eight." That's how I got into grade eight. And I came first in my class.

MARGARET ATWOOD
You worked, finally.

VICTOR-LÉVY BEAULIEU
To stay in grade eight, yes. One of my brothers was in that class. The teacher – we really weren't lucky – had just come from the military college in Kingston. He was the one, of course, who taught us English. In Saint-Jean-de-Dieu and Trois-Pistoles, we'd had no direct contact with the English language. The only anglophone I saw in the whole of my childhood was in Trois-Pistoles: every fall, [Planter's] sent Mr. Peanut on tour around the province.

MARGARET ATWOOD
Yes, yes, yes, we had him too, with the hat and monocle and black gloves. But we anglophones sometimes had two Mr. Peanuts at the same time.

VICTOR-LÉVY BEAULIEU
Oh! We only had one. (Laughs.) So this Mr. Peanut guy arrived in Trois-Pistoles and he did his little number on the steps of the food co-op – as I

recall, he sang – and handed out little bags of peanuts. We wanted to know if he was the real Mr. Peanut or just someone disguised as a peanut. With two or three of my little friends, I followed Mr. Peanut inside the co-op without him seeing us. He went down to the cellar, where he changed, and we were completely stunned to discover that Mr. Peanut was black, an anglophone, and he said I'll never know what to us in his language.

MARGARET ATWOOD
What a shock for you!

VICTOR-LÉVY BEAULIEU
Culture shock, yes!

MARGARET ATWOOD
Did you read bilingual cereal boxes?

VICTOR-LÉVY BEAULIEU
That also gives you culture shock. (Laughs.) One day, the teacher from Kingston asked me to read a passage in English from *Robinson Crusoe*. My brother and I had learned to speak English the French way: "on the table" was "on *de* table." Obviously, when you speak like that to English-speaking people, it's very hard for them to know what you're saying. So I might have been from the country, but I wasn't dumb enough to do what the teacher was asking. I refused to read. And after that, it was my brother's turn. And he read. The French way. The whole class laughed, including the teacher. Then the teacher, mimicking my brother's accent, asked where he was from. My brother answered, "From Saint-Jean-de-Dieu, sir." At that time, Saint-Jean-de-Dieu was not only the name of a little village near Trois-Pistoles, it was also an asylum in Montréal, which is now called Louis-Hippolyte Lafontaine. The teacher said, "You're from Saint-Jean-de-Dieu? Well, you'd better go back there. I think that's where you belong." I didn't understand why everyone was laughing, because I didn't know that Saint-Jean-de-Dieu was a psychiatric hospital. It was only when we got home that night that my brother and I found out that Saint-Jean-de-Dieu was a big grey house on Sherbrooke Street where they locked up lunatics. That made

me realize that words don't mean the same thing for everyone. And maybe, in a way, it brought me to writing.

MARGARET ATWOOD

Very interesting! I see other possible meanings in that little story. "Saint-Jean-de-Dieu is where you belong." Later we'll get to the theme of madness in your work. (Laughs.) Was the move traumatic for you?

VICTOR-LÉVY BEAULIEU

You're at home somewhere, and then you're thrown into an unfamiliar place where people don't speak the same language as you do. They don't understand many of your expressions. You have the feeling of being nowhere. It's painful. You withdraw a little into your shell. My favourite activity then was taking the bus and going downtown. By fourteen I had visited every street in Montréal. At the same time I would go to the library, where you could borrow three books a week.

MARGARET ATWOOD

You started to read a lot at the age of fourteen?

VICTOR-LÉVY BEAULIEU

Yes. Before that, as I told you, we used to read the books at home and the ones we won at school at the end of the year, and also the little dime novels from Québec that one of my uncles brought us: *X-13*, *Pit Verchères*, things like that. But in Montréal, I discovered the library. First I read all the poetry from Québec.

MARGARET ATWOOD

At fourteen?

VICTOR-LÉVY BEAULIEU

At fourteen or fifteen, I read Alain Grandbois, Anne Hébert's first collections of poems, Émile Nelligan, Saint-Denys Garneau, just about all the poets. But I had a problem. From my home in Rivière-des-Prairies and then Montréal North, to the Montréal municipal library, it took about three hours by bus, both ways. I would leave the library, and by the time I got home I had practically finished the books of poetry. Each trip cost fifty cents return. That meant having to pick up a lot of empty bottles along the streets. I had a brilliant idea. I looked in the catalogue of the library and started choosing only books of more than five hundred pages. With three five-hundred-page books, I had enough reading for a week. The first big book I read was Victor Hugo's *Les Misérables*. After that, I started on Alexandre Dumas.

MARGARET ATWOOD
Did you cry?

VICTOR-LÉVY BEAULIEU
Oh, yes. I was a very involved reader.

MARGARET ATWOOD
I also read *Les Misérables* in my teens and I cried a lot.

VICTOR-LÉVY BEAULIEU
It was sad and it also had a sinister element in the character of Javert, the police chief. I would amuse myself by following people in the street, saying to myself, "That's Jean Valjean. I'll wait for him at the corner and arrest him." Things like that. It was the first novel I read. I didn't know anything about Victor Hugo except what it said in the biographical note at the beginning of the book. After that, I read my first biography. And I learned that, in the Québec literature of the time, as in French literature, writers were always represented as sick.

MARGARET ATWOOD
They had to be.

VICTOR-LÉVY BEAULIEU
Writers had to suffer a lot. If you didn't suffer, you couldn't be a writer. In Québec there was a whole literature on it. We got those books at home. They were published by religious publishers, and my parents got them by subscribing to the good works of Sainte-Anne-de-Beaupré or something, so we had things like *Thérèse Gélinas*; *Ludivine Lachance, des infirme, sourde, muette et aveugle*, [Cripple, deaf, dumb, and blind], or *Le Journal de*

Gérard Raymond, who had lived in Trois-Pistoles, and who flagellated himself and kept a diary because he wanted to be a saint.

MARGARET ATWOOD
Suffering was necessary.

VICTOR-LÉVY BEAULIEU
Yes. It was a literature in which suffering was essential in order to become a writer. A great writer took what was experienced in the ordinary world, beneath the surface, and transformed it into something definitive. In *A Season in the Life of Emmanuel*, Marie-Claire Blais makes Jean-Le Maigre a poet who will end up dying of TB. This was typical of Quebec literature up until the mid-sixties. The best example of a writer who suffered a great deal, who was sort of the martyr of all Québécois writers, is Saint-Denys Garneau, a very handsome boy, gifted, talented, from a rich family, but who had mental-health problems. He was so tormented by those problems that he became a writer. And having become a writer, he had to die of a heart attack in his thirties.

Reading Victor Hugo was fantastic for me. For the first time in my life, I discovered a writer who wrote prolifically and apparently without suffering too much, who had a very good time, had several mistresses, and was never sick. I read his biography and I said to myself, "He's going to end up getting sick. Or else he's not a real writer." But Victor Hugo was practically never sick, he wrote like nobody ever before, and he died at eighty-five. That discovery was very liberating for me. It was perhaps the thing that marked me the most at the time when I was really getting to know writing.

MARGARET ATWOOD
The equivalent for English-speaking writers is Charles Dickens. For women who wanted to become writers, however, the models were discouraging, because in the nineteenth century all the women in literature were sick, and in the twentieth century they had to commit suicide. Like Sylvia Plath.

VICTOR-LÉVY BEAULIEU
In the nineteenth century, it was the men who were killing themselves. When he wrote *The Pickwick Papers*, Dickens was, I think, twenty-five. He

was deeply affected by the suicide of his illustrator, who had killed himself because two of his engravings were refused. At that time, more men than women committed suicide. The situation was reversed when women really started to write.

MARGARET ATWOOD

In the nineteenth century, women had so many physical illnesses that they didn't need suicide to die. But in the twentieth century, medicine had improved, so they had to make an effort. (Laughs.) We got the idea that we couldn't live an ordinary life. A woman writer couldn't have children or a husband, she was sort of a nun, and if she was serious, she had to end in suicide. That model declined with the advent of writers like Margaret Laurence – two children – and Alice Munro – three children. The suicide of the author is no longer a criterion of the quality of her work.

VICTOR-LÉVY BEAULIEU

Well, that's something, at least. Gabrielle Roy, Anne Hébert, and Claire Martin lived cloistered lives. Because of the social and religious structure in Québec, for a woman merely to write was extreme defiance. And to write you need free time. To have free time, you need means. Most women writers didn't marry, because tradition would have kept them at home doing nothing but taking care of children. Under those conditions, a woman who wanted to write had to remain unmarried or to live a hidden life. Some had secret lovers. Fortunately, the social conditions of the practice of literature have changed a lot.

MARGARET ATWOOD

Let's go back to high school. You were fourteen, a schoolboy, and you went to the library. Did you do anything artistic? Had you started writing?

VICTOR-LÉVY BEAULIEU

I really started writing at fourteen or fifteen. The writer Yves Thériault had an advice column in the paper *La Patrie*. I wrote him a letter saying I was unhappy in the city and asking him what to do. He answered in the paper. I kept his answer. He explained that people who feel out of place are not always wrong and said I should continue my studies so that, if I wanted, I could go back to the country and be better equipped to face life's demands. When I sent the letter to Yves Thériault, I was sure it would never appear in the paper. I hadn't told anyone about it except some of my friends at school.

MARGARET ATWOOD
Did he put your name in the paper?

VICTOR-LÉVY BEAULIEU
The letters were published under pseudonyms. It was the first time I saw my writing in print. It was a shock.

MARGARET ATWOOD
A pleasant shock?

VICTOR-LÉVY BEAULIEU
Yes. But it seemed to me that Yves Thériault wrote so well that my letter looked a bit foolish. Still, it allowed me to envision the possibility of writing, and that my writing could interest someone else. We were fourteen living in a four-and-a-half-room apartment on the second floor. With so many people around all the time, I took advantage of every free moment, every minute of peace, to scribble.

MARGARET ATWOOD
Did you show the letter to your family?

VICTOR-LÉVY BEAULIEU
Never! My parents wouldn't have agreed. They would have found it dangerous.

MARGARET ATWOOD
You were wise.

VICTOR-LÉVY BEAULIEU
I'd say I was cunning! And I started to read Thériault's novels, which I hadn't been familiar with.

I'm a faithful and humble servant. I make out a bill in Madame Monalesco's name; I get a cardboard box, put the twelve Molson in it together with the loaf of bread and the cigarettes. I ask Jack for the keys to the yellow truck and leave. Madame Monalesco lives two blocks from the store. She's a harmless old maid who's looking for a man. But since half her face is covered with a birthmark, and a moustache covers her upper lip, her seductive smiles tend to leave something to be desired. My God! Jos's route is full of hopeless cases! Foolish swell-heads, and those with no head at all! My poor, tiny country blasted by alcohol and stupidity and physical deformity and ignorance: is it worth the trouble to spend one's whole life denouncing you? And in the name of what future? Too many lost hours, too many circumstances from which we failed to profit, too many fears buried deep inside us, too much irresponsibility. Were Mom's parents right to exile themselves to Lowell, working fifteen hours a day in textile mills where the cotton ate up their lungs? Were Mom's parents right to become pot-bellied, White Owl-smoking, white nigger Americans in Lowell?

— Victor-Lévy Beaulieu
Jos Connaissant [*Jos Connaissant*],
translated by Ray Chamberlain

MARGARET ATWOOD
At what age did you write your first novel?

VICTOR-LÉVY BEAULIEU
At fourteen, a year after coming to Montréal.

MARGARET ATWOOD
How long was it?

VICTOR-LÉVY BEAULIEU
About two hundred pages. I still remember the title: *Who's Afraid of the Ghost?* It was a detective story. I did the illustrations myself, and I typed it

with two fingers on a typewriter I rented for five dollars a month from the Christian Brothers. I typed the whole thing on the balcony at the back of our house, after school, in the evening, because my father worked nights and we weren't allowed to make noise in the house during the day. I read my novel to my friends at school, but I never submitted it to a publisher. But I did submit the next one, *Ti-Jean in His Darkness*.

MARGARET ATWOOD
Written at the age of fifteen.

VICTOR-LÉVY BEAULIEU
Yes. And it was the first time I was invited to a publishing house to meet with a publisher.

MARGARET ATWOOD
What did he say?

VICTOR-LÉVY BEAULIEU
That's quite a memory. I didn't know the publishing houses. I had sent my manuscript to Fidès in Montréal, a house controlled by the church. Imagine – I get a call from the head of the company that publishes Félix Leclerc and Léo-Paul Desrosiers. It was what I had dreamed of. On the phone, he says he finds my manuscript interesting and he's made about eight pages of notes on it. I had made a lot of little mistakes, and he'd corrected them. He was very kind. He told me I should continue writing and all that. I didn't have a lot of clothes, so I borrowed a shirt and a pair of houndstooth pants from one of my brothers. That was the style then. When I walked into the publisher's office, I realized that he'd had no idea I was fifteen years old. That was my first meeting with a publisher.

MARGARET ATWOOD
Did he offer you coffee?

VICTOR-LÉVY BEAULIEU
No, not that time. But the second time, he did. And the third time . . .

MARGARET ATWOOD
That was progress!

VICTOR-LÉVY BEAULIEU
Yes, it progressed all right. I don't know if it was because of the quality of my manuscripts, but he invited me to his house. A private dinner with a publisher! But the dinner ended very badly, because I realized he was homosexual. Imagine what it was like for a kid just out of the country to find himself in the beautiful apartment of a publisher who was also quite a well-known writer and to suddenly realize that the guy was homosexual. I fled in a panic. I left so fast, I even forgot my overshoes. I never went back to Fidès.

MARGARET ATWOOD
Did he proposition you?

VICTOR-LÉVY BEAULIEU
Not directly, but at a certain point you feel it, and I left. I submitted the next novel to another publisher, who also invited me to his office. He was quite a character, and unlike any other publisher I've ever met, a very tall fellow whose pants stopped halfway down his calves and who talked to me about my book while rocking in a big chair. His gestures were broad and sweeping, and he moved towards me, asking, "Are you homosexual?" What? Were all the publishers in Montréal obsessed with that?

I chose the next one from the telephone book. He was Michel Beaulieu of Éditions Esterel. *Mémoires d'outre-tonneau* [Memories from beyond the barrel] was my first published novel.

MARGARET ATWOOD
And how old were you when you wrote it?

VICTOR-LÉVY BEAULIEU
I was eighteen or nineteen. By the time it was published, I was twenty-two or twenty-three. The publisher had to put off publishing it for lack of funds.

MARGARET ATWOOD

Let's talk about your view of writers when you were in your teens. Did you see the writer as a mystical romantic, an inspired prophet with a social vision – like Victor Hugo, say – or as a scholar, or as an artistic genius – art for art's sake, like Edgar Allan Poe or Baudelaire? Or as someone like Shelley, who said poets were the unacknowledged legislators of the world.

VICTOR-LÉVY BEAULIEU

It wasn't very clear in my mind. The only thing that was clear was, up to the age of fifteen, a desire to do research in nuclear biology. There was a lot of talk about that, and I was impressed. Then in grade ten I started writing my first novels. It quickly became obvious that I would be a novelist. I liked poetry a lot, I was reading a great deal of it, but that universe with its resonances remained a secret to me. I've written two poems in my life, and I didn't exactly find them inspired. The pace of the novel was much more suited to what was in me.

In big families where no one has ever had anything much to do with writing, memory remains buried, unused. Maybe my family entrusted its memory to me. For someone who carries this collective family memory, everything unexpressed from the past wants to come to the surface; it's like digging in the ground for water and striking a spring so strong that it fills the well. You have to use it, whether you want to or not. Maybe this collective family memory was what made me – without even knowing why – choose to write novels, which are better suited to it, I think, than poetry or non-fiction. One year I wrote nine two-hundred-page novels.

MARGARET ATWOOD

A writer is sort of an archaeologist.

VICTOR-LÉVY BEAULIEU

That's true. At least for the type of novels I'm thinking of, a writer has to be something of an archaeologist and a great archivist. I started searching through the family records and making connections among the facts. For example, why did my grandmother learn calligraphy to write accounting documents for her husband? Why didn't she use that beautiful calligraphy

TWO SOLICITUDES : TROIS-PISTOLES   155

for private writing? When you start to make connections among documents, what is implicit in them passes through your memory and becomes explicit.

MARGARET ATWOOD
So you become the voice of silence.

VICTOR-LÉVY BEAULIEU
I think so.

MARGARET ATWOOD
Did you wonder, when you were fourteen or fifteen, what your family would think if you wrote all those things about them?

VICTOR-LÉVY BEAULIEU
No, I didn't wonder, because I was sure I knew the answer.

MARGARET ATWOOD
Which was?

VICTOR-LÉVY BEAULIEU
That they wouldn't like it. And I was right, as I found out when I published my second book, *Race de monde* [What kind of creatures], which was fiction but with autobiographical elements – part of our childhood in Trois-Pistoles, the move to Saint-Jean-de-Dieu, and the big move to Montréal – which, obviously, I recounted in my own way, a bit ironically, with a few sordid details. Not necessarily what we had experienced in my family, but there was a connection. Any writer takes elements of his deeper experience and transforms them. It could be a simple little cut on the finger, which transposed in the novel becomes a huge wound. When *Race de monde* came out, my publisher, Jacques Hébert, had a launch, and I invited my whole family to it.

MARGARET ATWOOD
My goodness!

VICTOR-LÉVY BEAULIEU

They didn't come, except for one, who then went back to my parents with the book. And they held a sort of family council and read the book together.

MARGARET ATWOOD

Collective reading. Collective memory.

VICTOR-LÉVY BEAULIEU

Yes, a collective reading. The outcome was not very favourable for Mr. Author. Most of my brothers and sisters and my mother and father were very angry. They came from an oral tradition. They were not accustomed to reading. It was the first time they saw words that might have some relation to them in print. In *Race de monde*, there were twelve children instead of thirteen. One of my sisters called me, offended. She said, "All the others are there. Why not me? Don't you love me? Do you hate me?" She would also have been angry if she'd been in it, like the others.

MARGARET ATWOOD

Why didn't you put that sister in it?

VICTOR-LÉVY BEAULIEU

Ah! Because it was a novel and I didn't feel obligated to put in thirteen children.

MARGARET ATWOOD

Did you perhaps combine two sisters in one character?

VICTOR-LÉVY BEAULIEU

Not really. The situation I set up, just for the fun of it, was that Steven was the poet of the family. Steven was very much inspired by Marie-Claire Blais's Jean-Le Maigre. *A Season in the Life* had made a very big impression on me, and I found that that image of the poet was how he was traditionally seen in Québec. I invented two brothers who were enemies, Steven and Abel, who were really Cain and Abel.

MARGARET ATWOOD
Let's go back to the family council over the novel.

VICTOR-LÉVY BEAULIEU
As I said, the book came out, and my family read it and didn't like it. We didn't see each other for a year because of it. The first time the Parti Québécois ran in the elections, I decided with one of my brothers to go persuade my father, who was an old Union Nationale supporter, to vote for the PQ. We went there with a quart of Geneva gin and we started bugging him to become a Péquiste, and finally he got mad and kicked us out. And at the door he said, "I'll never forgive you for calling your mother Mama Toothpaste in *Race de monde*." I had a character in the novel called Mama Toothpaste, based on a childhood memory, because, when you're a child, your mother tells you every night to brush your teeth. So I called the mother in the story Mama Toothpaste. I guess my father thought the character in the novel was really my mother. He felt it was disrespectful, blasphemous, to speak of your mother that way. He held it against me for quite a long time.

MARGARET ATWOOD
Why was he so hurt?

VICTOR-LÉVY BEAULIEU
He found it disparaging. He thought I was laughing at her.

MARGARET ATWOOD
I know. But why so hurt?

VICTOR-LÉVY BEAULIEU
Ah! It affected him deeply. (Laughs.)

MARGARET ATWOOD
In 1965 and 1966, you were a clerk at the National Bank of Canada. What was that like? Did you like it?

VICTOR-LÉVY BEAULIEU

Of all the banks, it was the one that paid the least. As a result, they were less strict about hiring at that bank than at the Bank of Montreal, for example, or the Bank of Nova Scotia.

When I finished high school, I didn't have the money to continue my studies. In those days, you could either go to Jacques-Cartier Normal School to become a teacher, which didn't cost anything, or learn a technical trade. Neither interested me. So I looked for a job. They talk about the lack of jobs now. When I left school, after the Parent reform of the education system, there were no jobs for people like us then either. So I reluctantly applied for a job at the National Bank of Canada, and, to my great surprise, I was accepted to work as a clerk. That was before computers. I was at a wicket, and I had to write the entries in the passbooks for the customers who came to make deposits and withdrawals. Apparently I had very poor handwriting. The manager told me I would have a future in the bank if I learned to write with my right hand. Which I didn't do. The result was that I was transferred to bills of exchange.

My branch's territory covered downtown Montréal between St. Denis Street, Sherbrooke Street, St. Lawrence Boulevard, and Mount Royal Avenue. I would make my rounds, visiting customers who had drafts and who had payments to make. I'd get them to sign their bills and I'd take them to the bank, and that would be that. I learned to do my rounds very quickly, and I would spend the rest of the day playing pool in the pool halls on St. Lawrence Boulevard. Working at the bank let me get to know Montréal better, to gallivant around and go into places you don't normally go at sixteen or seventeen. It also gave me a new experience of music. One of my co-workers was a saxophonist. At noon in the little kitchen in the bank, he'd play for us. In the evening I'd go listen to him play in the clubs on St. Catherine Street or St. Lawrence Boulevard. But besides the music and the walks, I'd have to say that, no, I didn't like the bank, except perhaps for one other thing: there was a hold-up at our branch. It was a pretty funny experience, quite ironic, and I've written about it in one of my books.

I left the bank not because I wanted to leave it, but because I got sick. I had polio, and I spent close to three months in the hospital lying on a board waiting for the doctors to let me walk again. Those three months and the recuperation for a year at home gave me time to continue to read, but to read with a little more purpose. It's possibly the only time in my life that I had something like an attack of mysticism. I was discouraged and depressed. I sent a letter to Jean Herbert in Europe, who had written all sorts of books on Sanskrit, Asia, India. I said, "I'm a Québécois who has no money but who is interested in all that stuff. Could you send me some books?" Two or three months later, I received two big crates of books on Mahayana, on Aurobindo and the Mother, and on the East, which I didn't know anything about. I spent seven or eight months reading them.

MARGARET ATWOOD
Where were you?

VICTOR-LÉVY BEAULIEU
I was living with my parents in Montréal North.

MARGARET ATWOOD
With the twelve other children?

VICTOR-LÉVY BEAULIEU
There were nine or ten of us at that time; a few had got married. I even wanted to study Sanskrit under Jean Herbert at the University of Strasbourg. But that little phase ended quite quickly.

MARGARET ATWOOD
What brought on that mystical experience?

VICTOR-LÉVY BEAULIEU
I found Aurobindo extremely interesting. He says the human body and the universe have a similar structure. The cells of our bodies are connected by a fluid that constitutes a sort of aura. The same is true for all the elements of the universe. From a certain point of view, it's true that matter doesn't exist. As a writer I drew a parallel between his vision and reality and fiction. Because of that parallel, Aurobindo was a great discovery for me. But emotionally, I didn't at all get into his world, which was foreign to me. Intellectually, that reading satisfied me and taught me a lot, but emotionally, I was resistant.

MARGARET ATWOOD

In 1967, you became a columnist for *Perspective*, and you also wrote for *La Presse*, *Le Petit Journal*, *Digeste Éclair*, and *Liberté*. How did that come about?

VICTOR-LÉVY BEAULIEU

All that happened by chance. After spending a year at home with polio, I had to do something. I had to work, but I didn't want a nine-to-five job. That limited my options. One morning I took the bus to *Le Petit Journal*, which was run by Jean-Charles Harvey, the author of *Les Demi-Civilisés* [*Fear's Folly*], which was banned by the clergy because Harvey really slammed them in it. When I found out that Harvey ran *Le Petit Journal*, I went there. After making me wait a day, he finally saw me. I told him I wanted to be a journalist. And he said, "Do a piece for me and I'll see." My first piece was about all the incredible stories that telephone operators at Bell heard from madmen and morons and the like. I gave it to him and he published it. That's how I started doing journalism.

Shortly after that, I read in the paper that Radio-Canada needed a writer. I got the job. It paid very well compared to the little pieces I did for *Le Petit Journal*. My parents were very proud, very happy. So I took the bus to go to Radio-Canada. I got off at the first stop and went into a restaurant, and I said to myself, "No, I can't see myself working at Radio-Canada from nine to five." So I went back home and told my parents. They were devastated. They asked me, "What do you want to do?" I answered, "I want to write." And for me, writing could just as easily mean journalism as anything else, as long it was the actual writing that predominated. That was why I played the reporter, and why I worked on a magazine like *Digeste Éclair*.

As chance would have it, the editor of that publication was fired and the owner asked me to edit it. It was there that I met the first Québécois writers who were really contemporary: André Major, Yves Thériault, Gilles Archambault, Claude Jasmin. I'd call them up: "Do you have a piece? We'd like to publish you." Other writers sent me pieces and I published them, but without knowing the authors. That got me a lot more interested in Québec literature. Until then, I mainly knew Jacques Ferron. To me, *La nuit* [*Night*] was the first novel that portrayed Québec reality, but in a language that was both very Québécois and very universal. Other than that, I read Samuel

Beckett. I thought he was the greatest writer of the twentieth century. He had created a metalanguage that fascinated me.

MARGARET ATWOOD
That was in 1967.

I also had two other reading sources. The sixteen volumes of *L'encyclopédie de la jeunesse* [The young people's encyclopedia] from Grolier, which my father, in a noble gesture – since it was during the Depression – had bought shortly after his marriage. Almost my entire childhood is in that encyclopedia. As for my other reading, I owed it to my uncle. Every year he would come to the house, and because my parents gave him vegetables and boxes of clothes, he would bring us boxes full of *X-13*, *Albert Brien*, and *Pit Verchères* books. As soon as my uncle left, my mother would send us up to the attic with the big box, which we would rip open as fast as we could. The *X-13* books especially fascinated me. I remember that I was particularly disturbed by the story of the screwdriver torture.

– Victor-Lévy Beaulieu
Pour saluer Victor Hugo [In tribute to Victor Hugo]

VICTOR-LÉVY BEAULIEU
Yes, the year of the big international get-together in Montréal, Man and His World. I had heard about a literary contest sponsored by Larousse bookstores in France and Hachette bookstores here. They were asking Québécois and English Canadians to write an essay on the writer they felt had best defended human rights. The prize was a trip to Paris for at least six months, all expenses paid. I submitted an essay on Victor Hugo, whose concept of Europe as a single big country called the United States of Europe, which would be based on a confederal model, had impressed me a lot. They sent me a telegram from Paris saying I'd won the competition, along with an English Canadian named Rosa Rose Fedorus, who was of

Ukrainian origin and had written an essay on Voltaire. She came from a little hamlet in Saskatchewan and she had never been out of her little corner of the country, and I came from Montréal North and I'd never left my part of the country either. So the two of us went to Paris for six months. I worked for Larousse as a trainee, I saw French and foreign plays, I visited museums. It was an immersion in culture.

MARGARET ATWOOD
Did you feel isolated there?

VICTOR-LÉVY BEAULIEU
When I got to Paris, the Parisians took me for an American. That proved they didn't know what an American was! Strangely enough, I acquired my knowledge of written English in Paris, thanks to an American woman from Oregon who was staying at the same hotel as I was.

MARGARET ATWOOD
Which hotel?

VICTOR-LÉVY BEAULIEU
The Panthéon, right near the Place du Panthéon. I became friends with the American. When we were together, she spoke French to me in order to learn French, and I tried to speak English to her in order to learn English. It was very symbolic – being a Québécois in Paris, and getting along well with Americans, having fun with them – because, in spite of everything, we're on the same wavelength as they are, more so than with the French. What bothered me about the French was that they considered us philistines. You're a Québécois, you've read, maybe even more than a lot of the French, but as soon as they open their mouths, they're the only ones that under-stand books, they're the only ones who know what's what. And when you take them up on it, when you say, "But no, that's not what Victor Hugo wrote, he wrote such-and-such," they look at you and make a face. That side of the French annoyed me a lot.

MARGARET ATWOOD
That's only true of Parisians.

Montréal North, 1970.

VICTOR-LÉVY BEAULIEU

Of course. In Brittany and Normandy and with the rest of the French, it's much better. Anyway, in those six months, I also discovered some writers that are important to me: James Joyce and Norman Mailer.

MARGARET ATWOOD

Here's a very personal question. In your teens, did you have any girlfriends?

VICTOR-LÉVY BEAULIEU

I should hope so! The very first one was in Montréal, and I must have been fifteen. She was a girl from Montréal North. Her father was a Créditiste. And he had some funny ideas about family life and what his daughter could or couldn't do. So the main thing I remember about that first love, if I can call it that, was that, in the evening, I would be with her in the basement of her father's house, and regularly at eleven o'clock, the Créditiste father would come in with his alarm clock and make it go off to tell me to leave.

MARGARET ATWOOD

Good idea! I'll use that now.

VICTOR-LÉVY BEAULIEU

But as I was a bit hard of hearing for that kind of thing, I'd bug the guy by leaving at four o'clock in the morning (Laughs.) It's a great memory.

MARGARET ATWOOD

Maybe it wasn't that he was a Créditiste, but just the father of a young girl.

VICTOR-LÉVY BEAULIEU

Yes, but a father who's a Créditiste to boot. That's even more incredible.

MARGARET ATWOOD

Did you go to the movies with your girlfriends?

VICTOR-LÉVY BEAULIEU

Oh, yes. I remember a movie theatre in Montréal North called the Regal. We used to go there and try to find the darkest, least crowded corner. We'd go see

Elvis Presley movies, because that was about all they showed at that theatre, apart from Westerns. But we had some very good times in that movie theatre.

MARGARET ATWOOD
Another personal question. When did you start smoking?

VICTOR-LÉVY BEAULIEU
That depends on what kind of smoking you're talking about! If you're talking about tobacco, I started smoking cigars when I was fourteen. When we were in Saint-Jean-de-Dieu, my uncles would come to visit from the United States or from Montréal, and they'd act like big shots – nice cars, nice hats, nice clothes, and constantly puffing on huge cigars and making clouds of smoke. When I was fourteen, I came across a box of White Owls and I started smoking. The first time, it made me a little sick, but I got used to it very quickly. So I started smoking White Owls, like my Uncle Hervé from Montréal. He also wore an enormous ring with his initials on it. The White Owls had rings too. Smoking cigars also involved wearing the cigar rings. You'd take the ring off and stick it on your finger, and it would make you feel dashing, like you were someone else, a character in a movie. For us, those people from the city were like the movies; it was as if they made us part of a movie. My mother hated cigars, because the smell got into everything, into the curtains, into the furniture. That's why I switched to a pipe.

MARGARET ATWOOD
We've talked about your life up to the age of twenty-three; that is, until about 1967. When you came back from Paris, you became a script writer at a radio station, the editor of *Digeste Éclair*, and a columnist at *Le Devoir*. During the same period, you published *Pour saluer Victor Hugo* [In tribute to Victor Hugo] and your first novel, *Mémoires d'outre-tonneau*, and a radio documentary on Jack Kerouac, and another novel, *La Nuitte de Malcomm Hudd*. How did you do all that work in such a short time?

VICTOR-LÉVY BEAULIEU
By not sleeping much, obviously. Let's say that I was pretty lucky, I could go a long time without sleep. Also, I was lucky to get into various organizations without really trying. For example, I got a job at CKLM completely by chance.

When I came back from Paris, I had enrolled at Collège Sainte-Marie to do a humanities program. But I didn't have any money, and the good Jesuit fathers, who were very parsimonious, let me tell you, didn't let me finish my year. I didn't tell my parents. Every morning, I'd leave the house with the little lunch my mother had made me, take the bus downtown, and walk around Montréal. One day I saw a sign on a big building on St. Catherine Street near Peel: "CKLM Radio Station." I'd never seen a radio station, so I decided to go in and take a look at it. Like a lot of people, I had the impression a radio station was huge, immense. In fact, CKLM had two or three very small studios, a little newsroom, and two or three offices.

I went in and asked if I could visit, and they said yes. They gave me a tour guide, an old gentleman by the name of Antoons, who showed me the whole place in fifteen minutes. Afterwards, he took me into his office and chatted with me a bit, and then he asked if I would be interested in writing advertising copy. He put me in front of a typewriter, gave me some examples of ads, and asked me to write fifteen-, thirty-, and sixty-second spots. I did it, and then I went home. A few days later, my mother says to me, "You had a call from CKLM. Did you enter a contest? Maybe you won a radio. Call them back." I called back the old gentleman and was told that if I wanted to work at CKLM, I was hired.

Many of their announcers and hosts were actors. That's how I met Jean Duceppe and Roger Lebel. Jean Duceppe had a summer theatre. He asked me to work there. Roger Lebel asked me to write for him for a small paper in Montréal. So I got into all these fields without really intending to. At the same time, I continued to write. But I did my writing between five and nine o'clock in the morning. At nine o'clock, I'd put down my novel and go to work, either at the radio station or at a newspaper, to earn my living.

MARGARET ATWOOD
Were you still living with your parents?

VICTOR-LÉVY BEAULIEU
No. By that time I wasn't with my family any more. When I came back from Paris, I got married.

MARGARET ATWOOD
Right away?

VICTOR-LÉVY BEAULIEU
Almost right away. Maybe six months later. I got married and I had a wonderful honeymoon in the United States.

MARGARET ATWOOD
Is that the trip you tell about at the end of *Jack Kérouac*?

VICTOR-LÉVY BEAULIEU
That's it. I didn't speak English, but I could read all right. During my honey-
moon, I went to just about every bookstore in the eastern United States.
Everywhere I went, I bought piles of books – I didn't know much about
American writers – and, in the motel where we were staying, I'd look at
them. One night all the books fell on down on my wife and me. Maybe it
symbolized that literature was going to end up destroying us both. When
I came back from that trip, I proposed a series of programs to Radio-
Canada on American literature. That's how I came to write about Kerouac,
James Baldwin, John Updike, Allen Ginsberg, all those authors I had just
discovered. Some of their writing was quite complicated for someone
who hadn't mastered English. A friend, Pierre Turgeon, helped me with
the translation of certain passages that I had trouble understanding. That
allowed me to get to know American literature and to keep on reading a
lot of it.

MARGARET ATWOOD
You entered the publishing world as literary editor of the Éditions du Jour
and, a little later, as co-founder of the literary magazine *L'Illettré*. That led
you, in 1976, to found your own publishing house, VLB Éditeur. In the mid-
sixties, a lot of writers in English-speaking Canada got into publishing
because of the lack of publishers willing to publish new, experimental,
nationalistic books. They founded publishing houses like House of Anansi,
Coach House Press, Talon Books, Quarry Press. Did your presence in publishing have a similar political dimension?

VICTOR-LÉVY BEAULIEU

In a way, yes. In 1968, I was editing *Digeste Éclair*, a small magazine that belonged to Berthold Brisebois, one of the magnates of the yellow press in Québec. He published stuff like *Allô Police*, *Photo Police*, really sensational-istic papers. He wanted something a little more cultural, so I began editing this magazine that a lot of Québécois writers wrote for. But it happened that I published a piece by a member of the National Assembly, Yves Michaud, denouncing the concentration of the Montréal press in the hands of a few companies, such as Power Corporation. What I didn't know when I published that piece was that the owner was in the process of selling his business to Power Corporation. So I was given my pink slip. That coincided with the writing of my second novel, which I'd taken to Jacques Hébert at Éditions du Jour.

One day, I brought him the proofs that I'd just corrected. I hadn't found a title for the novel yet. One of Jacques Hébert's specialties was thinking up titles when the authors couldn't. The title of the novel had to mean some-thing to him and it had to be commercially viable. He was in his office with J.-Z.-Léon Patenaude, a good friend of his who was president of the Book Council. The two of them were talking, and Patenaude said to Hébert, "*Cré race du monde!* [What kind of creatures!]" I told Jacques Hébert that would make a good title for my novel, and he agreed. (Pierre Turgeon was not so lucky with the title of his book, *Faire sa mort comme faire l'amour* [Making one's death like making love], which was rather banal.)

So that day, I brought Jacques Hébert my proofs and he asked me, "Would you be interested in working in a publishing house? My assistant is going back to school." I was writing very early in the morning, so I told him I could work part-time in the afternoon. He said, "Come in the morning instead. I do most of my work in the morning." At that time Jacques Hébert would spend his afternoons working in radio and television all over the place, and then he'd disappear into the woodwork.

So I went there one morning at nine o'clock, and I left that night at ten o'clock. My job, which was supposed to be part-time, quickly became full-time. I ran the publishing house with Jacques Hébert until 1973. And then I resigned, because Jacques Hébert was a federalist and a good friend of Pierre Trudeau and Gérard Pelletier and that whole bunch, who all pub-lished with Éditions du Jour. I decided the collusion with the federalists had gone on long enough, and, with Léandre Bergeron, I founded my own publishing house, L'Aurore, which closed its doors after a year and a half or two years.

L'Aurore belonged to Montreal anglophone Jewish financial interests. They had founded the publishing house to support their distribution company. When problems arose with Léandre Bergeron and two or three other writers, I created VLB Éditeur, which is still in existence. I sold it in 1985, because I'd decided to move back to Trois-Pistoles and because a publishing house is a lot of work. At first it goes well, because you only have a few authors to take care of. But then the number increases, and you find yourself with sixty-five or seventy authors who often mistake you for their mother and think they can phone you at eleven o'clock at night or come see you at four in the morning, because they need you while they're writing, which is understandable.

I had a choice between writing and leaving writing for publishing, and I chose for a while to do nothing but write, because I found that I was behind on my writing program. But in 1994, I decided to come back to publishing, because there's a lot of pleasure in publishing books the way you want to publish them. There's a lot of pleasure in publishing when you can find nice papers and beautiful formats, and go against the current of what's being done these days, with publishers tending to put out cheaper and cheaper books – not bad books but cheap – supposedly because they're trying to reach a broad audience, and to do that you have to make books that don't cost too much. So I decided to create another small publishing house, in order, as the French publisher Bernard Grasset said, to add the books I was missing to my library.

MARGARET ATWOOD
It's a lot of work. I've done it myself. It's a bit like the Red Cross: you give your blood, you give more blood, and then they ask you for more blood.

VICTOR-LÉVY BEAULIEU
You have to be a bit of a vampire! (Laughs.)

MARGARET ATWOOD
It's other people who are the vampires.

VICTOR-LÉVY BEAULIEU

Yes, it's a problem. Publishing requires self-denial, because authors are not always easy.

MARGARET ATWOOD

Did you do it with a lot of idealism? For Québec literature? For writing? For young people?

VICTOR-LÉVY BEAULIEU

In Québec, in the seventies, 90 per cent of the book market was controlled by our dear French imperialist friends. A little like the big American companies controlling three-quarters of the English-Canadian market. For a national literature to prosper, it has to have control of its publishing and distribution structures. If you've got to depend on foreigners to do your distribution, you'll miss the boat; they won't pay much attention to you. It was a major problem in Québec. It seemed important to me to create a publishing house that would really be Québécois and that would be completely devoted to Québec literature.

I was critical of the publishers, even the Québec publishers – there were a few of them – because they produced cheap, poorly made books. The first manuscript that landed on my desk at Éditions du Jour, for example. I read it, I had it read, and it was accepted. Then I went to see Jacques Hébert and I said, "We've received a manuscript that we're going to publish."

He said to me, "Leave me the manuscript, no problem, I'll take care of the printing." And he sent it to the printer with a little note: "Dear printer, make me a hundred-and-sixty-page book from this manuscript." It was the printer who chose the typeface, the layout, the illustrations, if there were any, so that the printed book you got was not terribly professional.

I thought it was crazy, in a society that had access to technology, that we were making books with no illustrations, no photographs, nothing, supposedly because they cost too much. At VLB Éditeur, I tried to emphasize the choice of typeface and the layout, to make books that would first of all be interesting to look at, because books are objects. For example, when I published Shakespeare's *Macbeth*, translated into Québécois by Michel Garneau, I did some digging into Elizabethan literature, to find out how they printed at that time, so I could publish a *Macbeth* that was very Québécois and at the same time that looked like the books of Shakespeare that you might see in that period.

On the other hand, yes, it's certainly true, publishing is the Red Cross. An author can call you any time with a writing problem or a copyright problem he hasn't been able to sort out. It's also a wonderful trade, because you have the opportunity to add your own creation to someone else's.

MARGARET ATWOOD

But you always have to struggle with the problems of the market. France is big; Québec is small. Your market, from the financial point of view, is always limited. It's the same thing in English Canada; compared to the United States and Great Britain, it's small.

VICTOR-LÉVY BEAULIEU

The francophone market in Québec is at most six million people. But even in a market of six million, if things were done properly, there would be more possibilities for distributing this literature and making it profitable. But we've created bodies like the central lending libraries, which now supply the small municipal libraries in villages and neighbourhoods and which control the distribution of books. And most of these central lending libraries buy books on the basis of the media. So, if your book is a bestseller, you've got a chance it will be in the central lending libraries and the bookstores and the small municipal libraries. If not, it will go unnoticed. At least 80 per cent of Québec literature published is not distributed anywhere. I don't know if it's the same in English Canada, but here it's even more of a disaster than it was in the seventies, because all the French publishers have offices in Montréal and they control powerful distribution organizations. They're in a position to influence things like the big book fairs in Québec City and Montréal. If they're not happy with the locations assigned to them, they boycott the book fair, and there's no more book fair. They call the shots, because they still control 80 or 85 per cent of sales in Québec publishing, or publishing done in Québec. And as long at that doesn't change, as long as the governments in both Ottawa and Québec City don't understand that, there's little chance of Québec literature – and this is equally true of English-Canadian literature –

doing anything more than barely surviving. When you're barely surviving, it's almost impossible to go abroad and say, "In Québec, we have authors that you might be interested in reading." Survival doesn't make a good export.

MARGARET ATWOOD

I have an idea, Victor. You should adopt the Inuit language as your official language. Then there'd be no more competition with France. I've been to Finland. That country has a population of four million, and every year they publish four thousand books and eighty newspapers. It's extraordinary. Finnish is an absolutely impossible language. You have to have an impossible language!

The mass, the coffin at the end of the aisle, the six burning candles, the statues and the stained-glass windows covered with violet crepe, grandfather's low voice as he sang the prayer for the dead, standing erect by the organ in the lower balcony. He had come to meet us at Trois-Pistoles and had followed the procession to Saint-Jean-de-Dieu where Mom's body was to be exposed for a few hours. Grandfather had wanted to buy a crown of flowers himself which he took from the trunk of the car and placed at the foot of the coffin. . . . Soon he would be dead too. Soon we would all be dead and there would be no more witnesses and no more remembrance and no more memories of life, not of the present, not of the past: it would be all over and because it would be all over, nothing would ever have been except the dark, silent dream, the dream of eternity's possible forms.

– Victor-Lévy Beaulieu
Jos Connaissant [*Jos Connaissant*],
translated by Ray Chamberlain

VICTOR-LÉVY BEAULIEU

That's not a bad idea, Margaret. Somewhat along the same lines, Yves Thériault once said our problem as Québec writers – and you have the same problem with the Americans – was that we wrote in French, and that if we wrote in Iroquois, for example, there would be no problem, we'd be translated all over the world. Your books have been translated into French, so you know. If you choose a French translator, the Québécois will say it's badly translated. And if you choose a Québécois translator, the French will say, "But that isn't French, we can't understand a word of it." There are words that mean completely different things in France than in Québec. We Québécois are used to negotiating these linguistic differences. When they send us San-Antonio, well, we read San-Antonio – and we manage to make sense of the Parisian argot. The French, though, with their imperialist way of thinking, won't reciprocate in this little semantic exercise. They want everything to correspond to *their* standards, which are often bastardized if you can judge by all the English words they now use. In this area, they could learn some very valuable lessons from Québec.

MARGARET ATWOOD

Let's get back to the story of your life. At the end of the sixties, you were writing your novels and you were publishing books for Jacques Hébert. But in 1970, there was the October Crisis. The government of Québec asked the federal government to intervene because of a supposed plot by the FLQ. Civil rights were suspended and a lot of artists and intellectuals were jailed without trial. Were you connected with all that, and if so, how?

VICTOR-LÉVY BEAULIEU

To the FLQ as such, no. I had no direct connection to it.

MARGARET ATWOOD

No, but to the crisis?

VICTOR-LÉVY BEAULIEU

A lot of the writers and intellectuals who came to Éditions du Jour were very sympathetic to the cause of the FLQ, if not actual sympathizers. Jacques Hébert had warned me that our line was tapped by the RCMP and that I should be careful talking to people. Even Jacques Hébert was wire-tapped by the feds! I was also visited by some RCMP officers, who on some pretext asked me for information on people I knew who they thought were connected to the FLQ.

I was pretty much of a sympathizer. Given the political situation in 1970, it was pretty normal that Québec go through the same thing they were going through in South America, Morocco, Algeria, and other places, with political groups deciding to arm themselves and take up urban guerilla warfare. The kidnapping of a foreign political official like James Cross by one of the cells, and then of Pierre Laporte, a Québec cabinet minister suspected of having ties to organized crime in Montréal, seemed kind of normal in the Canadian and Québec political context. And it may seem insignificant that, of an Englishman and a Québécois who were kidnapped, it was the Québécois who died, but I believe, on the contrary, that symbolically it was very important. In my view the FLQ blew it, either by not freeing the prisoners they were holding or by eliminating the Québécois instead of the one who really represented imperialism and colonialism for them. To me, that was, if not a strategic error, at least a really dumb thing to do.

Later I knew some of the felquistes who had been closely involved. Several were from Montréal North. One of them even lived three buildings away from me without my knowing it. I met those people later. Jacques Lanctôt, one of the felquistes who had taken part in the abduction of James Cross, became one of my employees at VLB Éditeur after he returned from exile in Cuba and Paris. Fine. What I know about the FLQ is that, with some exceptions, unless I'm mistaken, it was a pretty anarchic movement that began completely innocuously and, in the course of events, turned into what you could call a monster. They lost control of things. Once you get into what I call the real power, either Québec City or Ottawa, once you're caught up in that, you're no longer in control of the game. The inquiries proved that the federal government and the RCMP knew perfectly well what was going on but didn't intervene right away, for reasons that we can still speculate about even today. First of all, I don't think there can be a conspiracy of a little cell, no matter where in the world, without the complicity of the governments in power. And I have the impression that, when these things happen and they're not resolved immediately one way or the other, it's because it suits the governments, which use them in a certain way, first as provocation and then to impose repression.

MARGARET ATWOOD

Among the politicians, only the NDP opposed the suspension of civil rights. But the Québécois never vote for the NDP. Why?

VICTOR-LÉVY BEAULIEU

As you know, the NDP has a long history.

MARGARET ATWOOD

A history of nonexistence in Québec!

VICTOR-LÉVY BEAULIEU

There are various reasons for that. First of all, the NDP, like its predecessor the CCF, never understood a very simple reality, which is that, if Canada exists, there also exists in Canada two founding peoples, two languages, two distinct societies. And all the resolutions that have been presented for the NDP to recognize this simple little fact have always been rejected. And in any case, the party has always been controlled at the top by anglophones. Québec francophones who sought a role at the top of the hierarchy have never been able to achieve that. The NDP was very centralizing, just like Trudeau. Québec francophones were less so. It was a way of protecting their language and culture. And on these questions the NDP, following in the footsteps of Frank Scott, that great jurist from McGill University, who was involved in the NDP for a long time, was very centralizing, you might even say Rhodesian. The NDP's Rhodesian attitude to Québec meant that the Québécois always viscerally rejected the NDP in elections, even though, with regard to social democracy, the party was, so to speak, the older brother of what became the Parti Québécois. The linguistic attitude of the NDP with regard to Québec prevented it from getting elected. Today, for quite different reasons, Preston Manning's Reform Party has absolutely no chance of electing any members of Parliament in Québec.

MARGARET ATWOOD

Isn't it a bit of a chicken-and-egg question; that is to say, if there had been Québécois candidates running for the NDP, wouldn't francophones have had more influence in it?

VICTOR-LÉVY BEAULIEU

These things are pretty simple, but when they happen, there's a lack of understanding on one side of the fence. The people in the CCF were Westerners at first, and then English Canadians from Ontario.

MARGARET ATWOOD

I know all that, but civil rights are worth something, aren't they?

VICTOR-LÉVY BEAULIEU

The Québécois had no complaint with that. But to them, the defence of civil rights alone was not sufficient to make the NDP a more, shall we say, appropriate government – more to their advantage than a Liberal or Conservative government.

MARGARET ATWOOD

That's all in the past now. The NDP has practically disappeared. But who knows, it could come back.

VICTOR-LÉVY BEAULIEU

That would surprise me.

MARGARET ATWOOD

Would you prefer a francophone tyranny to an NDP democracy?

VICTOR-LÉVY BEAULIEU

What are you alluding to when you say a francophone tyranny?

MARGARET ATWOOD

Neither the [francophone] Liberals nor the Conservatives opposed the suppression of civil rights.

VICTOR-LÉVY BEAULIEU

No, they voted for it in the Commons. I've always thought that the Liberals and Trudeau were a caricature of democracy. Trudeau was never a democrat. All his life, all he thought about was power and how to get it. But that's characteristic of the Conservative and Liberal governments we've had.

Okay. Now, the NDP. Yes, Broadbent was a real good guy, somewhat sympathetic to Québec, but I'd call that sympathy a façade. Establishing policies isn't everything; those policies have to have genuine resonance for the people they're being made for. That's why I don't think the Reform Party has a very bright future in Québec.

MARGARET ATWOOD

In 1972, you published a novel entitled *Un rêve québécois* [*A Québécois Dream*], which has a connection with the events involving the FLQ. In it, the character killed, in reality or in imagination, is not a minister of the government but the mistress of the protagonist, and it's a personal act. For you, what's the connection between politics and art?

VICTOR-LÉVY BEAULIEU

I wrote *Un rêve québécois* the year of the October Crisis. To me, the Québécois experienced the October Crisis in a way I would call unconscious or underground. It was obvious that a very large majority of Québécois were against the kidnapping and murder of Pierre Laporte. On the other hand . . .

MARGARET ATWOOD

But why kill the mistress?

VICTOR-LÉVY BEAULIEU

Un rêve québécois was a way of questioning the phenomenon of the Québécois collective unconscious in 1970. It was from this perspective that I created the characters of Joseph-David-Barthélémy Dupuis and his mistress, Jeanne-d'Arc. All it had taken to make people crawl back into their holes was for Trudeau to send a few little tin soldiers into Montréal. When you can't decide politically who you are, when you accept a situation of inferiority, when you're terrorized by somebody bigger than yourself, the immediate response is that you want to terrorize someone weaker than yourself. Joseph-David-Barthélémy Dupuis is an alcoholic who's just left a detox centre when the October Crisis breaks out. He goes back to his neighbourhood, Montréal North, where there are a lot of army helicopters. Marked by these images of violence, he becomes a terrorist to his mistress,

Jeanne-d'Arc. He forces her into all sorts of sordid acts and ends up killing her without really knowing why. To me, it was sort of a parable for the October Crisis as seen and as created by the Québécois, who at the unconscious level absolutely failed to understand – were unable to understand – what was happening.

MARGARET ATWOOD
Someone had to be killed.

VICTOR-LÉVY BEAULIEU
Yes, someone had to be killed. Sort of the way the terrorists killed Pierre Laporte, who's like the abused brother of Québec, Joseph-David-Barthélémy Dupuis kills his mistress, Jeanne-d'Arc, without really knowing why.

MARGARET ATWOOD
With political material, there's a danger of preaching. How do you avoid it? Is that possible?

VICTOR-LÉVY BEAULIEU
I don't know if there's always a danger of preaching. That depends on the meaning you give to the word *politics*. Lots of writers, not just Québécois, not just English Canadians, but foreign writers, have lent their pens to the service of a cause that's expressed through a political party. In France, Charles Maurras wrote novels in support of the right, and there was Drieu La Rochelle during the war. At the time, those novels can have a great impact for or against, especially in their society, but that doesn't make very good literature. I don't write to be the scribe of a political party, or as a political activity at all. What is essential to someone who writes is the writing itself.

MARGARET ATWOOD
I'll turn my formulation around. If you're a writer and you use political material, that carries the risk of being read as preaching, especially in the United States. If you write a complex, artistic novel, but you're known as someone who supports this or that, it risks being read as preaching.

VICTOR-LÉVY BEAULIEU

Yes, that's true. In all communities, in all societies, there are writers who become prophets, literary gurus.

MARGARET ATWOOD

In spite of themselves.

VICTOR-LÉVY BEAULIEU

It's up to the writer to make sure that doesn't happen. James Joyce wrote a lot on Irish politics, but he didn't become a preacher or a guru serving Irish politics. I think, in fact, that the exact opposite was true, because Joyce wrote at the most important level, the symbolic level. When a writer writes symbolically, there's little chance of his becoming a prophet, a guru, a preacher, or whatever. It's the work itself that makes the difference. At the beginning of the century, some American writers wrote in support of trade unionism. Steinbeck's novel *The Grapes of Wrath*, in particular, was written to help the American union movement. That doesn't stop it from being a great novel. But reading it today, I find the trade unionism a bit tiresome. Still, when it came out, it helped workers and union members gain respect and it helped the labour movement grow throughout the United States. I have nothing against this type of literature, but I don't find it particularly interesting. There's not much chance that I'll write the great novel of the Parti Québécois or the great novel of the Québec Liberal Party. I'd be surprised.

MARGARET ATWOOD

Later we'll talk about the temptations of the Devil. (Laughs.) *Un rêve québécois* is remarkable for its extreme violence. At the end, you give a very graphic description of the rape of a woman and the dismemberment of her body. What do you feel is the value or the role of violence in art?

VICTOR-LÉVY BEAULIEU

If only by reading the newspapers, people are exposed to all this violence on a daily basis. But newspaper writing, by making it commonplace and talking about it in a banal way, destroys its meaning. In "art," if one writes well, the readers suddenly see the total monstrosity of violence in front of their eyes. I'm certain that if a page from *Un rêve québécois* were published in the *Journal de Montréal*, readers would be horrified. Novel writing does the opposite of making violence seem normal. A very violent passage in a novel can make the reader aware of the intolerable nature of a sadistic act. The media make violence practically acceptable. Art has to make it unacceptable again.

MARGARET ATWOOD

If that's the role of violence in art, what do you feel is the role of violence in political life? Does there come a point where you feel it's justified?

VICTOR-LÉVY BEAULIEU

I would say in the end all violence is unjustifiable, since it involves quite simply the domination of one person by another. Now, when we try to control or eliminate this violence, we become aware of the weight of two thousand years of Judeo-Christian tradition and we realize that Western civilization is built on violence. To eliminate this violence from society will take more than work; it will take an overall change in society. And after two thousand years of shameless exploitation of violence by the powers that be, it's a utopian illusion to think that violence can be eliminated. Far from curbing violence, modern society exacerbates it. You just have to observe how it operates: fewer and fewer people have access to wealth, more and more people are completely marginalized in a system that they have no control over, that they don't understand, and that has less and less room for them. Violence comes in part from our heavy Judeo-Christian heritage.

MARGARET ATWOOD

A lot of other religions and societies have been founded on the idea of sacrifice, on rituals involving blood and purification. I'm thinking of the Aztecs. Couldn't it be something in human nature, and not only in the West?

VICTOR-LÉVY BEAULIEU

In less populous societies, sacrificing a person was saying to the supreme creator, "You see, I'm making the greatest sacrifice I can to you. I am putting in jeopardy my very kind, my tribe." In our modern societies, where there are too many people, any human sacrifice becomes absurd, the very opposite of the symbolism that was originally attached to human sacrifice. Such sacrifices are a lot more dangerous in contemporary societies, because they have become collective.

MARGARET ATWOOD

I have another idea. Maybe novels and films have acts of violence in them because life is a process and death is a solitary event. Solitary events are easier to represent and they attract more attention. What do you think of that? Maybe violence is essential to narrative forms.

VICTOR-LÉVY BEAULIEU

I think art isn't very different from the society in which it takes form, and that it feeds on the society. Art deciphers what is encoded. Readers and critics found my first novels very violent, especially the sexuality in them. Why? For the very simple reason that Québec literature before my generation was completely silent about sexuality. It wasn't talked about because of the church. The most revealing major work in this regard is *Le Libraire* [*Not for Every Eye*] by Gérard Bessette. The character, a bookseller in a small country town, falls in love with his woman lodger. Bessette, like any Québec writer of the sixties, was well schooled in religious repression. He talks at length about the bookseller's trade and the books on the Index [of proscribed books] because they were deemed too daring in literary and sexual terms. He wrote the book partly to denounce this repression of reading by religion. But at the same time, he himself reflects this repression in the love scenes between the bookseller and his lodger. His characters have coffee together in the evening, then they climb the stairs to the lodger's room. But as soon as they go in, the door closes and the chapter ends. We next see them on the following morning, sitting at a table having coffee. As a young reader, I said to myself, "They spent eight hours in that bloody room. How come we don't know what went on in there?" Québec literature didn't talk about that violence, or that beauty, or whatever – about sexuality, period. Then in my first novels, from *Race de monde* to *Oh Miami Miami Miami*, I tried to describe certain sexual practices, acts of violence, deviant acts, in order to be able to say to myself, "I talked about it." Most of those books were banned in colleges and schools. I told myself that proved I'd struck a chord of truth.

MARGARET ATWOOD

Have you read *Beautiful Losers* by Leonard Cohen?

VICTOR-LÉVY BEAULIEU

Yes, of course. Leonard Cohen talks about the reality of Montréal, but from the point of view of an English-speaking Jew. His novel touched me a lot, and at one time I would have liked to write like him. I believe Cohen was the first Montréal writer to use the myth of Katherine Tekakwitha in a meaningful way. In *Beautiful Losers*, unlike all the monographs in French and English I'd read on her, and unlike the Catholic platitudes they used to make us read, Katherine Tekakwitha was raised to the level of a true myth. That novel taught me a lot about the stranger that lives within oneself. *Beautiful Losers* is one of the great classics of Canadian literature, and of Québec literature as well, I would say.

– Jack's problem was that he didn't believe in humanity, neither his own nor others, there was a lot of St. Paul in him – (Put a pair of wings on your back, bleach your hair with peroxide and fly over Lowell to announce the good news: "You're all going to die and if you don't know the right way to do it, hell will be waiting for you – Live in the Unique, live in the thought of the Unique" – Jack's system was like the angel Ti-Jean: he flew low (the old absurd Christian concept of a good death and of a Jewish Trinitarian God and of Paradise at the end of your life) – In his naiveté or his disgust Jack was an uncorruptible man of the right – (But perhaps he always had been –

– Victor-Lévy Beaulieu
Jack Kerouac: a chicken-essay [Jack Kérouac: essai poulet],
translated by Sheila Fischman

MARGARET ATWOOD

Since 1972 you've written an amazing number of books. Some are novels, others literary non-fiction, and still others a mixture of the two. And you've also written plays, radio broadcasts, and television series. I've made a list of

With his dog, Alfred.

some of your heroes who've made their appearance in them: James Joyce, Jacques Ferron, Jack Kerouac, Victor Hugo, Don Quixote, Herman Melville, James Joyce's Stephen Dedalus, Shakespeare's Hamlet, William Styron, Tolstoy, and James Baldwin. The most recent additions are Voltaire and Faust. Looking at those men – because they're all men – I tried to figure out what they had in common and what about them fascinated you.

They could perhaps be divided into categories: one, the transgressors, those that break laws other than moral laws and literary laws, like Jacques Ferron, Jack Kerouac, and Faust; two, there are the idealists, like Don Quixote and Tolstoy; three, the introverted philosophers, like Hamlet and Stephen Dedalus; four, those on a mystical quest, like Melville and his hero the mad captain; there are also the other madmen, drunkards like Satan Belhumeur, Jos Connaissant, and their buddy Malcomm Hudd. These categories sometimes overlap in a single character, but let's just say that none of them is what a psychologist would call well adjusted. (Laughs.) Many of them are writers, and, even when they're not writers, they fulfil the functions of a writer; for example, they criticize their society. Considering all that, what do you feel is the role of the writer? Could it be that the character who's well adjusted to society is actually the crazy one?

VICTOR-LÉVY BEAULIEU
Madness is very important, not only for society but also for the individual. I think that, if you take up writing one day, it's because there's no solution, either for yourself or others. Because you've realized precisely that the basis of society is arbitrary, and that people who are perhaps more sensitive than others are stuck with it. This world of ours cannot do otherwise than produce a certain number of eccentric, crazy, visionary, enraged, maladjusted people. As a writer, first of all, and as an individual, I've asked myself: "Is this true of all societies?"

Most of the books self-published by the authors in little villages in Québec were written by eccentrics. I've already mentioned *Ludivine Lachance*. There was also that dear P.P. Paradis, who wrote a collection of poems called *La fin du monde vue par un témoin oculaire* [The end of the world as seen by an eyewitness], which is an expression of a kind of mystical, manic-depressive madness. Larouche, a poet from Chicoutimi, spent his life going back and forth between Québec City and Chicoutimi on the bus and writing poems about clouds. You've got to be a bit crazy to do that.

And the poet Roger Brien, who for years advertised in the newspapers and published little brochures in which he'd say, "Victor Hugo spent his whole life writing one hundred and ninety-two thousand lines. Roger Brien has written two hundred and ten thousand in five years." As I recall, his *Prométhée* fills seven five-hundred-page volumes, and it's written in alexandrines. In it, Katherine Tekakwitha discusses philosophy with Hegel, and Jacques Cartier chats with Pope Benedict XII. You read it and you realize that it's not just a bit crazy, it's completely insane.

I asked Clément Marchand, the poet, journalist, and publisher from Trois-Rivières, who published Roger Brien's famous *Prométhée*, what it represented, and I found his answer very apt: "Writers like that are lightning rods. By writing what they do, they allow other writers to give up that kind of thing and move forward." And I think that was my interest in writers like Melville, Hugo, and Kerouac. Delving into a writer means getting excited by what he writes, it means practically becoming him. For a Québécois like me, who became a writer in the sixties, when foreign literature in particular was banned in the education system, to plunge heart and soul into Melville, even without really knowing English, was to discover a whole universe, to feel it and smell it – and to see myself as capable of making sense of it. For me living in a young culture – English-Canadian and Québécois culture are in fact very young in comparison with others – reading those books and making them my own was very important.

It happened in different ways, depending on the writer. My little book on Hugo was a testimonial. As I told you, Hugo is the first writer I read who showed sovereignty in his language, in his life, in everything. With Kerouac, it was first of all the writing that fascinated me. *Doctor Sax* is still the great novel of childhood fears, of all the imagery of childhood, and there's only one writer who could have expressed it so well. I was twenty years old when I read Kerouac, and I didn't understand how a guy who had the good luck to live with Burroughs, Ginsberg, Lowell, that whole bunch, could be unhappy, how he wasn't able to really become part of American society and always remained a little on the outside. I felt there had to be reasons for that aloneness. Digging a bit into Kerouac's past, his family, his childhood in Lowell [Massachusetts] – his roots were French-Canadian – the increasing importance of his mother throughout his life, I realized that basically Kerouac couldn't really integrate into America and become an American. He was too French-Canadian.

MARGARET ATWOOD

But Lowell was also very, very unhappy, and he spent a lot of time in mental hospitals. And Burroughs wasn't exactly the image of a happy man. And they're not Québécois. Maybe there's something else.

VICTOR-LÉVY BEAULIEU

The Naked Lunch is not the story of a happy guy, that's obvious. But Kerouac's unhappiness doesn't at all have the same meaning as that of Burroughs or Ginsberg. You could say that, in Kerouac, it's at a basic level. While in Ginsberg and Burroughs, in spite of everything, there's a way . . .

MARGARET ATWOOD

But in his mystical experiences, Kerouac expresses joy, rapture.

VICTOR-LÉVY BEAULIEU

He expresses that, yes, but from a very French-Canadian point of view that goes back to an idyllic vision of religion. For example, his spurts of enthusiasm for Zen Buddhism are more intellectual than truly felt, as they are, for example, in Snyder. It's not at all the same practice, the same application, the same way of seeing it. At any rate, Kerouac was the perfect image of what a Québécois could become if the economic, social, and cultural situation of Québec didn't change. At the time when I was reading Kerouac, the future for a Québécois bore a strange resemblance not only to his work but to his life.

As for Melville, I had a childhood memory of reading him in a little abridged edition. I went back to him, and through that nineteenth-century writer, who came from a very puritanical environment and whose father was of French origin, I discovered a whole society that I had been unaware of. That's what's important when you read, first of all your relationship to others, but also the differences between yourself and others. Melville's development as a writer fascinated me. Usually you start by writing poetry, then you write stories, and finally novels. In Melville's case, it was the opposite. He started by writing huge novels, then he wrote tales and stories, and he finished with poetry, some of which resembles Japanese haiku. His poems are just three or four lines long. I was intrigued by this evolution. I wondered, "How is it that he's one of the only examples like this that I know of in literature?"

MARGARET ATWOOD

There's also Thomas Hardy.

VICTOR-LÉVY BEAULIEU

Yes, but it's still quite a rare phenomenon. So I began to explore Melville, and with him the birth of American society. I was doing some publishing, so I was interested in all the publishing problems. In the nineteenth century, the British didn't recognize American copyright. To be recognized as an author, you had to be published in Britain. The emerging American literature – Hawthorne, Emerson, Thoreau, Melville – faced the same problems Québec literature did with respect to France.

Moby-Dick is in a way prophetic. That visionary book has got all kinds of symbolism. It's full of crazy prophets too, a lot of crackpot sailors. It's a great mythic novel, and the narrative is very lyrical. The sea shanties in it are superb. I've never understood why nobody has made it into an opera. I made a little pilgrimage to Nantucket, and I found a small hotel there that belonged to a Mr. Paradis, a Québécois who had become a harpooner for the Americans. I discovered that a lot of Québécois did whaling for the Americans. There were even native people from Québec, crews of Maliseet and Micmac, who hunted whales.

They've always presented the St. Lawrence River as an obstacle. When the colony came under English jurisdiction, the French who had founded it did not return to France. They believed they could no longer escape the river's grip – they were afraid of being shipwrecked – and they remained here to help create the image of the people of Québec as a people of peasants and farmers, secluded on their land. When I read Melville and did my research on all the Québécois who had left to go whaling in the South Seas for the Americans, it made me realize that the isolation of Québec that they always talked about in our schoolbooks never existed, and that a great many Québécois were seafarers. It did me a lot of good to read that.

MARGARET ATWOOD
And now it's okay to go to Miami in the winter. It's not anti-Québec.

VICTOR-LÉVY BEAULIEU
As they say, we all end up getting old.

MARGARET ATWOOD
But Victor-Lévy, you're not being very nice, you're evading the questions. I began with a question about madness. You like visionaries, you like inspiration . . . you must know that the word *inspiration* comes from Delphi, where they would burn narcotic substances, and when the prophetesses inhaled the smoke, it gave them visions. You're a writer, and you like the idea of vision. How do you get yourself into the mental state necessary to write the kind of visionary passages you've written?

VICTOR-LÉVY BEAULIEU
It's hard to say how I get there. I think that, for some writers, there's a medium at work deep inside them. I think Victor Hugo was one of those. Besides, for years he turned tables and talked with the spirits.

MARGARET ATWOOD
It was the fashion. Everyone did it.

VICTOR-LÉVY BEAULIEU
Except that the spirits that spoke to Victor Hugo and the way he had of noting what they said produced high poetry, unlike a lot of mediums for whom the spirits spoke quite plainly.

MARGARET ATWOOD
The spirits of our time usually utter incredible banalities. Victor Hugo was lucky!

VICTOR-LÉVY BEAULIEU
What the spirits dictated to Victor Hugo on dreams . . . we had to wait for people like Freud and André Breton to say as much about them.

MARGARET ATWOOD

But Victor-Lévy, do you turn tables? Do you talk to spirits? Or what? Is it just Molson beer and Clamato? What are your inspirations?

VICTOR-LÉVY BEAULIEU

No need to be inspired in the deepest sense of the word. You sit down at your work table, you write, and then, I don't know by what process, you go into a second state. By concentrating, you become what is spoken instead of the one who is speaking. Writers often have – I put this in quotations – "visions." It was the case for T.S. Eliot and Victor Hugo. Not everyone has them. And some can't communicate them. As Burroughs said, a lot of people have their names printed on book covers, but that doesn't make them writers. A genuine writer has to have a visionary side in the true sense of the word. You've shown that yourself in *Cat's Eye* and *Surfacing*.

MARGARET ATWOOD

Do you think it's a kind of self-hypnosis?

VICTOR-LÉVY BEAULIEU

Yes, probably. Scientifically that could explain it. You put a pendulum in front of you, and it hypnotizes you. But the pendulum can be inside you. Writing is a bit like playing with a pendulum. To attain something beyond writing, like Maupassant, for example, you have to reach that kind of state. Otherwise you produce a rational literature – a subject, a verb, and a complement, but nothing more. Joyce called it an epiphany.

MARGARET ATWOOD

Say a few words about two of your literary forebears, Émile Nelligan and Hubert Aquin.

VICTOR-LÉVY BEAULIEU

Émile Nelligan is the forebear of practically all Québécois writers. He was really the first poet here who tried in a sense to justify being a poet by going all the way to madness, and by accepting it totally. Hubert Aquin, fifty years later, was the other Québécois writer who embraced that madness to the point of no return; that is, to the point of suicide. I knew Hubert Aquin, I worked with him. He was an exceptional player – with words, with literature, with life. He was a fabulous inventor of psychodramas. He put the breaking down of language at the centre of everything. And for language to break down, you have to really grapple with madness.

Aquin's *oeuvre* was that of a forerunner. In *Prochain épisode* [*Prochain épisode*], in *L'Antiphonaire* [*The Antiphonary*] – the novel in which it is perhaps best expressed – Aquin grapples with madness and, using a mirror structure, tries to reflect it back onto others. Because of the mirror effect, that madness strikes you right in the heart, if not the head. You could say that Hubert Aquin was genuinely mad. But quantifying madness isn't really important. It's an attitude. By making himself crazy, Hubert Aquin was trying, I think, to elevate his individual character to the level of myth. One of the functions of madness is to make people and things mythic. *Prochain épisode* describes that process. A guy decides to become a revolutionary and he feigns madness. They lock him up, and he ends up getting everything from others by feigning. But when you read the novel carefully, you realize that it's not a pretence. The character is actually mad, but he's an inspired madman, because he's also a visionary.

MARGARET ATWOOD
Somewhere I read the saying, "Wanting to meet a writer because you like their books is like wanting meet a duck because you like pâté." You said that Jack Kerouac was lucky to know people like William Burroughs and Robert Lowell. But those people had very difficult personalities with regard to social relationships. If you had the choice of spending a week on a small island, say Martha's Vineyard, with any writer living or dead, who would you choose?

VICTOR-LÉVY BEAULIEU
I would be very tempted by William Burroughs.

MARGARET ATWOOD
Why?

VICTOR-LÉVY BEAULIEU
First, he's someone who was fundamentally crazy. He's someone who did

amazing things. Just the fact that he came from that big business-machine family. To make fun of them, he wrote quite a fantastic book, called *The Soft Machine*. He had a life that was pretty weird and insane. He killed his wife by playing William Tell. He tried to cut through linear language, to show that, in modern society, you can no longer think just in a horizontal way, chronologically, that a lot of things are happening at the same time, both in discourse and in life. Burroughs syncopated writing. To me, he was the writer who did the most important work in that direction.

Why is Shakespeare such a great writer? Because words were more important to him than anything else, and when words are more important than anything else, it's like finding yourself in front of a big expanse of rock that you're chipping at with a chisel so that what you are inscribing stays there forever. In front of those definitive words, each one can find his freedom and interpret it in his own way, because even carved in stone, words live when they speak of what, even of the moment, goes beyond the moment. There's a reason Shakespeare was the greatest dramatic writer of all time. It's because he believed that the word and what is expressed by it is everything.

– Victor-Lévy Beaulieu
Docteur Ferron [Doctor Ferron]

MARGARET ATWOOD

But Victor-Lévy, those are good reasons for reading his work, not for having breakfast with him for seven days.

VICTOR-LÉVY BEAULIEU

I'd like to be with Burroughs because he was a junkie, a loser. He lived for a while in Tangier. He told how he once spent at least a week – the amount of time that I would like to spend with him – doing nothing but looking at the end of his shoe. I admire him a lot because, in the sixties and seventies, he was the first writer to experiment with hard drugs, practically to the limit, and then he had the courage to say, Learn to do it without any chemical bullshit. Learn to be yourself; learn your madness without needing anything more than to experience it. I think I'd learn a lot by spending a week on a desert island with a guy like that. (Pause.) I said Burroughs in answer to your question, but I think if I were really given the choice, I'd want to spend that week with James Joyce.

MARGARET ATWOOD
That would be even worse.

VICTOR-LÉVY BEAULIEU
It wouldn't be a quiet week.

MARGARET ATWOOD
Would he help you with the dishes?

VICTOR-LÉVY BEAULIEU
I don't think Joyce would help with the dishes!

MARGARET ATWOOD
You'd have to do all the cooking, all the housework . . .

VICTOR-LÉVY BEAULIEU
I might get something in exchange. Joyce is the major writer of the twentieth century, the one who went furthest in experimenting with language, the use of myth, taboos, rituals. And reading Joyce is especially pertinent for a Québécois, because he came from a small country rife with religious conflicts, and then, exiled, he wrote in English. Joyce made this beautiful statement, the equivalent of which a Québécois could dream of shouting to all of France: "I have put the language to sleep."

With his extraordinary mind, I imagine he must not have been easy to live with, quite mad at times. But the writing is the very definition of genius. When I read *Ulysses* for the first time, at first I didn't understand half of what was written, like most people who read it. But I was carried by his writing, which welds all languages into a mythological structure. *Ulysses* draws a lot on Homer, as we know, and on scholarship. In his experimentation with just about every language in the world, Joyce creates new words. We Québécois create neologisms, but the French language police – Paris, that is – forbids it. There are similarities between what Joyce did and what a Québécois writer may dream of doing or aim to do. Then, when I discovered *Finnegans Wake*, for the first time in my life I wanted to really learn English, and I sat down to translate the beginning. But I realized it was damn hard. I didn't get through the first paragraph. And when the French translation was published, about ten years ago, by a Jean Lambert, I compared it a bit with the English version. The book obviously loses in musicality.

Another reason I'd like to spend a week with Joyce is because he was an opera buff, and I can't stand opera. Maybe he'd make me see why opera is good, beautiful, and interesting. Yet another reason is his encyclopedic mind. Joyce was a scholar, a bit like the Celtic monks he often talks about. Cooking for Joyce, at any rate, wouldn't be too complicated, because he drank more than he ate. It's easier to prepare a Scotch than to whip up a lobster à l'armoricaine. We'd probably get along quite well in that respect. And regardless of how Joyce was in his good moments and bad, I'm sure I'd come back transformed from my week with him. He turned the thermometer of culture up a degree, and if writers since haven't followed, it's probably because it's very difficult to move that thermometer up another notch. Borges said something great about that: "You know, it's very easy to write *Don Quixote*. You just have to be born in Spain, have read all the romances of chivalry, and be called Cervantes." What Borges meant is that, to write *Don Quixote*, you have to have been born in a certain country – in this case, Spain – at a certain time – that is, after the great social and cultural mixing and mingling introduced by the Moors, the Saracens, the Eastern invasion – and to have read all the romances of chivalry – which would mean mastering the whole of culture up to that period – and to be called Cervantes, finally – which is the value that was added to the existing culture. Small degree by small degree, the culture of humanity becomes a ladder whose rungs go up so high that it's very hard for any writer to climb to the top rung and reach an even higher degree in writing and thus in culture. In the twentieth century, it was Joyce who, by creating a body of work that is in many ways unreadable, pushed literature to this ultimate point.

MARGARET ATWOOD

Anarchism, Victor-Lévy. Do you know the story of the meeting between Joyce and Proust? A lot of work went into arranging that meeting, because people wanted to know what two great writers would have to say to each other. The meeting took place. "Good evening, Mr. Joyce." "Good evening, Mr. Proust." Everyone strained to hear great literary things. But Proust said, "I get horrible headaches." And Joyce said, "Oh, so do I, and my eyes are getting worse and worse." They spent the whole time talking about their ailments. I think great writers don't want to share their writing secrets. If you spent a week with Burroughs or Joyce on a little island, they wouldn't say anything to your advantage. And what's more, you'd have to do all the cooking. The other problem is translation. It's very difficult, I believe, to translate Joyce into French or Spanish. French has thirteen vowel sounds, and Spanish seven. Since English has thirty-two, it permits a lot more wordplay. And in *Finnegans Wake*, as you know, there's a lot of wordplay. Translating that into French is next to impossible.

VICTOR-LÉVY BEAULIEU

Anthony Burgess talked about this problem and explained it quite well in his little book on Joyce, *Joysprick*. Joyce can't be translated. The words have double, triple, and even quadruple levels.

MARGARET ATWOOD

Even for an anglophone, it takes a lot of deciphering. But here's another question, Victor-Lévy. You have a great affection for Jacques Ferron. What has he given you?

VICTOR-LÉVY BEAULIEU

I told you about my family, which comes from the world of oral culture. Jacques Ferron said it in a very simple little sentence: "I'm the last of the oral tradition and the first of the written tradition." He also said, "If I could have been a storyteller, like the people in my family, like my uncles, my aunts, my grandfathers, and my grandmothers, there's no doubt I would never in my life have written; I would have told stories out loud." But he also said, "Since I had no gift for speaking, I began writing." And he wrote sublimely. Ferron used a language that, curiously, while modern, is a lot more like the French of the sixteenth century than contemporary French. His style is a blend of the two. Ferron is also without a doubt the Québec writer I've known who had the most extensive knowledge of what you might call the provinces of Québec. He had read all of our sub-literature – the parish monographs, the self-published books, the works by mystics and religious martyrs. His writing encompassed the entire space of Québec.

When I met him, I was just beginning to write, and I didn't know much about literature. He and his books whetted my curiosity. He gave me a lot of material on the Québec beneath the surface. For a long time, he received me at his home almost every Sunday after High Mass and talked to me about writers that were completely unknown to me. Thanks to him, I read Charles Dickens and writers like Lucien Rebatat, a Frenchman no one knows today. I even read Jean de Rotrou, because he was reading him and I wondered what he could be getting out of it. He was also a writer who was deeply involved in the social and cultural reality of Québec, not least through his profession as a doctor, which he never gave up.

Ferron was a doctor at the Saint-Jean-de-Dieu psychiatric hospital and at Mont-Providence, where my father worked. He established a lot of connections that way. He was an incredible library, and a mentor in the true sense of the word. He opened my eyes to realities I had been unaware of. He's the Québec writer I've known who had the best knowledge of foreign writing. Often – I don't know if this is true in English Canada – Québécois writers tend to be completely unaware of what's being done elsewhere, for all sorts of reasons, if only out of a kind of bizarre nationalism. But Ferron read Lewis Carroll, Robert Burns, Tennyson, Nathaniel Hawthorne, and Emerson, as well as Céline and Proust, Kenneth White, and the Russian writers, Dostoevsky, Tolstoy . . . His culture was worldwide. He was the first Québec writer I knew who had such a knowledge of all literatures. When you've come from a little place in the country where reading wasn't something normal, when you've studied in Catholic schools where literature was considered harmful – just imagine, La nouvelle histoire de Mouchette [Mouchette] by Georges Bernanos was banned! – and you meet a writer who's conversant with the authors of the whole world as if they were his friends, and who talks to you about them, it's very stimulating, it opens your eyes and makes the world come alive with sensations and emotions. Ferron did all that for me.

And for Québec, he highlighted a lot of very important things that weren't talked about: he was the first to draw the map of Québec in literature. In his stories about the Gaspé, Acadia, the Canadian West, like "La vache morte du canyon," he told us about an America that in the beginning was French, and showed very well why, from being entirely French, it kind of shrivelled to the area of Québec. Jacques Ferron, I feel, was the first writer from here to create a mythology. For example, his novel *L'Amélanchier* [*The Juneberry Tree*] – with little Tinamer from Portenqueu and her father, Léon, and her mother, and the animals, which have very special names like Bélial – creates a whole mythology, which is something every country needs in order to establish not only its literature but also what it is socially. Ferron, in that sense, was a pioneer, the founder of contemporary Québec.

MARGARET ATWOOD

I think he would be more exciting to spend a week on a small island with than William Burroughs.

VICTOR-LÉVY BEAULIEU

I'm not sure, because I might have to make boiled eggs for Monsieur Ferron. (Laughs.) But with Burroughs, maybe I could bargain.

MARGARET ATWOOD

When you were little, your family controlled you. With writing, you can control them in your turn by remaking them. Is writing also a way to control history, geography?

VICTOR-LÉVY BEAULIEU

In large part, yes, writing is a way to take revenge on your mama, who was too strict, your papa, who didn't let you do the things you wanted to do, and your brothers and sisters. First of all, writing is revenge against your own family. After that it also becomes a way to change your whole world, starting with the family. And when you change the world of your own family, there's a good chance you'll change the wider world around you, and that will create little ripples to the furthest limits of the geography you live in.

MARGARET ATWOOD

Victor-Lévy, you said that violence is unacceptable. Isn't revenge a kind of violence?

VICTOR-LÉVY BEAULIEU

No, revenge is not necessarily violent. There's even a saying in French that revenge is sweet in the heart of an Indian. (Laughs.) And when you're a writer, you're always a bit of an Indian. Revenge is not necessarily violent. It can take the form of seduction.

MARGARET ATWOOD

In the Bible, it says, "Vengeance is mine, saith the Lord."

VICTOR-LÉVY BEAULIEU

That God was very totalitarian, very bloodthirsty. The power of the Judeo-Christian God was built on blood spilled in his name.

MARGARET ATWOOD

But being a writer is playing God a bit, isn't it?

VICTOR-LÉVY BEAULIEU

A very small god in comparison with the other one, and that's lucky in a sense! The powers of the writer are limited in the realm of reality, but they aren't when it comes to symbols. For me, a successful writer is one who makes you see everything not as reality but as fiction. I'm convinced that we live not in a world of reality but in a world of fiction.

MARGARET ATWOOD

You talked about that Mr. Peanut sent by [Planter's]. As a child, you were curious about him and you wanted to know what was hidden under his shell. Is one of the roles of the writer to open people's shells?

VICTOR-LÉVY BEAULIEU

That's part of the job, yes, to look and see what's hiding in the oyster, so to speak. Sometimes, it's surprising, you don't find much. Other times, it's like

Pandora's box – all sorts of things come out that look like monsters to us but that are ordinary to the person who experiences them. For the writer, reaching the unconscious is serious work, because people cover it up, camouflage it, so they won't have to face the brutal reality of it. Often, writing is a mirror that reflects people back to themselves. The mirror is obviously streaked and a bit distorting, since it's the vision of a writer, of one person looking at another. The interpretation of this vision changes according to the individual.

In a way, my relationship to poetry is very much like Philippe Couture's relationship to his dream. While I perceive poetry as sovereignty itself in writing, I cannot really write it. And I have a similar relationship to water, to the river and the sea. Although I've always lived close to either the St. Lawrence or Rivière des Prairies, I've never learned to swim, nor have I ever set foot in a boat. Water both fascinates and repels me. I like to have it in front of me but not under me. Maybe this is because my childhood was filled with tales of shipwrecks on the open sea, huge storms, and sailors swallowed up forever by the waters of the river.

– Victor-Lévy Beaulieu
Les gens du fleuve [People of the river]

MARGARET ATWOOD

The Irish poet and playwright Yeats said that every writer wears a mask that reveals and hides at the same time. A mask is a kind of shell. What do the shells of writers consist of? Can their writing, which is so revealing from one point of view, also be a shell hiding something? Do you have a shell?

VICTOR-LÉVY BEAULIEU

I hope I at least have a very little one. Otherwise, it would be very hard just to live. Everyone has a shell. Writers don't escape that. Before they are writers, they are first individuals born somewhere and determined by their birth. Yesterday we talked about madness. I've thought about it some more. If you write, it's because there's at least latent madness in you. We tend, in general, to cover madness, to put it in a shell and leave it there. I was thinking about some of my forebears in my family. Today they would be called schizophrenics, but back then they lived almost normally, because madness was part of the scenery, so to speak. When you write, you're always attracted to the losers, the delinquents. Why is that? Probably because there's something dormant in them, or awakening, or going to sleep, that observes them in a certain way.

As soon as you come into the world, society grabs hold of you and tries to mould you into a good little automaton in the system. When I went to school, it always amazed me that before we went in they'd ring a big bell like the siren in a police station. At recess, at the end of classes, they'd ring the same bell. I always wondered why it was organized that way. Then one day they took us on a tour of some factories. It was like that there, too. They had the exact same bell. Even today, the function of schools is to train people who are very docile, so that they're good employees in the factory, not too resentful, not too demanding, and who, like Pavlov's dog, salivate at the sound of the bell. The family teaches you to stay in your shell, school does the same thing, the factory does the same thing. It isn't surprising that some people, even by the time they're seventy, have never found out what's inside their shell. They've always been forced to repress it. A lot of so-called social problems come precisely from the fact that people have stayed in their shells all their lives. They're frustrated, they're unhappy, and they don't even know why any more, because they have been made to lose even their deepest sense of identity.

MARGARET ATWOOD

I saw your beret, a real Breton shell – or a half-shell that covers only the head. Do you know *Les métiers de la France* [The trades of France], a seventeenth-century series of engravings? The merchants lived in their merchandise: the fruit merchant in fruit, the sausage merchant in sausages, and so on. I imagine that the writer is clothed in words, and because words are invisible, there are always accusations of obscenity, aren't there? Do you always show yourself without clothing, without a shell?

VICTOR-LÉVY BEAULIEU

I think it would be impossible to really show oneself without clothing and without a shell. Writing, even so-called biography, is nothing more than choosing the lies you feed to the world. I think in every writer there's a ham actor hidden deep down or waiting in the wings, so I don't believe in sincerity in the act of writing, and when I read a novel, it's not really the author's sincerity that attracts me, because to me that's almost impossible to achieve, especially when you write. Writers are always liars and double-dealers, and what's much more important than sincerity is their way of seeing the world, their vision of the world.

It's not surprising that vision of the world is often considered obscene. Obscenity is blamed for a lot in Western societies, which are founded completely on puritanism, on the art of camouflage, on disguising yourself so you don't see yourself as you really are. The vast majority of trials throughout the history of literature have been about obscenity, such as Flaubert's trial for *Madame Bovary*, Henry Miller's, and Joyce's for *Ulysses*. Joyce described the intolerable situation of the Irish, and he was accused of obscenity. Morality is often the only point on which society can attack the writer. For society – which is completely amoral or immoral in its decisions – it's a way of filling in its own gaps. On the other hand, truths that people didn't want to hear have often come out through literary obscenity. I'm thinking, for example, of certain books by the Marquis de Sade, and of others that are perhaps more important, by Mirbeau. Those books forced French society to look at itself in a mirror other than that of [Dumas's] *La dame aux camélias* [*Camille*].

MARGARET ATWOOD

Your most recent book, *Le carnet de l'écrivain Faust* [The notebook of the writer Faust], which is half autobiography, half novel, describes certain obsessions and superstitions of the narrator, who is a writer. He has to write sitting at a certain table and carry his manuscript with him at all times. Do you share those superstitions with your narrator? Do you have others? All writers have rituals.

VICTOR-LÉVY BEAULIEU

I've known writers for whom it was in the choice of their paper, their pen, their typewriter, and later their computer, and of where they'd sit down to write. My own little obsessions might be a bit like those described in *Le carnet de l'écrivain Faust.* When he was asked why he'd written some of his books in longhand and others on the typewriter, Jack Kerouac said, "It's because when I write on the typewriter, I have the impression I'm writing profane books, and when I write by hand, like my poetry for example, I have the impression I'm writing something sacred." For him, the sacred could not come by means of a machine. He wrote his sacred books by hand, on beautiful paper.

I too have my compulsions. I never write two books on the same kind of paper. Every time I start a book, I change paper. I always write with felt-tipped pens, and usually with the same colour until a book is finished. I also always carry my manuscript with me when I'm travelling or when I'm away from home. I do that for the very simple reason that I once had a manuscript stolen. I've always written longhand. I've never used a typewriter, except to retype my texts. I write very poorly, and no one can understand my handwriting, so I retype them myself. Usually my first draft has nothing crossed out. I taught myself to write without crossing things out in a simple way. I wrote on long sheets of legal paper in very small writing. The page was very closely written. When it was typed, it made four or five regular-size pages. If I made a mistake or crossed something out on my page, I'd crumple it up and throw it in the wastebasket, and make myself rewrite the whole thing from memory. Obviously, when you just have a few lines left to write at the bottom of a page and you're obliged to throw it in the wastebasket and start over, you tend to be more careful in the future, to write a little more slowly and make sure there are no crossings-out, at least in the first writing.

So why write longhand? First of all, I really like the physical movement of my hand on paper. There's also another advantage in writing longhand as opposed to using a computer, because regardless what state you're in, what you write on the computer always comes out the same. You take a typeface, say twelve-point Elzevir on so many picas, and it always comes out the same. Whereas, when you write by hand, your writing changes depending on the state you're in. It kind of reminds you how you were. After working on a manuscript for a year, you look at it and you know that these four pages were written the day after you tied one on, and those ones were written when you were in good shape. When you're feeling well, the physical side of the writing goes well. It's an obsession I've always had, even when I was a journalist. The other journalists found it weird that I'd sit down at my desk and write every piece out in longhand and then retype it on my typewriter. It's a compulsion of mine. I learned to type like journalists in the old days, with the five fingers of the left hand and one finger of the right hand, and I learned to type very fast. I was so accustomed to using a typewriter only to type my finished pieces that when I tried to write on it directly I'd become furious, I'd have the impression my sentences didn't look right, that they were no good. That's why I always insisted on writing longhand and still do.

With regard to my other compulsions, well, I always like to write in the same place. I live in a big house, but strangely enough I like to write in an enclosed space. I've never written anything outside, in nature. Nature is too distracting. That's it.

MARGARET ATWOOD

Have you ever been the object of another person's obsession? Do you get love letters from strange women? Or hate mail?

VICTOR-LÉVY BEAULIEU

Both happen. The year I won the Governor General's Award of Canada for *Don Quichotte de la démanche* [*Don Quixote in Nighttown*], I went to Ottawa to state in the Governor General's beautiful hall that I was Québécois and *indépendantiste*, and I imitated General de Gaulle when he said in Montréal, "*Vive le Québec libre!*" My little action was described in Canadian newspapers, and I must have received about a hundred letters full of insults and hate from anglophones outraged that anyone would dare to commit such a crime of *lèse-majesté*.

Fine. That's one kind of letter, but there are also people who write really hatefully to you; I mentioned earlier the lady whose daughter was studying *La nuitte de Malcomm Hudd* in school, who sent me a vitriolic letter. And I also receive love letters. It also used to happen at every book fair that there was a young man who'd spend the whole afternoon in front of my stand doing nothing but staring at me. I told him he was taking up space, and he disappeared. Later, at another book fair, a gentleman of about sixty, a handsome old fellow with greased-down white hair came and said to me, "What did you do to my friend?"

Trois-Pistoles, 1993.

Gilles Gaudreau

I replied, "Who's your friend?" It was that young man, who had once sent me a letter in which he had written, "I like your books a lot, I know your books, I would like to know you personally and physically." I'd felt there was nothing to say and I hadn't answered that letter. He had been outraged. The poor boy ended up being committed, and that was when this old gent came to tell me I had acted badly toward his friend, that I had condemned him to psychiatric care.

Sometimes, yes, it's losers who write me. You know as well as I do that, when you write about criminality and madness, you attract readers who identify with what you write. For a year, I was pursued by a woman reader I'd never seen in my life. She'd telephone me – fortunately, I have an answering machine – and invite me to her place to listen to her read dirty poems by Verlaine, Baudelaire, and Rimbaud. She'd send me absolutely insane letters, and lovely little things she'd buy in the sex shop near her house. That went on for almost a year, and there was no way to get rid of her. Often, you don't answer, and after two or three letters or two or three phone calls, it stops. But in that case, it was two or three calls a day, a letter at least every other day, letters to friends and relatives telling them, "I send him beautiful letters. I want to see him. He doesn't answer. Is there something wrong? Is he sick?" That happens sometimes. I imagine it's the same for you.

MARGARET ATWOOD

It's the same for anyone who has a public life. But for a woman, it's mostly men who write. For you, it was both. You have the choice. (Laughs.) Here's another weird little question. Do you suffer from any physical ills resulting from your lifestyle? For example, backaches or trouble with your hands, like a lot of writers. Do you exercise?

VICTOR-LÉVY BEAULIEU

Someone said, "There are two ways to approach life. The first one is to train to deal with it. The second is to avoid the hard knocks." By nature, I belong more to the second category. I've always found it a bit ridiculous that people spend their time training and being careful about everything to finally end up in the same place. Maybe I've been lucky. I never get headaches. Backaches either, or pain in my hands.

MARGARET ATWOOD
You're young. It could still happen.

VICTOR-LÉVY BEAULIEU
Until I'm ninety, I don't think I have too much to worry about. When I'm ninety, maybe I'll learn to work on a computer!

MARGARET ATWOOD
Victor-Lévy, you've written in many forms and you've also edited poetry anthologies, including *Les gens du fleuve* [People of the river], which is organized around the subject of the St. Lawrence. The word *poet* coming from your lips is high praise. You've described Joyce as the poet of his generation and compared him to Homer. You've revealed to me that you've only written two poems in your life. Why? Is it because the poetic energy and maybe also the spirit of prophecy and the desire to play with words are used up in your prose?

VICTOR-LÉVY BEAULIEU
There are minds capable of infinitesimally crystallizing a story, a life, a situation, and others that are swept up in polyphonic movement. Writing poetry doesn't suit me. Like it or not, as soon as I attempt it, it leads, alas, to novelistic writing, which is profane in comparison to poetry, which to me is closer to the sacred.

MARGARET ATWOOD
Let's get back to those two poems. What was it like writing them? Different from the experience of writing novels?

VICTOR-LÉVY BEAULIEU
A very different experience, yes. I was in grade ten. One of my teachers was named Laurent Boisvert. He was a poetry nut, and he belonged to a Québec association of young writers. That association published an anthology of poetry every year, for which you had to pay five dollars per printed page. This teacher said, "You should write poetry. We'd publish your poems in the anthology with the other writers."

I'd begun writing novels, mainly inspired by Yves Thériault. I was studying the Iroquois language in order to write novels with Indians. In spite of all the time I spent in the library transcribing Indian words, all I remember now is *wambelikaleshka*, which means "spotted eagle." At fifteen, my models were Yves Thériault and Félix Leclerc, authors we read a lot in school. I'd never written poetry. We'd learned the rules of French prosody. I knew that an alexandrine was twelve feet, but I really didn't understand why. The caesura was completely beyond me. So I wrote two poems, yes, but I'd say they were in free verse. I remember the title of the first one was "Cybele," like the goddess. It spoke of velvet hands and steely eyes – as you can see, not terribly original images! Those two poems were published in a collective work called *Soleils multiples* [Many suns], and they made up four pages as I recall. A few years ago, the Hébert brothers, the publishers at Herbes Rouges in Montréal, threatened to publish those two poems in their journal. I said I'd just as soon they didn't. Writing those poems made me realize just how difficult it is to write poetry, because poetry calls on rhythm and sound.

After that, again because of a teacher who loved Victor Hugo, I went through all of Victor Hugo's poetry. And contrary to what a lot of people today think, some of Victor Hugo's poems are very much like Mallarmé. After Victor Hugo, I went on to Mallarmé, who said that poetry had to be ethereal. Through the magic of their complexity and their construction, you can be moved as much by the meaning of the sound as by the sound of the meaning, so to speak. Mallarmé described exhibitions of paintings in Paris in such a way that it was poetry. I've never read anything as beautiful as Mallarmé's writings on painting. But all that didn't make me become a poet, it didn't lead me to write poetry – which nevertheless is sovereignty of language. In Melville, I discovered a writer who was very prosaic at first, and who, because of the circumstances of his life and his study of language, later devoted himself exclusively to poetry.

MARGARET ATWOOD
And Rimbaud?

VICTOR-LÉVY BEAULIEU
Of course, I read Rimbaud. Like all Québécois who were into reading

then. You have to realize that in the late fifties and early sixties it was almost revolutionary to read Rimbaud in Québec. They made us read Sully-Prudhomme and François Coppée, who not only had nothing to say but were incapable of saying it properly. And Rimbaud and *Une Saison en enfer* [*A Season in Hell*], when you're between fifteen and twenty, is a revelation. But I can't say that Rimbaud marked me profoundly – in any case not as profoundly as a writer like Réjean Ducharme, who drew on Rimbaud a lot in his novels and who, I think, found in Rimbaud a rhythm of writing that he made his own and that became characteristic of his writing. My reading of Rimbaud didn't take me that far.

MARGARET ATWOOD

In that poem you wrote, why did you choose the goddess Cybele? She's very, very sinister, I think, from a man's point of view. Cybele was a goddess who demanded rather special sacrifices from men.

VICTOR-LÉVY BEAULIEU

I would have to reread the poem, which I wouldn't dare do!

MARGARET ATWOOD

She wanted her disciples to emasculate themselves in her honour.

VICTOR-LÉVY BEAULIEU

I wrote it after things went sour with my first girlfriend. At that time, yes, my idea of love could well have had certain similarities with the sacrifices demanded by Cybele.

MARGARET ATWOOD

I went with you to see the magnificent Notre-Dame-des-Neiges Church in Trois-Pistoles, with all its architectural ornamentation, and also, like the churches of the Middle Ages, all the little stories related to the big building that contains them. That structure of related stories must have influenced you, just as it did the great writers of the late Middle Ages, such as Chaucer in *Canterbury Tales*. In your work, the same motifs come back in different forms and the same characters come back more than once. For example, Satan Belhumeur is the narrator in *Mémoires d'outre-tonneau* and *Satan*

Belhumeur [Satan Belhumeur], and he's also a memory of the narrator in *Jos Connaissant*. Did the structure of the church of your childhood actually influence your method of constructing your whole body of work?

VICTOR-LÉVY BEAULIEU

Well! I don't know if the church of my childhood influenced me to that extent, but I can say I have some very special memories of it. As you saw, it's huge in relation to the village of Trois-Pistoles and its population. I've seen that church in almost all its forms over the years. When it was restored in the fifties, I was just a little guy, but I was there. You should have seen the scaffolding, and the painters – one Italian, the other French – who also did the gilding and who did such good imitations of marble that people thought it was all real. Out of patriotism, the painters drew the Italian boot and the French hexagon on the columns.

Among my most vivid memories of my childhood are the big religious celebrations that were held in that church. As we've already discussed, I grew up in a very ritualized world, in which life was marked by very important holidays and solemn celebrations around baptisms, planting and harvest, death. The church was a central gathering place, the one that bestowed order on everything, the alpha and the omega of every life. There was also the beautiful big organ built by the Casavant brothers from Saint-Hyacinthe. My uncle played it. On Saturday afternoons, we'd often go listen to him practise. When the organ started playing, the floor of the church would vibrate. The special shape of the building, the detail, and the organization of the ceremonies and conduct: the first pew was reserved for the lay officials, next came the prominent citizens, and further back, the little people. There were pews that you bought, pews that you rented, and pews for those who couldn't pay. In the loft, there were the brothers on one side, the nuns on the other, and the children's choir in the middle. It all had a powerful effect on me.

In "L'Héritage", when I wrote the scenes of the religious ceremonies in the Trois-Pistoles church, I respected the rituals of my childhood, and I even found out about the current ones, so I could match the two. We went to visit the church, and I showed you the pew where my parents and I sat on Sundays forty years ago. You found it very small for the thirteen children we were. But we didn't all go to mass together. There were five or six masses said on Sundays, low masses and a high mass. You always write from what you know. You always write from the emotions you experienced when you were young. That's what determines the kind of writer you become. It goes without saying.

MARGARET ATWOOD
Are you in the process of building a church of words?

VICTOR-LÉVY BEAULIEU
In a way, yes. Balzac said that the various novels of his *Comédie humaine* were each a brick of the big building he was constructing. In his case, it was a cathedral. He said each of his characters was a stained-glass window. I conceive of writing in the same way. It can take any form, but the writer, essentially, is an architect. Personally, I prefer high buildings, baroque structures with a lot of inscriptions, crosses, and windows, like the church of my childhood.

I carry within me a strange, silent, impersonal world. At night, dreams inhabit me that remind me of what can't be grasped. During the day, I dream that I am asleep, and my actions are full of sleep, my eyes are wells of darkness. Even my eyes and the whites of my eyes are black. I frighten everyone. Children say, "Here comes Old Man Satan! Run, he has the plague!" Is it my fault if my skin is the colour of wine, if I'm ugly, if I'm naked, if I stink, and if I'm dirty? People run away from me. I have nothing and no one. I'm alone. My name is Satan."

– Victor-Lévy Beaulieu
Mémoires d'outre-tonneau [Memories from beyond the barrel]

MARGARET ATWOOD
What is that takes you from one book to the next? Do you imagine the theme first and then the characters, or do the characters come first?

VICTOR-LÉVY BEAULIEU

It depends. I didn't start at the same point in all the novels I've written. For *Mémoires d'outre-tonneau*, which was the first one, I started with the first line in my head. As I recall, it was: "I carry within me a strange, silent, impersonal world." I didn't have a lot of ideas or a lot of references, but I'd read the story of Diogenes, the famous Greek who would walk half-naked through the streets of Athens holding a lantern, looking for an honest man. He lived, so they say, in a tub. I drew from that myth a character who went around in a barrel. The novel came from that, but I can't say that I started out with a lot of ideas on what I was going to write.

MARGARET ATWOOD

You had a voice and a character to say those words, didn't you? Do the words come first and the character after?

VICTOR-LÉVY BEAULIEU

Again, it depends. When I wrote *Les grands-pères* [*The Grand-Fathers*], I had the character. Radio-Canada, which wanted to revive the golden age of radio drama, had asked me to write a story that would be broadcast fifteen minutes a day for two weeks. One of my grandfathers had had a strong effect on me, so I simply described an afternoon at the general store with him. But that memory brought back a lot of other ones. So I started to write about three other times in my grandfather's life. I wrote in the morning. I wrote in the evening. I wrote at night. Once those four stories were finished, I took my scissors and cut them up – I was sort of thinking of myself as Marcel Proust – and pieced them together. That's what became *Les grands-pères*, which was far from what I'd planned at the start. Six months before, I never would have thought I'd write a novel like that.

For *La nuitte de Malcomm Hudd*, it happened differently. I had an alcoholic uncle who'd talk a lot when he'd been drinking. One day when he was in his cups, he said to me, "I wonder why they all laughed at me because I brought my horse into the house." I went home and started writing: "And then all of a sudden he wondered why they all laughed at him because he brought his horse into the house." I knew there would be a horse and an alcoholic in that story, but I had no idea what I was going to do with them. The rest was created as I went along. I wrote every morning from six to half past eight, and I stopped when I didn't know where I was going or what turn the story should take. I also stopped as soon as I had the impression I knew, as soon as I said to myself, "That's where it's going. It's going there, and that's how it will end." To represent alcoholic speech, the whole novel is written without any periods, without paragraphs, and with everything in parentheses. Day by day, it progressed, and seven or eight months later, it had taken its own form almost naturally.

For *Don Quichotte de la démanche*, it happened differently again. I had a friend, Raôul Duguay – who's still my friend, by the way – and we had the idea of writing a novel together. Raôul was stuck on the symbolism of the number three. Everything in his place was 3, 33, 333 . . . So we decided that we'd write a novel together with thirty-three chapters that would each contain 3,333 words. I began writing that novel, but Raôul, who was busy doing shows, dropped out of the project. So I wrote the novel alone. It actually does have thirty-three chapters, but they don't each have 3,333 words. It's tedious counting words, and you sometimes have to cut two or three to get the right number. And in the course of the story there came a point when I had to say to myself, "My story can't have thirty-three chapters, it's going to have thirty at most." That's why there's a sort of interlude right in the middle, also in parentheses, which constitutes the three missing chapters.

While I was writing *Don Quichotte de la démanche*, I read some of the great works of antiquity, including Homer's *Iliad* and Virgil's *Aeneid*. I also read *The Death of Virgil* by the Austrian novelist Hermann Broch. So when I had a transition to make from one chapter to the next or from one paragraph to the next and I didn't know how to do it, I'd amuse myself by picking a sentence from the *Iliad*, for example, and putting it into my narrative. Reading while you write is a way to nourish the writing. Since *Don Quichotte de la démanche* is the story of a writer struggling with a woman, with alcohol, and with his obsession with cats, I read everything I could find about cats, alcohol, and women, including Malcolm Lowry. Somehow or other, it's all in there, without being too obvious.

For *L'Héritage*, I had read a few parish monographs, and in one of them I'd learned that some Protestants had settled in the area of Trois-Pistoles, in Saint-Cyprien, and that they'd lived there for ten or fifteen years, until they were driven out by the Catholics of the area. So I wanted to describe the life of a family of French Huguenots who, forced to leave Saint-Cyprien, ended up in the country. That led me to do some research to find the names of my characters, especially their first names.

Writers – and I know you do – pay a lot of attention to first names. First names are often symbolic of the essence of the character. The Amerindians had a fantastic custom. When children were born they'd be given a temporary first name, and when they reached adulthood they had the right to choose the name that suited them. When writers name their characters, they often do as the Amerindians did. I might have a temporary name for a character, and then suddenly a light comes on and I decide, "No, that's not the name of my character. He'll be called such-and-such." For *L'Héritage*, I referred to literature I had on the origins and symbolism of first names. I tried to make up a family of Galarneaus. Why Galarneau? There weren't any in Trois-Pistoles, so there was no danger of people saying to me, "You used the name of my family to make fun of it," or whatever. Galarneau in Québécois language means "cock of the walk."

And for the first names, I tried to find favourable or unfavourable astrological signs for the characters. For example, the characters with an *X* in their first names didn't accept what they were. That *X* symbolized the cross, the crucifixion, condemnation of some kind. All this hidden alchemy by the author doesn't necessarily strike the reader, but all together it makes a novel, a literature. It's also one of the pleasures of writing, at least for me, and I think it's important, this digging beneath the surface to avoid having even what's implausible appear implausible. (Laughs.)

MARGARET ATWOOD

The pilgrimage, the quest, is very important in your work. Captain Ahab, for example, is on a quest, as is your Don Quixote, as is your Jack Kerouac, although in his case the object of the quest is more obscure. Are you interested only in the quests of others, or do you have a quest of your own, Victor-Lévy? What's your great white whale? Most literary quests end in disappointment or defeat. The giant is only a windmill; the whale kills the captain. What is the true object of a pilgrimage? Is it the pilgrimage itself, or something else?

VICTOR-LÉVY BEAULIEU

Making a pilgrimage is as simple as going to visit someone. To really visit someone, you have to know them. To really know them, you have to learn what they are. In learning what they are, there's a chance – it's sometimes a risk – that you'll learn a bit about what you are, too. That's what I tried to do with Melville, Jacques Ferron, and other writers.

MARGARET ATWOOD

You've made little pilgrimages to their homes, but do you yourself have a pilgrimage of your own?

VICTOR-LÉVY BEAULIEU

One pilgrimage for me is trying to find out just how far literature, or what I simply call writing, can go, what limits you can go beyond, and if writing, contrary to Captain Ahab in *Moby-Dick*, contrary to the end of Tolstoy's life, can be an empowerment rather than a deep disappointment like that experienced by Melville and many other writers, who made a pilgrimage in words but never found their Grail. The quest, the great dream of any writer, including me, is, like a knight of the Round Table, to finally find that Grail. There are no examples in literary history of a writer who really achieved this, but perhaps that's what makes for the pleasure, the fact that no one has ever reached it. In comparison, there's nothing very interesting in twenty-eight hockey players who've set the same record. In writing there's no danger of that happening. The process is exclusive to yourself, without any competition with other writers, and since the pilgrimage you make is really personal, no one can ever determine whether or not you've succeeded. In the end it doesn't much matter anyway. It's the movement itself that matters.

MARGARET ATWOOD

So writing is a kind of quest without a whale.

VICTOR-LÉVY BEAULIEU

The whale is always there. You can't avoid it.

MARGARET ATWOOD
But it's invisible.

VICTOR-LÉVY BEAULIEU
Just as in 90 per cent of Melville's book the whale isn't there.You have to read something like three hundred pages of *Moby-Dick* before the whale appears. The author sets the scene for the whale to appear, but it takes a long time to make its appearance. And when it does, it's only sporadically. They sail for three, four, five, six chapters in search of it, and suddenly, it makes a little leap, spouts from its blowhole, and then disappears into the water, and you go for another seven or eight chapters before seeing it again.

MARGARET ATWOOD
But finally, it's there.

VICTOR-LÉVY BEAULIEU
Yes, it's there at the end.

MARGARET ATWOOD
Maybe your pilgrimage, like St. George's battle with the dragon or Theseus' with the Minotaur in the Labyrinth of Knossos, is rather sinister.

VICTOR-LÉVY BEAULIEU
That depends on your point of view.

MARGARET ATWOOD
Dark and shadowy, let's say.

VICTOR-LÉVY BEAULIEU
There's no harm in being sinister in a society that is sinister but refuses to admit it. All that to say that it doesn't matter what you pursue in your life. For Ahab it was the whale, for St. Brendan it was also a whale, for St. George it was his dragon, and for Theseus it was a monstrous sow or else the Minotaur, eater of youths and maidens in the heart of the Labyrinth. It's pretty certain that, in the end, you'll find yourself face to face with it. The Bhagavad-Gita says the victim is the executioner and the murderer is

the murdered, but personally, I wouldn't like to be both the whale and the whaler. The French essayist and novelist Maurice Blanchot summed it up well in a sentence that I find inspired, but that I wouldn't say to all Québécois because they'd resent me for it: "You have to reach towards sovereignty, reach closer and closer, but never attain it, because attaining it means losing it." The great books of humanity, like the *Iliad*, the *Odyssey*, and James Joyce's *Ulysses*, are frightful quests for sovereignty, if only with respect to language. Joyce showed that, when you attain profound sovereignty over language, there's nothing left. You have to begin again, start from zero. And I think that can be extended to all quests. At any rate, I often say, "There's no desperate enterprise, only enterprising despair." For someone pursuing a quest, that's the very essence of the thing.

MARGARET ATWOOD
You know the philosopher Gurdjieff? That's his philosophy too. He said, "If you don't like the road, don't go there."

VICTOR-LÉVY BEAULIEU
It's true that, to have adventures, you have to like adventure. If you don't like adventure to start with, you don't go off to Nepal, you don't climb Everest.

MARGARET ATWOOD
A great-aunt of mine was dying. She was very old, paralysed and blind. We asked her if she found it hard being like that, and she answered, "No, because I'm writing the story of my life in my head, page by page. When I get to the last page, I'll close the book."

VICTOR-LÉVY BEAULIEU
That's exactly it.

MARGARET ATWOOD
After living in Montréal for a long time, you decided to return to Trois-Pistoles. It was a pilgrimage. Was your aim to recapture the past, your own past and that of Québec? I must say that for most of your characters the rural past, although preferable to the urban hell you describe in such

gruesome detail, isn't exactly paradise either. Is the past really preferable to the present, and if it is, in what way?

VICTOR-LÉVY BEAULIEU

I don't think the past is preferable to the present. I do think that the present is often uninhabitable because we've forgotten the past, because we don't use it as a lever to make the present conform more to our desires, needs, and dreams. The disintegration Québec went through in the fifties because of the rural exodus to the city meant that a large part of the past was forgotten. I'm not a devotee of the past the way some people are, promoting a return to the old values, the *ceinture fléchée*, oil lamps. That vision doesn't mean anything any more in the world we live in today. But the city – Montréal, Toronto, New York, Mexico – hasn't given us what it should have, it has not succeeded in becoming a true city in the traditional sense of the word. The problems of the big urban agglomerations come from the fact that they were built on speculation, anarchy. There was no structuring organization that would have enabled those cities to develop in a way that was, if not harmonious, at least acceptable and livable.

As for the country and the little villages, they were dismantled and turned into places where people were left to die. It makes no sense, it's an aberration. History has shown that there can be no revolution if the country is not considered an important cultural entity. To return to the concept of the village is to return to the concept of year one, to childhood, that's the truth. But why shouldn't we go back to childhood when the adults who govern us, who are in the major centres, have completely corrupted everyday life? What we most lack in Québec, English Canada, or elsewhere are structures that are living and not petrified by bureaucrats who've lost all sense of creativity. In the little villages, the small units, it's easier to achieve the global village proposed by McLuhan, with whom I'm in perfect agreement. Technology can work in our favour. When technology allows me to solve a problem eight hundred kilometres away by means of a phone call or fax rather than going there by car, when instead of spending twelve hours in a buggy I spend an hour in an airplane, I no longer have any feeling of isolation or remoteness. It's fabulous to be able to have one foot in the past and the other in the future, and at the same time not feel torn in the present.

The ideal life would be to be able to go into the past or into the future while living in the present. If modern society were well thought out, well structured, a lot of people could do that. But the stratification of our society forces some people to live only in the past, while others, a lot fewer, are able to live only in the future. Those who are confined to the present, whether in Montréal or Toronto or even in the country, aren't able to enjoy it. And since they can't enjoy anything, they become desperate. The desperate acts we see everywhere are proof that it's no longer possible to keep the lid on society. If this society allowed interaction among the three, we wouldn't have these problems; the current would circulate normally between them and they would enrich each other, which would give us a much better quality of life.

That's what I'd of liked to relate to you, my good folks. Of course, adding a few odds and ends of my own invention, because a story isn't a story if you don't slip in a few good fat fibs. But I know you won't do me violence and that you've no intention of taking me by the neck and giving me a good choking. Not right away, anyway. Not before I've shut my mouth about La Corriveau and her cage. Even these days, when there ain't so many Christians any more, they still tells all kinds of stories about her. My good buddy Roberge's isn't the only one. There's others. There's lots of others that'd have to be told, but it'd never end, and I'm too old now even to think about it. That's the reason I ain't gonna tell you nothin' about what happened to La Corriveau's cage. Nobody wanted to go to Pointe-à-Lévy any more, on account of they was afraid of the misdeeds of La Corriveau. So one fine morning, no more cage. Disappeared. Flown the coop, that cage. They didn't find it again anyway. It took all of fifty years before it was found. And d'ya know where they found it after all that? In the cimit'ry, in a little plot reserved for people executed or drowned. So folks wouldn't get alarmed, the authorities got rid of it again, something about national security they said!

– Victor-Lévy Beaulieu
Ma Corriveau [My Corriveau]

MARGARET ATWOOD
So then, returning to Trois-Pistoles was a kind of pilgrimage for you?

VICTOR-LÉVY BEAULIEU
Definitely. Everything in life is a pilgrimage when you look at it closely. My return to Trois-Pistoles was also a swinging back of the pendulum. When you leave your little corner of the country at fourteen years old – which you hadn't wanted to leave, where you'd thought up till then you would make your life and be happy – all life elsewhere is exile, like it or not. You can like your exile. I know Canadian ambassadors to Paris who like their Parisian exile. It's not that I didn't like Montréal. It's a very livable city. But my desire ever since the moment I left my little corner of the country was to go back there.

It's all symbolic. I'm one of those who, like Jacques Ferron, feel that, before being from a country, first you're just from a street, from a little neighbourhood, from a little village, from a little region, and then, maybe, from a country, if it works out that way. Coming back to my corner of the country is sort of revenge against the great white whale of my childhood that prevented me from living the dream that I wanted to live at that time. If dynamic cultural structures were set up in all the regions of Québec, I don't see what would be wrong with that. That's what exists in the United States. American culture doesn't come only from New York. That multiplicity of worlds is important.

MARGARET ATWOOD
This is very, very strange, Victor-Lévy. Northrop Frye said exactly the same thing, and he was an anglophone.

VICTOR-LÉVY BEAULIEU
But being an anglophone doesn't mean you know nothing at all!

MARGARET ATWOOD
He said all culture is regional.

VICTOR-LÉVY BEAULIEU
I've read Guy de Maupassant. I've read writers as different as Asturias, or

Borges, or Alejo Carpentier, who wrote about the Caribbean. Well, from Montréal or Trois-Pistoles, the Caribbean looks very regional. What's interesting in the work of Alejo Carpentier or Borges or any other writer is that he makes his little microcosm take on the magnitude of the world by putting his writing genius into it. Writing genius, contrary to what many people think, is not something individual, but collective. No great book was ever written that wasn't collective. Joyce's *Ulysses* didn't come to us because someone just pulled it out of the air. It was Irish culture that gave rise to *Ulysses*. That work is the fruit of a collective genius. If there hadn't been an Irish society, the Irish famine, the wars with the British, Joyce's *Ulysses* would never have seen the light of day. Joyce is the added value of the writing of the collective genius, period.

MARGARET ATWOOD

You should be in politics and become mayor of Trois-Pistoles, don't you think so?

VICTOR-LÉVY BEAULIEU

No! (Laughs.) I'd rather be number two in the parish than mayor of Trois-Pistoles!

MARGARET ATWOOD

I was once asked to run for mayor of Toronto. I refused because Mr. Gibson [Graeme Gibson] said it would be very Norman-Mailerish! Winning an election must be okay, but after that you'd have to be mayor! That wouldn't be much fun.

Here's another question. Alberto Manguel, who edited *The Oxford Book of Canadian Ghost Stories*, said he had a lot of trouble finding ghost stories from modern Québec. A Québec writer told him that the realities of life in Québec were so strange that writers didn't feel the need to invent any other strange things. What do you think? Perhaps the French Revolution and the spirit of rationalism eliminated ghosts from French literature, or perhaps the Catholic church itself contains all the supernatural. Why no stories about ghosts? You have ghosts in Trois-Pistoles. Why no stories or novels about ghosts?

VICTOR-LÉVY BEAULIEU

The explanation is very simple. There's no tradition of the short story in Québec until recently. If the short story was very prominent in English-speaking culture in the nineteenth century and the early twentieth century, it was first of all because there were outlets available. A lot of American and British magazines published stories. This was not the case in Québec. I can give the example of a Québec writer who wrote a lot of stories: Yves Thériault. He began his career writing short stories. He even learned English so he could do it better. Outlets were almost nonexistent in Québec, with the exception of some radio stations and two or three magazines. A writer couldn't live on that. So Thériault tried to sell his short stories in the United States and elsewhere.

We've got closets full of ghosts in Québec. I don't know if it's the vehicle that creates the need, or the need that creates the vehicle, but one of the two was missing, and Québec writers didn't get into the genre of ghost stories. But, since magazines like *Moebius* or *Imagine* have been in existence, more and more stories are being written, even about ghosts. Manguel should have someone send him those magazines; there are some very decent writers in them. It would be interesting to compare them with short stories written by English Canadians or Americans. All is not lost, even for ghosts.

MARGARET ATWOOD

I wonder if the ghosts of Québec are different from other ghosts. About fifteen years ago I talked with a woman writer from Québec. I told her the house we lived in at that time – it was a farmhouse – was haunted. And she said, "That's strange! In Québec, the ghosts are outside, at crossroads." In English Canada, they're in houses. Is it true what she said?

VICTOR-LÉVY BEAULIEU

Maybe that writer spent all her time outside of houses! In Trois-Pistoles in 1996, there are still people who believe – and who say so – that houses are haunted. Not very long ago, I went to the home of a lady, who told me, "Victor-Lévy Beaulieu, you're a medium. Can you tell me if I have ghosts in my house, if my house is haunted?" I said, "Why are you asking that question?" She replied, "Even my four-year-old granddaughter who comes here tells me she sees shadows passing. Other people tell me there are spirits. Are there ghosts or spirits in my house?"

When it comes to that stuff, I'm a bit of a nonbeliever, a sceptic. I told her I didn't see any, that I'd have to spend a few nights at her place to find out if there actually were any. That gives you an idea. If someone here told me that, I'm sure that there are a lot of people all over Québec who think there are ghosts in their house. It's possible. The situation in Québec when it comes to ghosts is probably not very different from that of English Canada or the United States. What about you? Why are you so interested in ghosts and vampires?

MARGARET ATWOOD

In Québec, you don't have any vampires, because you have the church. The proof that you were able to chase the vampires out of Québec is that they're now all in Ontario. (Laughs.)

VICTOR-LÉVY BEAULIEU

Do they look like Jean Chrétien? (Laughs.)

MARGARET ATWOOD

No. They look like Mike Harris! Some of your works, in particular the play *Ma Corriveau* [My Corriveau], have consciously drawn on Québec folklore. Others express the past in a less folkloric way but are full of detail – I'm thinking of the novel *Les grands-pères* and the television series "L'Héritage." In other works, such as *La maison cassée* [The broken house], you show the past at the time of its disintegration and dispersion. Our ancestors' tools become today's tourist souvenirs. Is this interest of yours part of a bigger cultural plan that could be entitled "In Remembrance of Québec Things Past"?

VICTOR-LÉVY BEAULIEU

It could partly be that. From colonization to modern times, folklore has been omnipresent in Québec. So much so that it was seen quite pejoratively, and people started to systematically disparage and discredit it, reducing it to macramé. I know many Québec writers who were born in small

In Front of VLB House, 1995.

villages, and who never mention in their biographical note that they were born in Saint-Polycarpe or Saint-Éloi, because they consider it demeaning. When you're a major Québec poet and you correspond with René Char, you're better off saying you were born in Outremont. Why? Because all anyone remembered of folklore was kitsch and tackiness. The whole invigorating wealth of the folklore that scholars like Marius Barbeau in Québec City made known to us, the oral literature, the musical literature, the crafts – but in the artistic sense of the word – was absent.

There's an important folklore that it is absolutely essential to know. Most of the major works of other societies that I've read came out of folklore. It's their popular dimension – not in the sense of vulgarity – that allowed those books to have an audience, and to attain universality. Living within our Québec folklore is important, whatever it is. Of course, in the seventies when I wrote *Ma Corriveau*, we had gone to the opposite extreme. After classical college in the sixties, after the Latin that we learned *ad nauseam*, after all that, there was a need to come back to things that were closer to home. During that time a lot of Québec works from the past were published. For example, they revived artists like Massicotte, and guys like Labrecque did field studies of the folk songs and all that stuff. In many cases, it allowed us to rediscover a past that had been totally buried, either by the priests or by those new professors from Europe in the schools and universities, who felt La Bolduc's songs didn't compare to those of Mistinguette and who set out to teach us about foreigners rather than about what we were.

That return to the folklore for the right reasons was what led me to write *Ma Corriveau*, a play that tells the story of a woman condemned to death during the French régime because she allegedly killed two husbands. I surrounded it with all the folklore of the story of La Corriveau, which includes elves, ghosts, will-o'-the-wisps, all manifestations of what we were talking about before. If it's understood and lived in, and if it continues, the wealth of folklore leads you to something else. If Andy Warhol had been familiar with the *ceinture fléchée*, he could have made a beautiful Pop Art painting of it.

A writer draws on anything he can for positive elements, and there are lots in folklore. I've read the correspondence of James Joyce with his old aunt in Ireland. Surprisingly, Joyce didn't ask her profound questions about eternity, the meaning of life, and all that. He asked her, "What did that man sing, who I used to listen to as a child, who lived three blocks from us? What was that song he used to sing?" The old aunt would answer his questions. Joyce brings this back to life in both *Finnegans Wake* and *Ulysses*. We still have major work to do on our folklore. It's in those things that you recognize yourself, and when you recognize yourself, you can go forward, you can do something else.

MARGARET ATWOOD

I've got nothing against that.

VICTOR-LÉVY BEAULIEU

No, I'm sure you don't, because you yourself looked at things very much in that way in *Cat's Eye*.

MARGARET ATWOOD

In a lot of your works, there's an archetypal family drama. It goes a little like this: Papa, the authority figure, is cold and distant, as in *La maison cassée*, or actively mean, as in *La nuit de la grande citrouille* [The night of the big pumpkin], or else he wants the son to leave home. Mama, who has to raise the family, is dead or dying. The children think everything would be different if she were in good health. The son is neurotic. He sometimes wears women's clothes and he has fantasies of murder, rape, revenge, and violence. He dreams of killing his father. If he has a mistress, he uses her body but hates her soul. If he has a brother, the brother's name is Abel, which by implication makes the hero a Cain and therefore fratricidal. The daughter has been damaged in childhood by something connected to her father or her brother. She is paranoid and neurotic. She cannot have healthy relationships with men. She's as cloistered as a nun, or in the most extreme case, such as *La nuit de la grande citrouille*, she's a lunatic. Are these narratives specifically Québécois? Or are we in the landscape of a family drama that's more universal, as in Greek tragedy? Or is this a very contemporary drama that comes out of twentieth-century alienation and social breakdown?

VICTOR-LÉVY BEAULIEU

The characters you mention are not only related to modern life. These kinds of people already existed in Québec society in the eighteenth and nineteenth centuries. You talk about the schizophrenic or neurasthenic daughter. In the stories I've read that have some connection with my family, there was that type of woman, and I drew on that. For example, one of my aunts spent thirty-five or forty years of her life shut up in her room, sitting in her bed on cushions. She had no television or radio or anything. I'd go visit her quite often and there was a whole ritual to follow: you couldn't go see her before three o'clock in the afternoon, and after five minutes she would say she was tired and you'd have to leave. She looked like Alice in Wonderland when she drinks the magic potion and suddenly has a long neck. My aunt had hair like Alice and a long thin neck. She was all white, so when you saw her the first time it was rather frightening. The only communication she had with the world was in the evening at nightfall. When the sun was setting, she would go out on her verandah wearing dark glasses, a big hat, and a long scarf. After five minutes she'd go back in. Those characters I describe in my novels certainly existed.

Québec society was formed on the basis of a handful of French settlers. Inevitably there was a lot of inbreeding. Families were very large – twelve, fifteen, eighteen children – and they all intermarried. Those marriages necessarily resulted in some children having defects that led to neurasthenia, claustrophobia. In my family, there aren't that many real schizophrenics like Perceval, for example, but some of them dealt with their schizophrenia by staying shut in, like that aunt.

As for the eldest son driven from his home and wanting his father's death, you just have to do a little digging to realize that this belongs to tradition since the beginning of humanity. We were saying earlier that Québec families of the nineteenth century were poor and that only the eldest son could stay on the family land, so all the other boys had to go live somewhere else as soon as they turned fourteen, fifteen, or sixteen. They'd go to western Canada or the United States. It happened sometimes that this tradition was reversed and it was the youngest son who inherited the land and supported the parents in their old age. This situation, which sometimes occurred in my family, led to a lot of quarrels among the children. That was sort of the problem I was looking at in my novel and television series L'Héritage. It's even happened that an eldest son, for all sorts of reasons, would end up abandoning the family farm to the youngest and going to live somewhere else.

And – this was kept hidden because of the religion – there was also an enormous amount of incest in these families. My writing of "L'Héritage" coincided with a story in the Québec media of some daughters who had been raped or abused by their father and who had taken him to court. Before the eighties, it was taboo to talk about this even in families where it had occurred. There's absolutely no mention of it in Québec literature of the nineteenth century, not in books or newspapers or in court transcripts. If a father or grandfather got a young girl pregnant, she was sent to the city and she had to leave the child in a orphanage. I didn't invent anything when I talked about incest. One of the best letters I ever got was from a lady in New Brunswick who said it was the first time she'd talked about it and that she had finally allowed herself to do so because she'd seen "L'Héritage" on television. Any writing about incest is like a Greek tragedy – with one little difference, which is that the tragedy ends with a symbolic death that's a sort of resurrection. To convey the horror, the writer has to use descriptive language, which makes the thing even more odious.

MARGARET ATWOOD

And why all those dead or dying mothers in your work? Is that also simply the reality?

VICTOR-LÉVY BEAULIEU

If you read Québec novels from before 1970, the mother is omnipresent and the father is powerless and inept. In *Les Plouffe* [*The Plouffe Family*] by Roger Lemelin, the mother controls everything, all day and even at night. In Michel Tremblay's plays it's even more striking. The father is not only absent, vanished – he's become a ghost. In *En pièces détachés* [*Like Death Warmed Over*], he ends up just sitting in front of the TV, watching cartoons and drinking beer.

I was absolutely opposed to this vision of things. It wasn't at all the image I got of my grandfathers, great-uncles, and uncles. I felt I had to set the record straight. A lot of mothers in Québec died very young, and unlike Antoinette, the grandmother in *Une saison dans la vie d'Emmanuel*, they were far from omnipresent in the family. With a few exceptions, like Didace, the father in *Le Survenant* [*The Outlander*] by Germaine Guèvremont, our literature doesn't show a lot of important, authoritarian men like those in my family. That's why I created the character of Xavier Galarneau, who puts the law above everything else. Normally in a traditional family, there's the law, but there's a more redistributive justice for the children, for this and that. In other families I've known, the law takes precedence – the law says such-and-such, there are no exceptions for anyone, and feelings don't enter into it. On my father's side of the family especially, my ancestors were much more on the side of law than of justice. You could say that law appeals more to masculine concepts, so to speak, and justice to feminine concepts – or so some people say.

MARGARET ATWOOD
And I think justice is for men and grace for women.

VICTOR-LÉVY BEAULIEU
Yes, I would agree. Writing not only reflects a society, but it also plumbs the depths of what that society represents.

Too many texts go on dying in the awfulness of liquefied words. And that never makes a country come except in what is only the relentlessness of beginning again. This blindness and all the ink black of the Québec darkness to span it in wasteful life. So many illusions and dreams, so many disenchantments and sorrows, and yet why? For an undertaking that's creaky and obsolete, unnamed because it is unnameable. Nothing more than sparse fragments that, even gathered together, would not have the thickness of an anecdote. Family, I hate you. And so what? Family, I tell your story anyway.

– Victor-Lévy Beaulieu
La jument de la nuit [Night mare]

MARGARET ATWOOD
I have a question for you that will be impossible for you to answer from your personal experience. Do you think being a male writer is different from being a female writer? If so, what are the differences? Do you think they're biological or due to social conditioning, and have you learned anything about this from Québec women writers?

VICTOR-LÉVY BEAULIEU

It's quite different being a male or a female writer, but I don't think the reason is biological. When you look at how society is set up, how it's structured, how and by whom it's controlled, like it or not, whether you're a man or a woman, you're forced to admit that it's men who hold the power. And men's power is in their image. For a woman, I imagine that must be difficult. It hasn't been centuries that women have been able to take part in institutions as they do now. In Québec in the fifties, for example, Gabrielle Roy was considered a revolutionary, and we were advised not to read her books, because she was supposedly a Communist. A man would have had less of a problem with that than a woman.

Today society has changed somewhat, and fortunately women play a larger role in all organizations. The fact remains, however, that they are obliged to find their niche in a system that is still run and controlled by men. In the Québec government, women make up only 10 per cent of the ministers and members of the National Assembly, and it's the same in the federal government. In all institutions, in education, the economy, social life, women are still very much in the minority in terms of power to decide, to do things, to act. And as long as power is held by men alone, well then, nothing's going to change. Anyway, to me, it's not male power that has to be changed but power, period.

MARGARET ATWOOD

There's also a difference in audiences. For example, women read more novels than men. And they read novels written by men and novels written by women. On the other hand, men who read novels read more novels written by men. It's a little like with clothing: women can wear pants, but if you're a man and you wear a dress, it's something very special.

VICTOR-LÉVY BEAULIEU

Unless you're a Scot! (Laughs.) I'm not crazy about statistics, but they show that 80 per cent of purchases in Québec bookstores are made by women. You could say that 80 per cent of literature, or just about, is bought and read by women. It's clear that women will buy books that are about women and are written by women. I have nothing against that. That gives women writers a definite advantage. On the other hand, that conclusion is a bit ambiguous, since the majority of women read according to the codes they have been taught to recognize, which are men's codes. Even in a great novel like *Bonheur d'occasion* [*The Tin Flute*], which was written by a woman, the coding of the characters is men's. Gabrielle Roy's vision comes mainly from the father, not the mother. The mother is only there to support a description that is basically very masculine.

Women's incursion into the field of literature is a fairly recent phenomenon, and so is that of heroines taking up all the space and the foreground. In *The Robber Bride*, you find a woman's view of women, whereas before, we had men's views of women. *La voix* [The voice], by Roger Fournier, is the story of a guy harassed by a woman who calls him constantly to invite him to her place. It's obviously a novel written by a man, with male stereotypes pasted over female desire. What you now find in novels written by women is female desire. Before the sixties, that literature didn't exist.

MARGARET ATWOOD

Things have indeed changed a lot. You said in an interview that you found Tolstoy's relationship with his wife, Sophia, which was not at all happy, very modern. What does that modernity consist of?

VICTOR-LÉVY BEAULIEU

Tolstoy was a nobleman who, as the youngest son, in accordance with Russian tradition, was heir to an estate, and who in his youth had led a rather depraved life. And then, when he reached his thirties, he felt the need to be like just about everyone else and, in order to have full social status, to get married. He chose a young girl from the minor Russian nobility, Sophia Bers. From what I've read about it, it wasn't really a marriage of love for Sophia.

It turned out that Sophia and Leo were both very domineering, and with each trying to dominate the other, conflicts were inevitable. And the children amplified the conflicts. Sophia Bers is a marvellous character. Her story is very modern, because, being a domineering woman, she wanted to take charge of her husband's affairs. He wanted to keep his freedom, which he couldn't, and at the same time he tried in every possible way to dominate his wife and children, to impose his ideas, his way of living, of eating . . . Sophia Bers was neurasthenic, a bit schizophrenic, and when her husband pushed her too far, she'd throw herself into the pond on their estate. She wouldn't die though, as in today's stories. She'd be rescued in time, Tolstoy would ask her forgiveness, and it would start all over again worse than ever. What's interesting and at the same time surprising about the couple is that they lived like this for such a long time. Tolstoy constantly threatened to leave her, but he never did. Until finally one morning at the age of eighty, he decided to leave his home. He never returned, because, as we know, he got to a little Russian train station, fell sick, and died there.

And here you see just how modern they were. Tolstoy died in the stationmaster's house. They sent for his wife, but he obstinately refused to speak to her. She remained outside waiting in vain and never saw him alive again. It surprised me that a guy like Tolstoy, with his great freedom of thought, should be so limited in his marital relationship. You can find that kind of behaviour every day, you just have to glance through the tabloids. And that's why I became interested in their story. To someone who writes, there's a whole social, cultural, and personal drama already there, which I discussed in the book I wrote on them, with one part on each of them, back to back.

MARGARET ATWOOD

Jack Kerouac had his vision of the ideal woman: she's always ready for sex, she nurtures the man when he needs it, she doesn't make any demands, she never complains, and she smiles all the time. The women in your writing aren't exactly like that. What's your view of the ideal woman?

VICTOR-LÉVY BEAULIEU

Kerouac was born of rural French-Canadian parents. He spent his early childhood in an environment where the mother saw to everything: language, education, culture, religion. He had a special attachment to his mother, and as he got older, it became stronger. As you know, he ended his days in St. Petersburg, in the bungalow next door to hers. In the United States, in the narrow circle of French Canadians, Kerouac spoke only French as a small child, whereas his father was very Americanized. Very sensitive and a touch neurasthenic, he felt lost in the big world of America and played up the image of his *maman* always at his side, kind, saying her rosary, feeding him. Men who have such a special attachment to their mothers often see other women as nothing but objects that can be obtained quickly with no problems, and also gotten rid of easily. Things weren't simple for Kerouac. He had a lot of problems with women. That was too bad for him, but maybe he deserved it. For me, the ideal woman would be . . .

MARGARET ATWOOD
Good?

VICTOR-LÉVY BEAULIEU
Good? Not necessarily. Good women don't necessarily make for good relationships. If I had to make a comparison, she'd be a bit like Simone de Beauvoir was for Jean-Paul Sartre. Simone de Beauvoir was the better half of that couple.

MARGARET ATWOOD
But it was hell!

VICTOR-LÉVY BEAULIEU
It was hell, yes, but hell isn't a problem for me!

MARGARET ATWOOD
You prefer hell to heaven.

VICTOR-LÉVY BEAULIEU
I prefer the hell that Sartre and de Beauvoir had, together but sometimes separated. I prefer that to the hell of the Tolstoys, together but stuck to each other. To me, the ideal woman would be a companion in emotions and feelings, and at the same time, in reason. I don't know if that explains much to you. Even to me it seems pretty complicated, thank you very much!

MARGARET ATWOOD
People speak of Mother Russia and see Paris as a woman. As imaginary characters, countries and cities have their traditional dramas constructed

by their citizens. The word Québec is masculine in French, but I have the impression it's considered a woman.

VICTOR-LÉVY BEAULIEU

It's probably not that simple. But if I had to describe Québec in those terms, I'd draw on the plays of Michel Tremblay and say Québec is neither woman nor man, but homosexual.

MARGARET ATWOOD

(Laughs.) You've spoken about Québec's dark shadow, its hysterical nature. Is it a tragic figure, as in Greek tragedy, or is it a kind of hero fighting the forces of external evil, as in melodrama? And if you had to relate the history of Québec as a dramatic character in a very short film, what would the story be?

VICTOR-LÉVY BEAULIEU

First let's establish our concepts. I don't think Québec is an historical society.

MARGARET ATWOOD

But that's what you said.

VICTOR-LÉVY BEAULIEU

Sometimes, when I see the Québécois reacting to everything, I find our foundations are downright hysterical, not historical. The historical appeals to reason, to something that was founded and that you use as the basis for going higher or farther, whereas the hysterical is like a spiral, always beginning again. After all the business around Meech Lake, the vast majority of Québécois were in favour of sovereignty. Fine. Then a few weeks later, something else happened, and they changed their minds. Québécois are not just hysterical, but spiraloid – making waves at the top and waves at the bottom, and going back to the centre and then moving away from the centre again. It's also cyclical, which is the opposite of any history. If I had to write about that – that's part of what I try to do in *La grande tribu* [The great tribe] – I'd show that it's natural that the Québécois experience a kind of schizophrenia.

The very foundations of Québec, the first settlers, the first priests and nuns, were marked by schizophrenia, by hysteria. In the pages of Blessed Catherine de Saint-Augustin's diary, she tells how she went into a trance and talked to a statue of the Blessed Virgin with the baby Jesus in her arms, and how the Blessed Virgin told her that she had big breasts and she had too much milk for baby Jesus, and so Catherine of Saint-Augustin offered to drink the milk to relieve the poor Virgin Mary. That's part of hysteria in the original sense of the word. We know that, in France, devil possession, witches, all those problems, ended when the colonization of America began. I have the impression that the Old World deported everyone it had locked up to the New World, and that, in a way, that marked the origin of Québec.

Québécois still have an anarchist streak. They can happily support Lucien Bouchard in Québec, and do exactly the opposite at the federal level, or vice versa, like a Meccano set or a game of tic-tac-toe: I put my X there if you put your O there, and then I put my O there if you put your X there. There isn't really any continuity, either in action or in thought. This unpredictability has its good sides, but also very bad ones. You can't build a proper society in such a changing context. When René Lévesque was sick, the doctors held a press conference to talk about his illness, and they said he was suffering from transient global amnesia. That was the medical term they used. At the time, no doctor explained what it meant. Well, if you consult medical books a bit, you find out that transient global amnesia is pretty much the state of someone who's undergone I don't know how many electroshock treatments, if not a lobotomy. This could provide an historical explanation of why Lévesque got a bit hysterical after the referendum.

MARGARET ATWOOD

I had an aunt like that. Nothing to do with the referendum.

VICTOR-LÉVY BEAULIEU

In a politician like René Lévesque, the transient global amnesia was perhaps more symbolic. I'm interested in symbols, and I see a continuity in history and in events. Québécois often show signs of transient global amnesia. It's difficult to get over, for a lot of reasons. To me, what we're dealing with here is modern archetypes. We often have too much of a tendency in literature to use the archetypal only in relation to the past, and we don't alter it. In your poetry, you took ancient characters, archetypes, and transformed them. That's what literature should do. There is no new truth, and there's no hope but what we create.

MARGARET ATWOOD

We also suffer from global amnesia, but it's not transient. It's a permanent disease. (Laughs.) We forget everything! The critic Northrop Frye said that the central question in American literature was "Who am I?", that is, the quest for individual identity, and that the central question in English-Canadian literature was "Where is here?", a question from which the I is absent, a quest for the definition of a place. What is the central question in Québec literature? Is it something like "Who are we?" or perhaps "What house do we have to burn to free ourselves from the past?"

VICTOR-LÉVY BEAULIEU

It could be "What house do we have to burn to free ourselves from the past?" but that house refers – much more than to something external built of brick, stone, or wood – to that well-locked little house one has at the centre of oneself, which should perhaps be burned, yes, to get to something new, healthy, wholesome, if I may say so.

MARGARET ATWOOD

It's not "Who are we?"

VICTOR-LÉVY BEAULIEU

No. The question "Who are we?" doesn't seem to me to be a basic question for a Québécois.

MARGARET ATWOOD

You know that already.

VICTOR-LÉVY BEAULIEU

In many cases, unfortunately, we know only too well who we are. We'd like to be some other place, some other way, different, but we don't know how to get there. I can't blame the Québécois for being like this. In various ways, just about all the people in the West are like this. But if Québec is like this, it's not because it's part of a division of the empire called the United States, or because it supposedly belongs to a nation-state like France or the remnant of an empire like the British Empire. For contemporary man, problems present themselves differently depending on whether he's in a country that is dependent, interdependent, confederal, or whatever. You can go from level one, which is the nation-state, to level two, which is something else, and then to level three . . . in the end, it comes down to the same thing. Instead of "Who are we in the world?", the typical question of the Québécois of today could be, "What are we doing in the world and why are we doing it so badly?"

The writers whom I'm instinctively drawn to – perhaps because I project myself into their all-encompassing, total undertaking – share Melville's sense of urgency. Even Virgil, in whom it appears in reverse. Why didn't he want to finish the *Aeneid*? Torturing himself over it, almost undone by it, setting about it, backing off, growing more feverish as the thing took shape; a truly exemplary effort at retreating from the task which left him not knowing which way to turn. And wasn't Joyce responding to the same sombre anguish when, fearing blindness, he searched desperately for someone who could continue his work, a writer like himself – with the same initials, who was born the same day, the same hour as he in that magical Dublin where Anna Livia Plurabelle lived? And Victor Hugo, who forced his family to shut him up in his study and stash his clothes in a closet under lock and key so he could exist solely within the singular space of the book he was writing?

They were all like Melville furiously writing *Moby-Dick* in less than a year, rushing towards the final sentence, becoming neurasthenic at the thought of not having enough time.

– Victor-Lévy Beaulieu
Monsieur Melville [*Monsieur Melville*],
translated by Ray Chamberlain

MARGARET ATWOOD

You're not doing so badly. Others do worse. Plato would have banned poets from the ideal Republic, because they always lie. I read an anthropology book that put forward the idea that the origin of humanity was not man the hunter or man the toolmaker or man the great warrior, but man the liar. It seems that even chimpanzees lie. What is the role of lies in art? Do writers lie more than other people, or in some way less?

VICTOR-LÉVY BEAULIEU

I'm not sure writers lie more than other people. We live in a society built on lies. There's something amazing about lies, something fascinating. People are able to lie only because they are capable of negotiating differences. It's a choice. And when you're able to choose, you're in a way sovereign over yourself and others. The whole game consists of being able to lie and being able to answer lies with other lies. In a sense, living is lying all the time. Faulkner or somebody – I don't know who – said that to live was to compromise oneself. I would say rather that living is lying to others and to oneself.

MARGARET ATWOOD

If the world was going to end tomorrow, would you continue to cultivate your garden?

VICTOR-LÉVY BEAULIEU

It's hard to answer that. I don't have the soul of St. Gonzaga or St. Dominic Savio, who, when he was asked what he would do if the end of the world was at hand, answered, "I would continue to play ball." It's easy to say that before, but during, I'm not sure that answer would hold up. I can't really answer your question.

MARGARET ATWOOD

One of the seven deadly sins is envy. I have a joke for you. It comes from Cuba and it's about writers. In hell, there are some cauldrons that are used for boiling souls. Each cauldron is for an occupation. You've got all the lawyers in one cauldron, all the dentists in another, and another for the writers. And for each cauldron there's a devil who throws coal on the fire and who pushes the souls down when they come up to the top. One day the devils, finding the work too hard, decide to call a strike. They get together and protest, they sign petitions. But the devil who takes care of the writers' cauldron is absent. They wonder why. They go see him and say to him, "Your work is very hard. Why don't you join our strike?" And the writers' devil answers, "But my work isn't as hard as yours, because when the souls of the writers come up to the top, the other writers grab their legs and pull them back down."

Here's my question. You've been very successful, Victor-Lévy Beaulieu. Have you experienced a lot of envy from other writers – or is it heaven here in Québec?

VICTOR-LÉVY BEAULIEU

Writing in Québec isn't very different from writing elsewhere. For a North American like me, it was a shock to see the tentacles of the octopus of writing in Paris. All the sycophancy inherited from the Enlightenment, all the obsequiousness of writers towards critics and publishers. Québec writers are lucky in comparison to that. We aren't very numerous, so there's a lot less competition, which changes the problem. I don't know if it's the same in English Canada. The six million Québec francophones who read or who buy books by Québec francophone writers don't constitute the kind of market in which I'm going to start a war because, if I get ahead of someone else, I'll sell a million or two million copies. Whether you get ahead of, or go behind, or stay even with them, you'll sell your five thousand copies just the same. For there to be competition among writers as there is in France or the United States, there have to be enough people for it to make a difference. For example, as a Québec writer, I can't sit down in front of my typewriter or my computer and write the first line of a book, and say to myself, "If my novel interests people, if it's good, I'll sell three or five million copies, and I'll get rich and be able to do what I want." It's impossible for a Québec writer to think like that. It wasn't like that for James Jones. After going through the Second World War in the Pacific, he settled in his little trailer in Florida, and he started writing his novel, typing it with two fingers because he didn't know to type. This American with a market of two hundred million potential readers said to himself, "If I write my book and people are interested in it, I could sell one or two million copies and become a millionaire, and then I could do what I want."

This situation makes the practice of literature in Québec very different from what it is in France or the United States or Russia. Practically no one in Québec can really live from their writing. You can count the exceptions on the fingers of one hand: Antonine Maillet, a guy like Michel Tremblay – because his plays are translated, presented, and published all over the world – and a few other writers who can manage because they also work for television. I would compare the Québec of culture or literature or writing to a kind of co-operative, in which, unlike many countries in the world, the writers tend more to help each other than to shoot each other down.

And then, there's some consolation for me in the actual practice of writing, in knowing there are so many holes in our past to fill and there are very few writers to do it. Unlike the case in the old society of France, a writer here can create just about anything. He just has to look around a bit and reach out to the past and pull it back. There'll be all kinds of characters, all kinds of situations, because the culture hasn't got to that point yet. You can be very optimistic, because there are lots of holes to fill. For the French, it's hard to write something new. The whole field of the past is occupied.

I mean, you go into the National Library in Paris and you take the section of French books since Francis I, and there are so many it'll give you hives. But in Toronto, you say to yourself, "I want to write about the 1837 Rebellion," and there's nothing stopping you from doing it, because very few people have touched that subject. In France, you'd have hundreds. Just on Victor Hugo, there have been something like eighty-five hundred books written in France so far. You'd have to get up pretty early in the morning to say something that would seem a bit new, because everything's already been said. Whereas here, for a poet like Émile Nelligan, who's considered, in quotation marks, the "founding father of Québec poetry," you go into bookstores or libraries and if you find five books on Émile Nelligan, it's exceptional.

MARGARET ATWOOD
And an opera.

VICTOR-LÉVY BEAULIEU
And an opera, yes. Now that's even more exceptional. So, for a Québec

writer, there's the problem of knowing you'll never sell a million copies because there isn't the market, but at the same time, you tell yourself that you can do something new because there are a lot of holes in Québec's past that have to be filled with writing.

MARGARET ATWOOD

I find French writing very different from Québec writing, especially the poetry.

VICTOR-LÉVY BEAULIEU

It's not done in the same sense or with the same goal. And it doesn't talk about the same things either. Today, after Du Bellay, Ronsard, Mallarmé, Rimbaud, and Verlaine, it's very hard to write French poetry that's any good. And then, the French have lost that rhythmic sense, that sonority, that guys like Mallarmé and Ronsard had. The Québécois have not only preserved but developed it. In Claude Beausoleil and in earlier writers like Paul-Marie Lapointe, there's a dwelling in words that makes Québec unique. The Québécois were able to preserve that truly poetic side that belongs to dream and magic, but the French weren't. But we can do that – and so can English Canada – because our countries are new and exploration both of language and of life is still possible here.

MARGARET ATWOOD

The French use the expression "Anglo-Saxon humour" for things that are at the same time serious, very dark, and funny. The origin of this humour is more Scottish than Anglo-Saxon, but I have the impression that you share this type of humour. It's true, isn't it? What's the role of humour in writing?

VICTOR-LÉVY BEAULIEU

Black humour is important to me. I've already said in a novel that wordplay saves you from disintegration. When you're able to play with words, to make up jokes, even corny ones, it shows there's another level that exists, and that means you can get beyond even the most horrible thing, because you're able to negotiate differences through language. Jewish humour in particular has framed or encircled that thing very well. Historically, the Jews were often victims of absurd situations. They got through them, particularly in literature, by means of mastery of language, that very special Yiddish humour that the uninitiated often have trouble understanding – because it's so intrinsic to the Jewish spirit that, if you're not Jewish, it may be a bit hard to grasp. I find Anglo-Saxon black humour healthy. When I reread the story of Adam and Eve retold by Mark Twain, I can't help laughing. It's a very pointed humour, not that broad or gross humour on the most basic level that television gives us examples of every day. As a reader, I'm attracted by the types of humour that draw on my intelligence. You don't find that in all literatures, obviously.

MARGARET ATWOOD

Have you been criticized for joking about serious subjects?

VICTOR-LÉVY BEAULIEU

Yes, certainly. There are people who think of writing in one way only – it has to be heavy – and who can't understand when you depart from that norm and make certain things comical or absurd through laughter or the way you write about them, which is the essence of humour. In "L'Héritage," there were a lot of humorous scenes, but it was a black humour that went beyond the basic level. At the beginning, I often had disagreements with the people producing the show, because they didn't understand that it was black humour. They wanted to make it into heavy metal.

MARGARET ATWOOD

Is there nothing you would consider in bad taste?

VICTOR-LÉVY BEAULIEU

Bad taste is everywhere in everyday life. There are a lot of things in bad taste that I try to avoid, but there's one in particular that I'd want to avoid at all costs – that I do avoid at all costs – and that's personal insults.

MARGARET ATWOOD

Do you think that God has a sense of humour?

VICTOR-LÉVY BEAULIEU

No, not at all.

MARGARET ATWOOD

Not at all? But He created man!

VICTOR-LÉVY BEAULIEU

Yes. And I think man acquired a sense of humour when he aspired to become a god.

MARGARET ATWOOD

Now let's talk about the Devil, who's very important in your work. I have a little joke for you. The Devil goes to a writer's home. He says, "I'll make you the best-known writer in the world. You'll be rich and famous, and your books will live forever. In return, you only have to give me your grandmother, your mother, your children, and your soul. Sign here." The writer says, "Great! I agree. Give me the pen." And then he adds, "But what's the catch?"

In your most recent work, *Le carnet de l'écrivain Faust*, you show Faust as a writer. Traditionally, Faust is the German writer who sold his soul to the Devil in exchange for material possessions, knowledge, and good sex. He was a very common hero in popular theatre in the early Renaissance, before his more literary incarnation in Christopher Marlowe's *Doctor Faustus* and before Massenet's opera. He's clearly the ancestor of both the mad scientist and the inspired artist of the nineteenth century. Your Faust is a Québec writer who has also sold his soul to the Devil but who may not have got knowledge in return, or even material possessions. Do artists sign a pact with the Devil or with their own diabolical side in exchange for artistic gifts? And if the Devil appeared before you, how would the negotiations go? What would you ask for in return for your soul? If you still have any . . .

VICTOR-LÉVY BEAULIEU

If I still have any? Of course I do! That was exactly the question I was asking myself!

Faust is an old myth of humanity. The artist is forced to sell what he is in order to be able to continue to write, to be able to continue to be an artist. In the kind of society we live in, it's perhaps even harder than it once was to preserve your freedom. In former societies, the artist often had a more obvious reason for existing. For example, Genghis Khan razed Asia, massacred everybody, and the only prisoners he took were scientists and artists – the scientists to create better weapons of war for him and the artists to glorify him and his régime. Today's powers-that-be have established a different order of priorities. Now they have their own propagandists. There are a lot of Canadian writers who have been hired by prime ministers to write speeches. For years Jean Lemoyne, in Québec, wrote Trudeau's speeches.

For me, power is the Devil, and the Devil no longer needs to go to see someone to buy his soul, because he's found other ways of obtaining what he needs, which is his glorification. Advertising agencies have nothing to do with the integrity an artist may have. The advertising agency exists to sell a product, and the soul counts for nothing in the sale of that product. Herman Melville said you can't write if you don't have free time, and you don't have free time if you don't have any money. The problem of the contemporary artist belongs to that perspective much more than to the ancient mythologies. Today's artist can no longer sell his soul to the Devil, because the Devil is power, and he uses polling firms and professional propagandists, who have no souls.

MARGARET ATWOOD

But, Victor-Lévy, if the Devil is power, and if you're an *indépendantiste*, and if Québec separates and the government of Québec gains power, will that government be the Devil?

VICTOR-LÉVY BEAULIEU

Regardless of all that, I feel power should be abolished. But perhaps in abolishing power, we'd abolish the Devil, too, which would be too bad in a way, because in that famous Devil-God duality, only the Devil is interesting, if only for his black humour, which God doesn't have. At least you can play with the Devil who's in power by using humour. But finally, that doesn't change anything for me; it's power that must be abolished.

MARGARET ATWOOD

There are many kinds of power. Writing is also a kind of power. I think you use the word *devil* in two senses: the external devil you were talking about, but also another devil that you could call the good devil. And maybe it's the good devil that provides the genius you draw on if you want to be a creator.

VICTOR-LÉVY BEAULIEU

Yes, but there again, if you look at the myth of Faust, even at its origins, that power of the good devil never was able to be abolished, precisely because it represents creation in the narrow and the broad sense of the word, total creation, and the impetus that causes someone to create cannot be abolished by any power. And that's quite heartening in a sense, because no matter what kind of society you might live in, there's no devil now that could abolish that. There will always be someone somewhere capable of demonstrating his freedom by writing. And that was how Thomas Mann solved the problem in *Doctor Faustus*, long before our time, since the novel dates back to 1949. And I find that comforting.

MARGARET ATWOOD

But you've evaded the question. What is the true price of your soul, Victor? Is it a secret?

VICTOR-LÉVY BEAULIEU

A soul has no price, since it's not material. It's a bit of a false question to try to put a price on the soul.

MARGARET ATWOOD

But you have a writer in your work who thinks he's sold his soul to the Devil.

VICTOR-LÉVY BEAULIEU

Yes. Maybe he's right to think that.

MARGARET ATWOOD

It's not autobiographical?

VICTOR-LÉVY BEAULIEU

There's always autobiography everywhere, but let's say, from the perspective of *Le carnet de l'écrivain Faust*, that the writer in that book makes creation a totalitarian act. To be capable of creation in one way or another, he has to separate from his wife and even his children to a certain extent, to experience being alone, in order to be able to write in his own way, as he wishes to and as totally as he wishes to. It's putting yourself outside life to be able to describe life. There's something absurd in that, but at the same time he can't escape it, because he feels it's what he must do. But you need peace to write – those who've lost it while writing become like Nietzsche – so, to have some peace to write, he says to himself, "You have to have money to have peace to write, so I have to negotiate what I am in a way – but as little as possible to be able to do what I want to do; that is, to keep my freedom as a creator."

MARGARET ATWOOD

One last question. I'm not asking you the question about the separation of Ontario, because I know your answer: "Why not? Yes, if you want!"

VICTOR-LÉVY BEAULIEU

You've understood perfectly! (Laughs.)

MARGARET ATWOOD

Should the writer offer hope to the reader? If so, what kind of hope? Simply the hope of knowing more?

VICTOR-LÉVY BEAULIEU

I don't think one writes to give people hope. Perhaps that's the role of some writers, but I started writing because I found there was no solution, either for people in general or for myself. Since I still feel the same way, I would find it a bit dishonest to mislead people into thinking I'm an optimist.

MARGARET ATWOOD

You agree with Camus: dirty hope!

VICTOR-LÉVY BEAULIEU

Yes, I'm pretty much in agreement with Camus about that. I think that our society, to make room for hope, would have to disappear altogether and become something completely different. I'm for change much more than for hope. But with change, you can never say in advance what will come. Often it takes completely unpredictable forms. The only thing I still hope for is that man will become a mutant in the good sense of the word.

MARGARET ATWOOD

Writers are necessarily optimists. They spend a lot of time producing their books. They surely must hope that someone somewhere will read all that work.

VICTOR-LÉVY BEAULIEU

If not, there would be nothing but absurdity.

MARGARET ATWOOD

You're an optimist. Admit it!

VICTOR-LÉVY BEAULIEU

Living, in any case, means forcing yourself to be optimistic. Do we really have any other choice?

BIBLIOGRAPHY

Margaret Atwood

MAJOR PRESS EDITIONS

Novels

The Edible Woman. McClelland & Stewart, 1969; André Deutsch, 1969; Atlantic-Little, Brown, 1970.

Surfacing. McClelland & Stewart, 1972; Simon & Schuster, 1973; André Deutsch, 1973.

Lady Oracle. McClelland & Stewart, 1976; Simon & Schuster, 1976; André Deutsch, 1976.

Life Before Man. McClelland & Stewart, 1979; Simon & Schuster, 1980; Jonathan Cape, 1980.

Bodily Harm. McClelland & Stewart, 1981; Simon & Schuster, 1981; Jonathan Cape, 1981.

The Handmaid's Tale. McClelland & Stewart, 1985; Houghton Mifflin, 1985; Jonathan Cape, 1985.

Cat's Eye. McClelland & Stewart, 1988; Doubleday, 1989; Bloomsbury, 1989.

The Robber Bride. McClelland & Stewart, 1993; Doubleday, 1993; Bloomsbury, 1993.

Alias Grace. McClelland & Stewart, 1996; Doubleday, 1996; Bloomsbury, 1996.

Short Fiction

Dancing Girls. McClelland & Stewart, 1977; Simon & Schuster, 1977; Jonathan Cape, 1979.

Murder in the Dark. Coach House, 1983; McClelland & Stewart, New Canadian Library, 1997.

Bluebeard's Egg. McClelland & Stewart, 1983; Houghton Mifflin, 1985; Jonathan Cape, 1987.

Wilderness Tips. McClelland & Stewart, 1991; Doubleday, 1991; Bloomsbury, 1991.

Good Bones. Coach House, 1992; Bloomsbury, 1992; Doubleday, 1994; McClelland & Stewart, New Canadian Library, 1997.

Poetry

The Circle Game. Cranbrook Academy of Art, 1964; Contact Press, 1966; Anansi, 1967.

The Animals in That Country. Atlantic-Little, Brown, 1968; Oxford University Press, 1969.

The Journals of Susanna Moodie. Oxford, 1970.

Procedures for Underground. Oxford, 1970; Atlantic-Little, Brown, 1970.

Power Politics. Anansi, 1971; Harper & Row, 1973.

You Are Happy. Oxford, 1974; Harper & Row, 1975.

Selected Poems. Oxford, 1976; Simon & Schuster, 1978.

Two-Headed Poems. Oxford, 1978.

True Stories. Oxford, 1981.

Interlunar. Oxford, 1984.

Selected Poems II: Poems Selected and New, 1976-1986. Oxford, 1986; Houghton Mifflin, 1987.

Selected Poems 1966-1984. Oxford, 1990.

Margaret Atwood Poems 1965-1975. Virago, 1991.

Morning in the Burned House. McClelland & Stewart, 1995; Houghton Mifflin, 1995; Virago, 1995.

Children's Books

Up in the Tree. McClelland & Stewart, 1978.

Anna's Pet. Lorimer, 1980.

For the Birds. Douglas & McIntyre, 1990.

Princess Prunella and the Purple Peanut. Illustrated by Maryann Kovalski. Key Porter, 1995; Workman, 1995; Barefoot, 1995.

Non-Fiction

Survival: A Thematic Guide to Canadian Literature. Anansi, 1972.

Days of the Rebels 1815-1840. Toronto: Natural Science of Canada, 1977.

Second Words: Selected Critical Prose. Anansi, 1982.

Strange Things: The Malevolent North in Canadian Literature. Oxford, 1995.

Anthologies

The New Oxford Book of Canadian Verse in English. Oxford, 1982.
The Oxford Book of Canadian Short Stories in English (with Robert Weaver). Oxford, 1986.
The Canlit Foodbook. Totem (Collins), 1987.
The Best American Short Stories 1989 (with Shannon Ravenel). Houghton Mifflin, 1989.
The New Oxford Book of Canadian Short Stories in English (with Robert Weaver). Oxford, 1995.

ART AND SMALL PRESS EDITIONS

Poetry

Double Persephone. Hawkshead Press, 1961.
Kaleidoscopes Baroque: a poem. Cranbrook Academy of Art, 1965.
Talismans for Children. Cranbrook Academy of Art, 1965.
Speeches for Doctor Frankenstein. Cranbrook Academy of Art, 1966.
Marsh, Hawk. Dreadnaught, 1977.
Notes Towards a Poem That Can Never Be Written. Salamander Press, 1981.
Snake Poems. Salamander Press, 1983.

Fiction

Encounters with the Element Man. Ewart, 1982.
Unearthing Suite. Grand Union Press, 1983.

FRENCH TRANSLATIONS

Novels

Faire Surface (Surfacing). Éditions Grasset, 1976; Le Serpent à plumes Éditions, 1994.
Lady Oracle (Lady Oracle). Éditions L'Étincelle, 1976.
Marquée au corps (Bodily Harm). Éditions Quinze, 1981.
La vie avant l'homme (Life Before Man). Éditions Quinze, 1981.
La femme comestible (The Edible Woman). Éditions Quinze, 1984.
La servante éclarate (The Handmaid's Tale). Éditions Robert Laffont, 1994.

Œil-de-chat (*Cat's Eye*). Éditions Robert Laffont, 1988.
La voleuse d'hommes (*The Robber Bride*). Éditions Robert Laffont, 1994.
Captive (*Alias Grace*). Éditions Robert Laffont, 1998.

Short fiction

L'œuf de Barbe-Bleue (*Bluebeard's Egg*). Éditions Libre Expression, 1985.
Les danseuses (*Dancing Girls*). Éditions Quinze, 1986.
Meurtre dans la nuit (*Murder in the Dark*). Éditions Remue-Ménage, 1987.
La troisième main (*Good Bones*). Éditions de la Pleine Lune, 1995.
Mort en lisière (*Wilderness Tips*). Éditions Robert Laffont, 1996.

Poetry

Politique de pouvoir (*Power Politics*). L'Hexagone, 1994.

Children's Books

Sur arbres perchés (*Up in the Tree*). Pierre Tisseyre, 1979.
Princesse Prunelle et le pois pourpre (*Princess Prunella and the Purple Peanut*).
    Illustrated by Maryann Kovalski. Éditions Phidal, 1996.

Non-Fiction

Essai sur la littérature canadienne (*Survival*). Éditions du Boréal Express, 1987.

BIBLIOGRAPHY

Victor-Lévy Beaulieu

Novels

Mémoires d'outre-tonneau. Éditions Esterel, 1968.

Race de monde. Éditions Stanké, Québec 10/10, 1986.

La nuitte de Malcomm Hudd. Éditions du Jour, 1969.

Jos Connaissant. Éditions du Jour, 1970; Éditions Stanké, Québec 10/10, 1986.

Les grands-pères. Éditions du Jour, 1971; Éditions Robert Laffont, 1973; Éditions Stanké, Québec 10/10, 1985.

Un rêve québécois. Éditions du Jour, 1972.

Oh Miami Miami Miami. Éditions du Jour, 1973.

Don Quichotte de la Démanche. Éditions de l'Aurore, 1974; Éditions Flammarion, 1978; Éditions Stanké, Québec 10/10, 1988.

Una. VLB Éditeur, 1980.

Satan Belhumeur. VLB Éditeur, 1981.

Steven le Hérault. Éditions Stanké, 1985.

L'Héritage (I. L'Automne). Éditions Stanké, 1987.

L'Héritage (II. L'Hiver). Éditions Stanké, 1991.

Le carnet de l'écrivain Faust. Éditions Stanké, 1995.

La jument de la nuit. Éditions Stanké, 1995.

L'Héritage. Éditions Trois-Pistoles, 1996.

Short Fiction

Blanche forcée. VLB Éditeur, 1976; Éditions Flammarion, 1976.

Moi Pierre Leroy, prophète et un peu fêlé du chaudron. VLB Éditeur, 1982.

"La boule de caoutchouc," in *Dix nouvelles humoristiques.* Quinze, 1985.

"Docteur l'Indienne," in *Aimer.* Quinze, 1985.

"La robe de volupté," in *Premier amour.* Éditions Stanké, 1988.

Non-Fiction

Manuel de la petite littérature du Québec. Éditions de l'Aurore, 1975.

N'évoque plus que le désenchantement de la ténèbre, mon si pauvre Abel. VLB Éditeur, 1976.

Monsieur Melville. VLB Éditeur, 1978; Éditions Flammarion, 1980.

Célébration du yogourt. VLB Éditeur, 1981.

Entre la sainteté et le terrorisme. VLB Éditeur, 1984.

Chroniques polissonnes d'un téléphage enragé. Éditions Stanké, 1985.

Pour saluer Victor Hugo. Éditions du Jour, 1970; Éditions Stanké, Québec 10/10, 1985.

Jack Kérouac: essai poulet. Éditions du Jour, 1972; Éditions de l'Herne, 1973; Éditions Stanké, Québec 10/10, 1987.

Pour faire une longue histoire courte (interview with Roger Lemelin). Éditions Stanké, 1990.

Docteur Ferron, Pèlerinage. Éditions Stanké, 1991.

Gratien, Tit-Coq, Fridolin, Bousille et les autres (interview with Gratien Gélinas). Éditions Stanké, 1993.

Monsieur de Voltaire. Éditions Stanké, 1994.

"Lettre à un ex-ayatollah en pantoufles," in *Trente lettres pour un oui.* Éditions Stanké, 1995.

Chroniques du pays malaise 1970/1979. Éditions Trois-Pistoles, 1996.

Trois-Pistoles et les Basques: Le pays de mon père. Éditions Trois-Pistoles, 1996.

Le Bas Saint-Laurent: Les racines de Bouscotte. Éditions Trois-Pistoles, 1997.

Québec Ostinato. Éditions Trois-Pistoles, 1998.

Theatre

En attendant Trudot. Éditions de l'Aurore, 1975

Ma Corriveau. VLB Éditeur, 1976.

Monsieur Zéro. VLB Éditeur, 1977.

Sagamo Job J. VLB Éditeur, 1977.

Cérémonial pour l'assassinat d'un ministre. VLB Éditeur, 1978.

La tête de Monsieur Ferron ou Les Chians. VLB Éditeur, 1979.

Discours de Samm. VLB Éditeur, 1983.

Votre fille peuplesse par inadvertance. Stanké/VLB Éditeur, Éditions Stanké, 1990.

La maison cassée. Éditions Stanké, 1991.

Sophie et Léon and *Seigneur Léon Tolstoï.* Éditions Stanké, 1992.

La nuit de la grande citrouille. Éditions Stanké, 1993.

Le bonheur total. Éditions Stanké, 1995.
La guerre des clochers. Éditions Trois-Pistoles, 1997.
Beauté Féroce. Éditions Trois-Pistoles, 1998.

Anthologies

Les gens du fleuve. Éditions Stanké, 1993.
Écrits de jeunesse 1964/1969. Éditions Trois-Pistoles, 1996.

ENGLISH TRANSLATIONS

Novels

The Grand-Fathers (*Les grands-pères*). Translated by Marc Plourde. Harvest House, 1973.
A Québécois Dream (*Un rêve québécois*). Translated by Raymond Chamberlain. Exile Editions, 1978.
Don Quixote in Nighttown (*Don Quichotte de la Démanche*). Translated by Sheila Fischman. Press Porcepic, 1978.
Jos Connaissant (*Jos Connaissant*). Translated by Raymond Chamberlain. Exile Editions, 1982.
Satan Belhumeur (*Satan Belhumeur*). Translated by Raymond Chamberlain. Exile Editions, 1983.
Steven le Hérault (*Steven le Hérault*). Translated by Raymond Chamberlain. Exile Editions, 1987.

Short Fiction

The Rubber Ball ("Le boule de caoutchouc"). Translated by Ray Ellenwood. Penguin, 1985.

Non-Fiction

Jack Kerouac: A chicken-essay (*Jack Kérouac: essai poulet*). Translated by Sheila Fischman. Coach House, 1975.
Monsieur Melville (*Monsieur Melville*). Translated by Raymond Chamberlain. Coach House, 1984.